CHRISTMAS PLAYS
for
YOUNG ACTORS

Christmas Plays
for
Young Actors

*A Collection of Royalty-Free
Stage and Reading Plays*

Edited by
A. S. BURACK

Publishers   PLAYS, INC.   *Boston*

Copyright © 1950, 1969 by

PLAYS, INC.

Reprinted 1977

Library of Congress Catalog Card Number: 70-86850

ISBN: 0-8238-0008-3

MANUFACTURED IN THE UNITED STATES OF AMERICA

PREFACE TO THE REVISED EDITION

The success of the original edition of *Christmas Plays for Young Actors* has encouraged me to issue this revised edition, with timely changes suitable for modern young audiences and actors. As editor of PLAYS, The Drama Magazine for Young People, I have been aware of the perennial demand for dramatic material which points up and illuminates the spirit and significance of Christmas—both in terms of the traditional Christmas story and the meaning of this holiday in the setting of today. In an attempt to meet this expressed need and continuing interest, I have brought together a variety of the most popular Christmas plays published in our magazine.

The types of plays range from comedies and fantasies to serious dramas, suitable for all age levels—Junior and Senior High, Middle Grades, and Lower Grades, with a special section of plays for radio-style reading. Both modern and traditional subjects and themes are included to provide a balanced assortment of plays.

Suggestions for staging, lighting, properties, and other effects have been given in detail under the Production Notes at the end of the book. Simple equipment and flexible casts make all of the plays easy to perform. It is possible to adapt any of the plays to include specialty numbers and the singing of carols.

I am happy to present these worthwhile, production-tested plays in permanent book form and hope that they will continue to please actors and audiences of all ages.

A. S. Burack

T A B L E   O F

CONTENTS

CHRISTMAS PLAYS

for

YOUNG ACTORS

Pink Roses for Christmas

by Josephine E. Campbell

Characters

JOHN ARNOLD, *genial, elderly man*
LYDIA, *his wife*
JANIE⎱
JIM ⎰ *their children*
TILLIE, *middle-aged "hired girl"*

TIME: *Late afternoon of the day before Christmas.*
SETTING: *Dining room in the Arnold home.*
AT RISE: LYDIA *enters from the kitchen, carrying a centerpiece of pink roses which she places in the center of the table, then standing back, admires the effect.*

LYDIA: Oh, Tillie?

TILLIE (*Offstage*): Yes ma'am?

LYDIA: Can you stop basting that turkey long enough to see how lovely the roses look?

TILLIE (*At kitchen door, wiping her hands on her apron*): My! They do look scrumptious, Mrs. Arnold. You'd never think there was snow a foot deep outside! Smells more like June!

LYDIA: You haven't seen the candles yet, Tillie—(*Hurries to buffet and brings the two candles to the table and places right and left of the centerpiece*) There! Aren't they a perfect match?

3

TILLIE: I'll say they are! You'd think that florist grew the roses to match the candles, wouldn't you!

LYDIA (*Happily*): That isn't all—(*Gets four place cards from buffet*) See? Place cards. . . . With pink rosebuds on them!

TILLIE (*Admiring them*): Heavenly days! You're doing things up brown!

LYDIA: Doing them up "pink" you mean. Oh, I know it's silly, having place cards for my own children, but I want this dinner to be perfect. And I know Janie will notice these little details. After all the college luncheons and dinners she has gone to—

TILLIE: Land, Mrs. Arnold, I don't think it's silly. And neither will Jim and Janie, I'll bet. Those two kids—away from home for the first time—they'll appreciate everything you do.

LYDIA (*Fondly*): I know they will—the dears! Tillie, if anything went wrong now, I couldn't stand it!

TILLIE: I'll keep my fingers crossed, Mrs. Arnold. . . . Heavenly days! I smell those mince pies boilin' over. . . . (*Exits*)

LYDIA (*Calling, as she places silverware on the table*): Never mind, it's a nice spicy smell. (*Hums to herself happily*)

JOHN (*Offstage*): Lyddy! Oh Lyddy!

LYDIA (*Hurrying to stair door*): Yes, John—what is it?

JOHN (*Shouting*): Where the Sam Hill is that new tie?

LYDIA: Just where I told you, John. In the right-hand top bureau drawer. . . . And John, don't upset things.

JOHN: I got it. Won't upset a thing— Tie it in a jiffy. . . .

LYDIA (*Goes to table, murmuring*): That man! (*Moves things about on table critically*)

TILLIE (*At kitchen door*): Mrs. Arnold, think this sauce looks O.K.?

LYDIA (*Inspecting it*): Why, yes—it looks just right to me. Tillie, the children will never have anything at college like your cooking . . . and everything has turned out so beautifully—(*Both women exclaim as there are a series of loud thumps heard.*)

LYDIA (*Rushing to stair door*): Mercy! John has fallen down stairs!

TILLIE (*Rushing to door*): Heavenly days—I knew somepin' would happen—

LYDIA (*At door*): John! Did you fall?

JOHN (*Enters brushing his clothes and grinning*): Nope . . . Thought I'd save time coming down head over heels. . . . Spoke too soon about not upsetting anything, it seems.

TILLIE (*Giggling*): The way you joke, Mr. Arnold—(*Exit to kitchen.*)

LYDIA: Well—turn around and let me brush you off. Did you tear your suit? (*Gets brush from buffet drawer.*)

JOHN: Didn't know you wanted me to—

LYDIA: Stand still, John. Goodness! One would think you had bumped all the way down on your shoulder blades!

JOHN (*Hand on hip*): Ouch! Think you got the wrong location, Lyddy—

LYDIA (*Instantly concerned*): John, dear—you *are* hurt! I'll get the liniment. . . .

JOHN (*Stopping her*): Hey! I'm all right, honey. Anyhow, think I want to buy cut-flowers in December and then smell up the room with liniment? How's my tie look, Lyddy?

LYDIA (*Straightening it*): Looks like you needed more practice turning somersaults down stairs, my dear! Oh John, in just a little while we'll light the Christmas candles for the children!

JOHN (*Tipping her face up, fondly*): Seems to me the Christmas candles are already lighted in your eyes, honey.

LYDIA (*Earnestly*): Every minute of this Christmas Eve with the children will be precious. Even if they have only been away since last fall—I have missed them so!

JOHN (*Soberly*) : I hope they haven't changed.

LYDIA : Of course they haven't changed—bless them !

JOHN (*Turning to the table*) : Well, the old dining-room table looks quite festive. But I always thought Christmas candles were red.

LYDIA : Oh, I have the red candles in the front room with the Christmas tree. I wanted pink decorations in here because Janie loves that color. . . . And after all, can you think of anything more artistic? (*Stands admiring the table centerpiece and candles*)

JOHN (*Grinning*) : Sure. A big platter of turkey with all the trimmin's.

LYDIA : Oh—you men !

JOHN (*Picking up a newspaper and looking through it*) : What would you think of our driving out south tonight after dinner—past that big Stanton estate? I read they're opening the house for holiday guests from the East. Here it is— (*Reads aloud*) "There will be lighted wreaths in every window of the huge Stanton mansion tonight, as well as several lighted Christmas trees outside—" Be quite a sight for the kids, eh?

LYDIA : Oh, they'd love it, John . . . And afterwards we'll have our Christmas tree and our presents, and the children will sing "Silent Night" for us—just as they have ever since Janie was in pigtails and Jimmy in knee-pants. Oh, John, (*Leans her head against his arm*) this is going to be our happiest Christmas. . . . (*Telephone rings. Both start*)

LYDIA : Oh—what if that should be bad news—

JOHN (*Taking down receiver*) : Shucks—it's probably Ed, down at the depot—I asked him to let me know if there was any change in train time (*Speaks into receiver*) John Arnold speaking. . . . Hi, Ed. . . . What's that? (*Louder*) It did! For Pete's sake— Yeah—thanks Ed—(*Replaces receiver.*

Greatly excited.)— That was Ed, Lyddy. . . . He forgot to telephone. . . . He says the train is in three sections. . . . Where's my hat—(*Scrambles about.*)

LYDIA: You mean—the train's *in!*

JOHN: Yes, doggone it, Ed said he saw Jim and Janie getting into some flashy car— Hey, Tillie, seen my hat? (*Throws things about*)

TILLIE (*At door*): Heavenly days! Are they coming now! There's your hat—Mr. Arnold—under those newspapers—

LYDIA: Oh dear—where's my shoulder shawl—(*Searching frantically.*)

TILLIE: You put it in the buffet— Here 'tis (*Gets shawl and puts it about* LYDIA's *shoulders.*) I'll start dishin' up right away. (*She goes out. The door is flung open. Two smartly dressed young people rush in. They throw the packages they have on a table and exclaim while embracing their parents*)

JANIE: Mom—oh Mom! We're really here—

JIM: Hi, Dad! You're looking fine. Get away from Mom, and give me a chance, Janie—

LYDIA (*Tremulously*): Darlings—

JANIE: Dad—you fraud! Don't pretend you are wiping your eyes!

JOHN: Me? Just showing off my clean handkerchief. . . .

TILLIE (*At kitchen door wearing a white apron*): Merry Christmas!

CHILDREN: Hi, Tillie. (*They shake hands.* JANIE *kisses her.*)

JIM: Is the cooky jar filled, Tillie?

TILLIE: Yes *sir!* All the cookies you like—both of you. Well— I'll start dishin' up now—(*Dashes out to kitchen*)

LYDIA: Tillie has been working so hard—getting things ready to eat the minute your train was due—

JANIE: Oh, Mom, we can't eat dinner now!

JOHN: Don't tell us you're dieting, young lady!

JANIE: We have the most gorgeous news! Jim, you tell them now—

JIM (*With mock dramatic gestures*): Folks! Brace yourselves! We're to have the Arnold Christmas Eve tomorrow night, because—get ready for the shock—because—we are invited to the Stanton mansion for the big Christmas Eve party!

JANIE: Isn't it wonderful! Jim—they're struck dumb! (JOHN *has gone to stand beside* LYDIA *as if to protect her.*)

JOHN: But how—I don't understand—

JIM: It's this way, Dad . . . Bill Stanton is a cousin of these Stantons and he was invited here for the holidays. . . . Well—Bill's got a crush on Janie—

JANIE: Oh, he has not. . . . We're just good friends—

LYDIA: But—the Stantons themselves didn't invite you—

JIM: Yes, they did—it's a blanket invitation. They told Bill to bring anyone he liked from the college—

JANIE: Why—we thought you'd be delighted! We kept it for a surprise.

JOHN (*Grimly*): You certainly achieved your object.

LYDIA: But children—you mean—you won't be here on Christmas Eve?

JIM: Oh sure, Mom—we'll just shove the date one day ahead. See? (*Loud honking outside.*) That's the Stanton station-wagon. . . . They've got a load of guests. . . . We said we'd only keep them waiting five minutes—

LYDIA: *Five minutes!*

JANIE (*Uncertain now*): We thought you'd be thrilled—having your children invited to the Stanton mansion. . . . But, Jim, maybe we'd better not go—(*More loud honking outside*)

JIM: We'll have to decide. Can't keep the Stantons waiting!

LYDIA: Of course, you must go, children. We wouldn't want you to miss such a wonderful opportunity—would we—John?

JOHN (*Briefly*): They must decide for themselves.

JANIE: I don't believe you understand, Mom. It's just for tonight. We'll be back tomorrow morning and have our Christmas tree tomorrow night—(*More honking.*)

JIM: Gosh, if the President can shove holidays around, so can we. 'Bye, Mom—see you in the morning. . . . 'Bye, Dad— (*Rushes out*)

JANIE: Mom, if you don't smile—I won't have a bit of fun. 'Bye—(*Kisses both parents good-bye and rushes out after* JIM. *There is the sound of voices outside and of a car starting.* LYDIA *and* JOHN *stand in the open door.* LYDIA *waves a hand-kerchief up and down mechanically until* JOHN *draws her away*)

JOHN: It's cold with the door open, honey—(*Closes door*)

LYDIA (*Slowly walks to table, stands looking at it*): Janie . . . didn't notice the place cards . . . or the roses—

JOHN: Didn't have time. Wait until she gets here tomorrow.

LYDIA (*Sadly*): Not after the Stanton dinner. Ours will be commonplace.

TILLIE (*Looking in*): Heavenly days! Where are they?

JOHN: They are invited to the Stanton blow-out tonight.

TILLIE: Yeah—fat chance of that! Are they outside?

LYDIA: Mr. Arnold is not joking, Tillie. Jim and Janie are invited to the Stanton Christmas Eve party. Of course we want them to accept. It is—(*Clears throat*) it is an honor. They'll be home tomorrow.

TILLIE (*With consternation*): Heav-un-lee days! What about dinner?

JOHN (*Briskly*): Go right ahead and serve dinner. I've got appetite enough to make up for two absentees.

LYDIA: Yes—you may as well serve dinner, Tillie. You've worked so hard.

TILLIE: O.K. I'll start dishin' up. Takes a few minutes— (*Exits*)

JOHN (*Making a determined attempt to be jovial*) : How about lighting up, Lyddy? I want to see how my girl looks by pink candle-light.

LYDIA (*Lifeless tone*) : Just as you wish, John. (*Stands beside table watching* JOHN *as he rather clumsily lights the two candles.*)

JOHN (*Offering his arm with mock ceremony*) : May I seat you, Madam?

LYDIA (*With faint smile*) : Thank you, dear. (JOHN *seats* LYDIA *at left. Then sits opposite her at right. Silence for a moment. They look at each other.*)

LYDIA (*In panicky tone*) : John—it's so empty . . . Let's ask Tillie . . .

JOHN : Of course we'll ask Tillie. (*Calls*) Hey—Tillie—

TILLIE (*Appearing in door*) : Just about a minute more, Mr. Arnold—

JOHN : No—we're in no hurry, Tillie. We want you to sit down with us.

TILLIE (*Astonished*) : Me? Land sakes, Mr. Arnold—I'd just be jumpin' up an' down all the time—

JOHN : Well—that sounds real interesting—

LYDIA : It doesn't matter—your serving dinner, Tillie. We— we want you to sit down—(*Bites her lip*) It's sort of lonesome—

TILLIE (*Suddenly understanding*) : Why, sure, Mrs. Arnold, I'll be proud to sit down. I've got a clean white apron on. . . . I'll sit while Mr. Arnold asks the blessing, anyhow. Thank you, Ma'am.

TILLIE (*Sits down facing the audience. Shows by her manner her sympathy for the two parents*) : It isn't as if they won't be back, you know. . . .

LYDIA (*With an effort to appear happy*) : Oh, of course . . . it's foolish to miss them so—just for a meal. . . . (*There is a short silence. All bow their heads*)

JOHN (*Reverently*) : Our Father in Heaven, we ask Thy blessing upon the food Thou hast provided so bountifully. Bless
all within this house—(*Abrupt pause*)—and do Thou bless
those absent ones—whom we love—so dearly. Amen. (*The
last phrase in a husky low tone.* LYDIA *bows her head to
her folded hands and* TILLIE *raises her apron to her eyes.
Suddenly young voices singing "Silent Night" are heard.*)

LYDIA (*Starting up*) : John! It's the children—singing our
carol—

TILLIE (*Beaming*) : I knew those kids were only fooling. I'll
get started dishin' up—(*Hurried exit to kitchen.* JOHN *and
LYDIA take a few steps toward the door, then pause, tense as
they listen. After a few measures of "Silent Night" the door
is flung open and* JIM *and* JANIE *rush in, grab their parents
and whirl them around to the tune of "Jingle Bells."*)

JOHN (*Still cautious*) : What does this mean, children?

LYDIA (*Happy but breathless*) : Gracious—I'm too old to dance
—Jimmy—

JIM (*Arm about his mother*) : Mom! The farther away we got
the worse we felt about leaving you two alone on Christmas
Eve—

JANIE (*Interrupting, standing with her arm through her
father's*) : And finally I told Bill to turn around and take us
back home—I told him I wouldn't enjoy one minute of the
party—

LYDIA : But your friends, dear—what will they think?

JANIE : Bill Stanton will fix that, Mom. He said there's to be
a big mid-week party. We could *enjoy* that!

JIM : You needn't worry, Mom. Bill understands. He said if
he had a Dad and Mom, no darned party could keep him
from being with them, especially at Christmas—

JANIE : Bill's an orphan—

JOHN : Let's have him over while the kids are here, eh, Lyddy?

LYDIA : Of course we shall—the poor boy . . .

JIM: He's a grand guy—saw right away something was wrong when we drove away from here, with you folks standing in the door. . . .

LYDIA (*Radiantly*): But everything is all right now—

TILLIE (*Looking in from kitchen*): You folks better sit. I'm dishin' up. (*Exit. All laugh. From the kitchen sounds of rattling pans, etc.*)

JIM: Boy! Have I got an appetite!

JANIE (*Going down stage to table*): Oh, Mom! How lovely the table looks! (*Picks up a place card, exclaims*) And—place cards! How *sweet!*

JOHN (*Smiling*): Your mother was afraid you might forget where you belong—

JIM (*Soberly*): Gosh, Dad, I guess we came pretty close to forgetting. But—believe me—never again!

JOHN (*Hands on* JIM's *shoulders, evidently much affected*): Son! We know what you have given up for us—

JIM: "Given up"—nothing! We're where we *want* to be—

JANIE (*Hugging her father's arm*): *We* made the decision, Dad, remember. (*She draws* LYDIA *to her side, so they now stand in a half-circle facing downstage*)

LYDIA: Still, it was a test, my children—and you came through.

JOHN: Listen! (*Faintly, the strains of "Silent Night."*) It's the Christmas carollers—(*They hum with the carollers passing by, as the curtain falls.*)

THE END

No Room at the Inn

by *Emma L. Patterson*

Characters

THE INNKEEPER
TWO TRAVELERS (*Men*)
THE BOY, *servant to Innkeeper, about ten years old*
JOSEPH
MARY
FOUR SHEPHERDS
SERVANT TO BALTHAZAR

BALTHAZAR, *a young man* ⎫
MELCHIOR, *a middle-aged man* ⎬ *The Three Wise Men*
CASPER, *an old man* ⎭

SERVANTS *and* GUESTS *at the Inn*

TIME: *Eve and early morning of the first Christmas.*

SCENE 1

SETTING: *A section of the inn yard at Bethlehem.*

AT RISE: *It is late afternoon. There is a red cast in the sky more intensified at left. People entering the courtyard from the highway are framed in a red glow. Throughout the scene there is activity—servants coming from the inn with pitchers or jars to draw water from the well, people walking between the stable and the inn. If the stage is shallow, this activity should be omitted in order not to cause confusion. The INN-KEEPER is seated on the bench beside the door. TWO TRAV-*

13

ELERS *enter through left gate. The* INNKEEPER *rises and advances toward them. They meet at center.*

FIRST TRAVELER: Are you the keeper of this inn?

INNKEEPER: I am, sirs. How may I serve you?

SECOND TRAVELER: We wish lodging for the night.

INNKEEPER (*Rubbing his hands*): How many are there of your party?

FIRST TRAVELER: We are traveling alone.

INNKEEPER (*Hesitantly*): Oh, I see. And you left your pack animals outside?

FIRST TRAVELER: We have no pack animals, no baggage.

SECOND TRAVELER: The very simplest accommodations will do for us. We are not wealthy.

INNKEEPER: Gentlemen, I am sorry, but I haven't a bed left. People have been pouring into town all day, registering to be taxed, you know.

SECOND TRAVELER: Yes, that is what brings us. We have come quite a distance.

INNKEEPER: Yes? Well, you will have to try somewhere else for lodging.

FIRST TRAVELER: Is there another inn here in Bethlehem?

INNKEEPER (*Walks back to bench*): No, but you will doubtless find some place. Perhaps you have friends who live near.

SECOND TRAVELER: No, we are strangers.

INNKEEPER: Oh, too bad. (*Sits on bench.*) Well, good evening, gentlemen, and good luck to you in finding a place. (*The* TRAVELERS *hesitate an instant, then turn and go out by left gate.* INNKEEPER *claps his hands and calls*) Boy, where are you? Come here, boy. (BOY *enters at center gate.*)

BOY: Yes, master?

INNKEEPER: Come here, you lazy oaf. Why do you loiter in the stables when there is so much work to do?

BOY: Why, master, you told me to feed the horse of the guest who just arrived.

INNKEEPER: Umph! You took too long about it.

BOY: I am finished now, master. What shall I do next?

INNKEEPER: Go stand outside the entrance gate. If any wayfarers come past and wish to enter, tell them there is no more room in the inn.

BOY: But, master, have you forgotten? There is still a room vacant, a fine large one, the best in the house.

INNKEEPER: Silence, fool! Of course I know that, but I am not so stupid as to rent that to any common traveler for a few farthings when if I but wait an hour some man of wealth is sure to come along and give me a good price for it.

BOY: Yes, master.

INNKEEPER: Go, now. Stand outside the gate and note the travelers carefully. If they come on foot or with only a pack mule, tell them there is no room. But if you see a man on horseback with a retinue of servants, send for me at once. We will have room for him.

BOY: Yes, master.

INNKEEPER: There! Someone approaches now, a couple of peasants. See, he is lifting her down from the donkey. Go and meet them. Tell them there is no room. (*The* BOY *runs off stage left. The* INNKEEPER *sits on the bench beside the door, folding his hands on his stomach.* JOSEPH *and* MARY *enter left. She is leaning heavily upon his arm. The* BOY *runs in after them and circling around in front of them, bars the way so that they are forced to halt.*)

BOY: I tell you, sir, it is no use to come in here. There is no room. (JOSEPH *leads* MARY *to the well-curb and she sits down, leaning back wearily. The* BOY *crosses to right.*) I told them what you said, master, but they would come in. The lady is very tired.

INNKEEPER: Humph! Lady, is it? Woman is good enough for her. Just a peasant woman. (JOSEPH *crosses to right and stands before* INNKEEPER.)

JOSEPH: Is there not some small place somewhere that you could give us for the night? My wife is too exhausted to go further.

INNKEEPER (*With an extravagant show of patience*): The boy told you there was no room. Why, then, must you persist in intruding? Do you expect *me* to move out and sleep in the mire of this courtyard in order to give you a place? Move on, now, and don't annoy me further. (JOSEPH *turns away reluctantly.*)

BOY (*To* INNKEEPER): There is a vacant cattle stall. Perhaps we could—

INNKEEPER: Be quiet, boy. We will need that for the horses of the late-comers.

JOSEPH: But you have no room for late-comers. So you have said.

BOY: Horses can be picketed anywhere, master.

INNKEEPER: But these people would not wish to be lodged with the beasts.

JOSEPH: Indeed we would be very glad even of such a place.

BOY: I will put down some fresh sweet hay for a bed.

INNKEEPER (*Reluctantly*): Very well. The price will be the same as for the stabling of a beast—of two beasts.

BOY (*Capering toward the exit*): This way, sir. I will make it ready for you. (JOSEPH *goes to the well-curb and helps* MARY *up. Exeunt* BOY, MARY *and* JOSEPH.)

INNKEEPER: See that you get back here promptly. I am going in to my supper. (*Exit* INNKEEPER *right.*)

CURTAIN

*   *   *

Scene 2

Time: *Six hours later. It is after midnight.*

At Rise: *The* Innkeeper *is seated on the bench. The* Boy *enters at rear.*

Boy: Oh, master, the most wonderful thing has happened. A baby has been born, a little boy.

Innkeeper: A baby born! Where?

Boy: In the stable.

Innkeeper: Umph! A wonderful thing indeed. One more added to the already too numerous population of the poor and ignorant.

Boy: But this baby seems different. When I look at him, it makes me feel—well, I can't describe it. You come and see him, master.

Innkeeper: I? I go to look at a peasant child born in my stables? (*He gives a short, scornful laugh.*)

Boy: I can stay here in the courtyard and keep watch for travelers.

Innkeeper: Travelers! There are none abroad tonight. Here it is past midnight and my best room still vacant. In all my life I never had such bad luck at this season.

Boy: Someone may stop even yet. It is a good night for traveling, starlit and mild.

Innkeeper: Yes, I never knew it to be so light at midnight.

Boy: That one star seems to hang right over the stable. (*Enter* Four Shepherds *left. They pause and look about them, then cross to center.*)

Innkeeper (*Brusquely*): Well, what is your business, shepherds?

First Shepherd: Sir, could you tell me. Has there been a child born at this inn tonight?

BOY (*Eagerly*): Yes, there has, a wonderful baby! He is in a manger in our stable. Shall I show you—? (*He runs toward rear exit.*)

INNKEEPER: Stay here, boy. (*The* SHEPHERDS *draw together at center and talk among themselves.*)

SECOND SHEPHERD: This must be the place.

THIRD SHEPHERD: It is as they said—lying in a manger.

FOURTH SHEPHERD (*To* INNKEEPER): May we go and see the child?

INNKEEPER: A fine lot of shepherds you are, leaving your sheep in the middle of the night to look at a baby. I manage my business day and night and even so can scarcely make a living.

THIRD SHEPHERD: There are more important things than business.

INNKEEPER: Well, move on. Don't clutter up the courtyard. (*Exeunt* SHEPHERDS.)

BOY: How do you suppose they knew about the baby?

INNKEEPER: They are probably relatives or friends of the couple. They are the same class of people. I don't like to have such common trash making free about the place. It gives people wrong ideas about the sort of guests I keep.

BOY: Why, master, shepherds are very fine people. I know one named—

INNKEEPER: On second thought, perhaps you had better go to the stables and keep an eye on those shepherds. See that they don't hide some lambs under their cloaks on the way out.

BOY: Yes, master! (*He turns and starts toward rear gate. Stops at center and gazes out through left gate.*) Master! Master! There is a camel caravan at the gate. (INNKEEPER *leaps up and stares through left gate.*)

INNKEEPER: Horses too! Arabian horses and servants galore. (*There is the sound of hoofs in the dust and of men calling.*) Ah, my chance has come. Now if I only had three or four vacant rooms. Oh, such wealth! Such magnificence!

BOY: They are stopping. Some are dismounting. Shall I go out and greet them?

INNKEEPER: No, I will attend to this. You go into the stables and send those shepherds away. (*Exit the* BOY. *Enter left the* SERVANT OF BALTHAZAR. *He stands very erect just inside the gate, bows, then folds his arms.* INNKEEPER *advances and bows.*) A good evening to you, sir. My humble dwelling is at your disposal.

SERVANT (*In a deliberate, expressionless tone as though speaking in a tongue foreign to him.*): Is there a newborn babe in this place?

INNKEEPER: A newborn babe? Why—why—yes, there is— but—it is not—(SERVANT *bows and goes out left.* INN-KEEPER *stares after him, puzzled. He paces across the courtyard muttering.*) Newborn babe! What do they want of a newborn babe? There must be some mistake. (*Enter* SERVANT OF BALTHAZAR *left. He takes up his previous stand by the gate. Enter the* THREE WISE MEN *each bearing a small coffer. They cross to center.* INNKEEPER *bows very low.*)

MELCHIOR: Where is the child?

INNKEEPER (*With many bows indicates rear gate*): This way, my lords. (*The* WISE MEN *walk out at rear.* SERVANT *crosses and takes up position beside rear gate, arms folded.* INNKEEPER *starts to follow* WISE MEN *but comes face to face with* SERVANT *who has the attitude of standing guard.* INNKEEPER *halts, crosses back to bench, turns and goes back to face* SERVANT.) This child is no person of importance. His parents are ordinary peasants. They came here begging a place to stay only this afternoon. If I had not taken pity on them and allowed them in, the child might have been born right by the roadside. Oh, no, your masters must have made a mistake.

SERVANT: My master is a prince of India. The other two are

Oriental nobles. Their wisdom is great and infallible. They do not make mistakes.

INNKEEPER: But what do they want of this child?

SERVANT: There is for him a great destiny. They have read it in the stars. They wish to do him homage. They bring him gifts.

INNKEEPER (*Shrugs his shoulders*): All this sounds foolish to me. But then I am not a sage, only a simple business man—and speaking of business, these gentlemen will wish to stay overnight here, won't they?

SERVANT: I will ask my master when he returns.

INNKEEPER: But surely they would not think of starting on at this hour. Shall I have beds prepared?

SERVANT: I will ask my master when he returns. (*Enter the* SHEPHERDS. *They start toward gate at left.*)

INNKEEPER: Well, my men, did you find the child for whom you were searching?

SECOND SHEPHERD: Yes.

INNKEEPER: Is he a very remarkable babe, unusual in any way? (*The* SHEPHERDS *look at each other. They speak a few words in an undertone.*)

FIRST SHEPHERD: He appears like any other child.

INNKEEPER (*To* SERVANT): You see? (*To* SHEPHERDS) And why did you wish to see the child? How did you hear about him? (*Again the* SHEPHERDS *confer with each other.*)

THIRD SHEPHERD: While we watched our flocks we were told of it.

INNKEEPER: Ah, by someone who had been here and seen him perhaps?

FOURTH SHEPHERD: Perhaps. (*Exeunt the* SHEPHERDS *left.*)

INNKEEPER: You see, it is just the ordinary story of a very ordinary birth. It is remarkable how rapidly news gets around among the lower classes. I'm afraid your masters will have to seek further—tomorrow. (*Enter the* THREE

WISE MEN *rear.* SERVANT *approaches* BALTHAZAR *and murmurs something in a foreign tongue.* BALTHAZAR *looks sharply at the* INNKEEPER.)

BALTHAZAR: Is it true that you have a vacant room in your inn?

INNKEEPER: Yes, my lord, it is at your service, a fine large room. I have held it for you at great expense and inconvenience.

BALTHAZAR: Then why must this family whom we have just left be lodged on a bed of straw in a cattle stall?

INNKEEPER: But—but—my lord, I did not realize—I would have gladly—a boy, one of my servants, took them there. I did not know—(*His stammerings fade off into silence.*)

MELCHIOR: Innkeeper, this night you are host to a king. Your finest room, if hung with the rarest of our tapestries, would have been but a poor setting for his glory. And you entertained him—in a manger. (INNKEEPER *falls to his knees.*)

CASPER: Friends, your words of reproof are useless and worse than useless. It were better to leave this man in his ignorance. Come, let us journey on. (*The* THREE WISE MEN *turn left to depart.*)

INNKEEPER: Masters! Masters! Stay but a few moments and I will even now show homage to this king. I will prepare the room with my own hands and myself lift him from the straw to a bed of down.

CASPER: Do not disturb the child. All has taken place as it was destined to do since the beginning of time.

INNKEEPER: But a king lying in a stable!

BALTHAZAR: That is of no consequence to him. Yours is the loss, not his. Had you shown kindness to these humble people last evening, you would have been lauded and revered through all the ages to the end of time. You chose otherwise.

INNKEEPER: But, my lords, I have none of your great learning. How was I to recognize royalty in such a guise?

MELCHIOR: It is not a question of learning. The shepherds

knew him and so did your little errand boy. Those who have saved room for him in their hearts shall see him and know him. The rest shall go blind to their graves.

BALTHAZAR: You had no room for him in your heart or in your house, no room for anything but yourself, comfort for yourself, money for yourself. Is it not true?

INNKEEPER (*With bowed head*): It is true. My heart is as empty as that vacant room.

CASPER: Do not despair, innkeeper. You were thoughtless and selfish, but it is not too late for you to do this king a service yet.

INNKEEPER: What is it, my lord? Only tell me and it shall be done.

CASPER: It is this. Say nothing to anyone of our visit. Help the parents to escape with the child in secrecy from the country. Herod is seeking him to kill him.

MELCHIOR: The shepherds are pledged to silence. If you say nothing, the child is safe.

INNKEEPER: I shall keep silence, my lords.

CASPER: It is well. Let us depart. (*Exeunt left* THREE WISE MEN *and* SERVANT.)

INNKEEPER (*Rises from his knees, goes to bench and sits lost in thought. Enter the* BOY *from rear*): Come here, lad. Those Oriental princes who were just here told me about the babe, who he is. I think I should like to see him.

BOY: Oh, master, I am so glad! Come, I will show you.

INNKEEPER: Just a minute, son. You started once to tell me how it made you feel to look upon this child, but I would not hear it. Now I am ready to listen.

BOY: Well, master, it is a hard thing to describe. I forget about myself and my heart seems to swell within me. And I feel that the only important thing in life is being friendly and kind.

INNKEEPER: I need that. Yes, I need to see him. But I have no gift to take him.

BOY: You need no gift, master.

INNKEEPER: But those Eastern princes carried in rich coffers.

BOY: Yes, and, master, one box was heaped with gleaming gold.

INNKEEPER: But out of their great wealth those gifts were nothing. Their real service to him was in finding him and in recognizing him as king.

BOY: That is true, and we can do that also.

INNKEEPER: It will be easier for you than for me. All my life I have assumed that kings could be recognized by their fine raiment.

BOY: I will help you, master.

INNKEEPER: Good! With your help I shall succeed. And my gift will be the empty room, the room that was too good for a king.

BOY: How do you mean, master?

INNKEEPER: I shall never rent that room again. Hereafter it will be free each night to the one who needs it most.

BOY: He will like that gift the best of any you could make.

INNKEEPER: Come, lad. Morning will soon break. Lead me to the king. (INNKEEPER *rises and takes the hand of the* BOY *who leads him to rear gate.*)

THE END

Puppy Love

by Helen Louise Miller

Characters

MR. BRADLEY
MRS. BRADLEY
MIKE
VALERIE

JUDY
CRYSTAL AVERY
MR. WINTERS

TIME: *Christmas Eve.*
SETTING: *The living room of the Bradley home.*
AT RISE: JUDY *is addressing some last-minute cards and* VALERIE *is wrapping gifts.*

VALERIE (*Impatiently*): There! The string tore! I don't see how Mother manages to turn out such artistic packages. Mine always get lumpy and the string is either too long or too short. I think I'll leave this one for her.

JUDY: No fair! Remember, this Christmas we're doing things Dad's way. A job for everyone and everyone on the job! Mother's job is the dinner. Yours is gifts, and mine is cards. Let's each stick to her own department.

VALERIE: You get off easy compared with me.

JUDY: What's so easy about mailing cards for a family of five? I've worn my fingers off to the elbow and what do I get? Nothing but complaints.

VALERIE: And no wonder. You're sending the same cards to everybody. Dogs . . . nothing but dogs.

JUDY: I think dog cards are cute.

VALERIE: But they're not suitable for everybody, Judy. You should try to make cards suit the people.

JUDY: I do. Cocker spaniels for Mother's friends; hunting dogs for Dad's crowd; police dogs for Mike's gang; scotties for yours and wire hairs for mine. Besides, I get plenty of cards I don't like, so if some people don't like these, we're even. It has something to do with the law of averages.

VALERIE: You talk like Dad. Everything's system with Dad since he's after his new job. He even thinks he can systematize Christmas. (*Taking one of her packages to* JUDY's *table.*) Would it be too far out of your department to hold your finger on this string while I tie the knot?

JUDY: Oh, sure. That's just cooperation. There!

VALERIE (*As she ties knot*): Thanks. How are you coming with your cards? Why, Judy Bradley! You've sent a card to Crystal Avery from Mike.

JUDY: And why not?

VALERIE: Why not? You ask me "why not" when they haven't been speaking for a whole week!

JUDY: That's none of my business. Here's Mike's list, and there's Crystal's name, as big as you please. So naturally I sent her a card.

VALERIE: But that list was made out before the fight. Don't you think Mike will be mad?

JUDY: I don't think. I just follow orders. I stick to the lists. If they're not right, it's not my worry.

VALERIE: You're terrible.

JUDY: I am not terrible. I'm just practical. Besides, I think it's silly to be mad at your best girl at Christmas time. Now he won't get any present.

VALERIE: And neither will she. Oh, Judy, it *is* silly. Mike and Crystal always had such fun together. I wish they'd make up.

JUDY: Wishing won't make it so.

VALERIE: But what else can we do?

JUDY: Plenty.

VALERIE: Like what?

JUDY: Like sending Crystal a card—or a present.

VALERIE: A present! I wouldn't dare!

JUDY: It would probably fix everything.

VALERIE: But she'd find out Mike didn't send it.

JUDY: Maybe yes—maybe no. Anyhow, nothing ventured, nothing won, is the way I look at it.

VALERIE: But what could I get at this late date? The stores will close in another hour. What could you suggest?

JUDY: That's *your* department. Remember, I stick to cards.

VALERIE: Oh, Judy, you're so provoking. Now, you've put this idea in my head, and left me high and dry with it. (MIKE *enters with an armload of greens which he dumps on the floor.*)

MIKE: Well, here they are! Where do you want 'em?

VALERIE: That's not in our department. You're in charge of decorations.

MIKE: That only includes cutting and hauling. It doesn't mean I have to put them up.

VALERIE: Oh, yes, it does.

MIKE: Says who?

VALERIE: Says Dad. He's the boss. The rest of us just take orders.

MIKE: Oh, yeah?

JUDY: Yeah. And how about closing the door? It's wide open, and you know how Dad feels about heating all outdoors.

MIKE: Shut it yourself. That's not in my department.

JUDY: Oh, dear! I sometimes wonder if Dad's efficiency is all it's cracked up to be. Somehow it just doesn't go with Christmas.

VALERIE: Well, paying the bills is Dad's department, so somebody better shut the door. If he doesn't land his new job we'll all be out in the cold.

JUDY: Very well. I'll shut it. But you'd better get that mess cleared away before Mother comes home. (JUDY *exits.*)

MIKE: I'll take it down cellar and sort it out.

VALERIE: That's a good idea. The tree stand's down there some place.

JUDY (*Calling*): Mike! Valerie! Look! Look what I have! (*Enters carrying a puppy.*) Bless his little heart! Isn't he a darling?

VALERIE: Oh, Judy! He's precious! Where did you get him?

JUDY: Right on our doorstep.

MIKE: Gee, he's a cute little tyke. What's your name, fella?

JUDY (*To the dog*): Tell him you don't have a first name yet, but as of now, your last name is Bradley.

MIKE: Bradley! Ha! You don't think we're keeping him, do you?

JUDY: I most certainly do. All my life I've wanted a puppy for Christmas, and now I have one.

MIKE: And what about the rest of us? Don't you think I've wanted a puppy for Christmas, Easter, and George Washington's birthday ever since I was so high? But did I ever get one?

VALERIE: As long as we live in the Carlton Apartments, Judy, you might as well forget about pets. If Dad lands his new job maybe we'll move.

JUDY: But this is different. This puppy came straight from Heaven.

MIKE: Like fun! He walked up Milford Avenue.

JUDY: That's not what I mean. He was sent to us by Fate.

MIKE: Tell that to Mr. Carlton, and ask him about our lease.

VALERIE: It's no use, Judy. I'd love to keep the little fellow too, but it's out of the question.

JUDY: But what will we do with him? We can't put him out in the cold.

MIKE: Well, I know what I'm going to do with him. Give him to me. (*Reaches for dog.*)

JUDY (*Pulling away*): No, no. Keep away from him. What are you going to do with him?

MIKE: Feed him. Give him to me, Judy, and I'll see that he gets some chow. (*Takes dog.*) Come on, Poochie, we'll see if we can find you some nice warm milk. (*Exit.*)

VALERIE: He's darling.

JUDY: Oh, Val, can't we keep him?

VALERIE: I'm afraid not, Judy, but he sure would make a wonderful Christmas present for somebody.

JUDY: Yeah. For somebody who didn't live in a hateful old apartment house?

VALERIE: For somebody who liked dogs.

JUDY: Val! I've got it! Let's give him to Crystal. She doesn't live in an apartment. And she loves dogs!

VALERIE: We could tie a big red bow around his neck.

JUDY (*Getting card from table*): And here's the perfect card to go with it.

VALERIE: Here's the ribbon. There's enough for a good sized bow.

JUDY: What shall we write on the card? I guess we won't dare to sign Mike's name.

VALERIE: Mercy no! That would be forgery. Just write "Merry Christmas."

JUDY: I'll take it over, and she can draw her own conclusions.

VALERIE (*Watching as she writes*): Two r's in "Merry." You're a dreadful speller.

JUDY: Spelling doesn't matter at Christmas time. I'll go fix him up. (*Exit.*)

VALERIE: I know this isn't in our department, but Christmas

is a wonderful time to meddle in other people's business. (*Doorbell*) Now who in the world can that be? (*Goes to door.*) Why, Crystal Avery! This *is* a surprise!

CRYSTAL (*Entering with* VALERIE. *She carries two packages.*): Oh, Val, is Mike in?

VALERIE: Yes, do you want to see him?

CRYSTAL (*Drawing back*): Heavens, no! No, indeed! I'm just stopping by with this fruit cake. Mother wanted me to bring it over . . . and I thought if Mike were out, I'd stay for a few minutes. But since he's in, I'd better go.

VALERIE: Nonsense! He's down in the cellar fixing the Christmas greens. And what if you should run into him? It's high time you two made up.

CRYSTAL: Oh, I know, Valerie, I'd love to . . . but . . . you know how hard it is to make up, once you start not speaking.

JUDY (*Entering with puppy now wearing red bow and tag*): Look! Isn't he a picture? Oh, Crystal! When did you arrive?

CRYSTAL: Oh, how precious! Where did you get him?

JUDY: Well—er—he isn't exactly ours. He's a present.

CRYSTAL: A present? For whom?

VALERIE: For you, Crystal.

CRYSTAL: Oh, no! Not for me!

JUDY: Yes, for you. Do you like him?

CRYSTAL: Like him? I adore him . . . only . . . only . . . well . . . who sent him to me?

JUDY: Can't you guess?

CRYSTAL: Oh, girls! This is wonderful! Absolutely wonderful. Now I can give in and not be mad any more. I can even leave this present for Mike.

VALERIE: You have a present for Mike?

CRYSTAL: Of course, I've been expecting we'd make up any minute, and I wanted to be prepared. Here, (*Hands package to* JUDY) give this to Mike, will you?

JUDY: But he'll be up here any minute. You can give it to him yourself.

CRYSTAL: Oh, no. I don't want to see him just now. I have a feeling he'll be over later this evening.

JUDY: I have a feeling you're right.

VALERIE: It will be wonderful to have you back in the family, Crystal.

JUDY: And the puppy will be part of the family too.

CRYSTAL: The puppy! Oh, my goodness! How awful!

VALERIE: What's the matter?

CRYSTAL: Oh dear! This is terrible.

JUDY: What's terrible?

CRYSTAL: The puppy!

VALERIE: What's terrible about the puppy? I thought you liked him!

CRYSTAL: I do. I love him. But I can't take him.

JUDY: For heaven's sake, why not? You don't live in an apartment.

CRYSTAL: No, but it's Mother. She's allergic to dogs. Gets hay fever if one sets foot in the house. I've never been allowed to have a dog. (*Hands him back to* JUDY) Here, take him! And explain to Mike, will you? He'll understand. At least, I hope so.

VALERIE: At least, he'll understand you're not mad any more.

CRYSTAL: And that's the most wonderful thing in the world. Well, I must fly before he catches me here. Merry Christmas, everybody.

GIRLS: Merry Christmas.

CRYSTAL (*At door*): And Merry Christmas to you, Doggie. I'll send you the biggest bone I can find tomorrow. (*Exits*)

VALERIE: Well, what do you know about that?

JUDY: I know we still have this puppy on our hands, and I love it.

VALERIE: Better take him back to the kitchen till we can decide what to do with him.

JUDY: I've already decided. Of course, if somebody claims him, we'll have to return him, but for now, I'm keeping him!

VALERIE: I wish it were just that easy. It's a good thing, after all, that Crystal couldn't take the dog. We'd better advertise for the owner. (JUDY *exits.*)

MIKE (*Entering with small tree in stand*): There! How do you like the tree?

VALERIE: It looks nice, Mike. By the way, somebody was here just a minute ago.

MIKE: I thought I heard voices. Who was it?

VALERIE: Crystal.

MIKE: Crystal! What did she want?

VALERIE: She brought you a present.

MIKE: Oh, no. You're kidding.

VALERIE: No, I'm not, Mike. Honest. Here it is. (*Hands him package*) She left it for you.

MIKE: Well, I'll be doggoned! You mean to tell me she's not sore any more?

VALERIE: It doesn't look that way. You don't go around buying presents for people you're sore at.

MIKE: Oh, I wouldn't say that. I was sore at her, and yet I bought her a present.

VALERIE: You did?

MIKE: Sure. I've been expecting to make up and I wanted to be prepared. I'll take it right over. Gee, this is swell! This is great! I knew she couldn't hold out . . . not over Christmas. Women are always sentimental when it comes to Christmas.

VALERIE: And dogs.

MIKE: Dogs? What do dogs have to do with it?

VALERIE: Well, Crystal saw the puppy, and somehow, I just

can't explain how, but *somehow,* she got the idea you intended the puppy for her Christmas gift.

MIKE (*Laughing*): That's a good one! Mrs. Avery would sneeze her head off at sight of a dog. But the only thing that matters now is that Crystal and I have made up. If the puppy had anything to do with it, I'll buy him a bone as big as his head for his Christmas dinner. So long. . . . Tell Mother I'll bring Crystal along home to help trim the tree. (*Exit.*)

JUDY (*Enters*): The puppy is sound asleep. I made him a bed near the stove and he's good as gold.

VALERIE: Judy, dear, there's no use setting your heart on this puppy. Dad would never hear of it.

JUDY: What's the matter? Doesn't he have a department for dogs?

VALERIE: Oh, don't talk like that, Judy. Dad loves dogs as much as anybody else. It's just that we've always lived in apartments and there's no place for a dog.

JUDY: And besides, dogs aren't efficient. Dad has no time for anything that isn't efficient. Look how he has Christmas organized. You in charge of gifts. Mike in charge of decorations. Mother in charge of food. He's trying to run Christmas the way he runs the factory.

VALERIE: It's only because he wants to get the new job. If he can impress Mr. Winters with his efficiency he'll get to be the new superintendent and things will be much better all around. We might even get a house of our own.

JUDY: Oh, fiddlesticks on Mr. Winters. I hate him.

VALERIE: That's silly, Judy. You've never even seen Mr. Winters. (MRS. BRADLEY *enters in time to hear last sentence.*)

MRS. BRADLEY: Well, you're going to see Mr. Winters sooner than you expect. I just stopped at the factory to pick up your father and his secretary told me he's on his way out to the house with Mr. Winters in tow.

GIRLS: Good grief! Not on the day before Christmas!

MRS. BRADLEY: That's the way I feel about it . . . but it's too late now! If only he had called me. Good heavens! Look at this room. Judy, clear away that card table. Valerie, straighten up that sofa. I'll go make some tea. This house doesn't show much evidence of efficiency. Look at that tree! Not even trimmed. Where's Michael?

JUDY: He's made up with Crystal. I guess he's over at her house.

VALERIE: He said he'd be bringing her over later to help trim the tree.

MRS. BRADLEY: I hope it's much, much later, after Mr. Winters goes. Please, girls, try to make the room look decent. And as soon as you can, come help me in the kitchen. (*Exit*)

JUDY: This is awful! Poor Mother! Imagine Dad dragging Mr. Winters out here today of all days. Doesn't the man have a home?

VALERIE: Business is business, you know.

JUDY: Yeah, I know. And Christmas is Christmas! (*There is a scream from the kitchen and* MRS. BRADLEY *runs in.*)

MRS. BRADLEY: Valerie! Judy! Come quick! There's a strange dog in the kitchen. Help me get it out of here!

JUDY: Oh, dear! It's not a strange dog, Mother. It's the puppy.

MRS. BRADLEY: What puppy?

VALERIE: Judy found a puppy on the doorstep and brought it in out of the cold.

MRS. BRADLEY: Well, get it out of here. Your father will have a fit!

JUDY: I thought Dad liked dogs.

MRS. BRADLEY: Not in the apartment! It's breaking our lease. Old Man Carlton is just looking for a good excuse to get rid of us anyhow. Judy, you've got to get that dog out of here.

JUDY: But Mother! I can't put him out this minute.

MRS. BRADLEY: Yes, you can. Right this minute. Before your father . . .

MR. BRADLEY (*Off stage*): Just put your things in the hall closet, J. W., and make yourself at home.

MRS. BRADLEY: It's too late! They're here. (MR. BRADLEY *and* MR. WINTERS *enter*.)

MR. WINTERS: I hate to impose on your hospitality the day before Christmas, Bradley. I know how much confusion and extra work there is at this season of the year.

MR. BRADLEY: Oh, my family takes Christmas in its stride, J. W. A job for everyone and everyone on the job, I always say. Mary, this is Mr. Winters, President of Winters, Incorporated.

MRS. BRADLEY: How do you do, Mr. Winters?

MR. WINTERS: I was just telling your husband I hate to intrude at this time, Mrs. Bradley, but he assures me you always have everything under control.

MRS. BRADLEY: Well, you know how things are at Christmas, Mr. Winters.

MR. WINTERS: Exactly. And are these young ladies your daughters?

MRS. BRADLEY: Yes, this is Valerie, Mr. Winters.

VALERIE: How do you do, Mr. Winters?

MR. BRADLEY: And this is our youngest, Judy. Judy, this is Mr. Winters.

JUDY: Good afternoon, Mr. Winters.

MR. BRADLEY: We believe in division of labor at this house, J. W. Judy is in charge of the cards this year. Valerie has the gifts and Mike has the decorations. (*Notices the tree*) Er— I see Mike hasn't finished his job. Where is he?

MRS. BRADLEY: He and Crystal will be in later, dear, to trim the tree. It's still quite early, you know.

MR. WINTERS: And that last minute hustle and bustle is all part of the Christmas excitement, isn't it?

MRS. BRADLEY: It certainly is. If you'll excuse me, I'll see about the tea things.

MR. WINTERS: Now don't go to any trouble, Mrs. Bradley.

MRS. BRADLEY: Just some tea and fruit cake, Mr. Winters, in honor of the occasion. (*Exit*)

MR. BRADLEY: Sit down, J. W., and make yourself comfortable. Well, girls, is everything ready for the big day?

JUDY: Not quite, Dad. I still have some last minute cards.

MR. BRADLEY (*Frowning*): Quite a few I should say.

MR. WINTERS (*Chuckling*): I always get a flock of cards the day after Christmas. And I see you're still wrapping Christmas packages.

VALERIE: Yes, there's no end to it with such a large family. (MIKE *and* CRYSTAL *enter,* MIKE *pulling* CRYSTAL *by the hand.*)

MIKE: Sure you're going to stay for supper, and we'll trim the tree afterwards. Oh, excuse me, for bursting in like that, Dad. I didn't know you had company. We just came in to tell you the good news: Crystal and I have made up. We're going to all the Christmas dances together.

MR. BRADLEY: I'm glad to hear it. It's nice to see you again, Crystal, after a whole week. J. W., this is our little neighbor and my son's girl friend, Crystal Avery.

CRYSTAL: How do you do, Mr. Winters?

MR. WINTERS: Merry Christmas, Crystal, and Merry Christmas to you, young man. I suppose this is Michael?

MR. BRADLEY: Yes, this is my son. Mike, you better run out in the kitchen and see if you can help your mother bring in the tea things.

JUDY: Val and I will help too. (*All the young folks exit except* CRYSTAL.)

CRYSTAL: I brought a box of tree lights, Mr. Bradley. Mike said yours were on the blink. I'll see if I can plug them in.

MR. BRADLEY: Do you need any help?

CRYSTAL: Oh, no, thanks, I can manage. (*Wraps string of lights around tree and plugs them in.*)

MR. WINTERS: These modern girls are real mechanics.

CRYSTAL (*As tree lights go on*): Well, that's fine. They actually work.

MR. BRADLEY: They look very nice, although it's not like Michael to let the tree lights go till the last minute.

MR. WINTERS: Now it really looks like Christmas. (MRS. BRADLEY *and young people enter with trays of tea and cakes.*)

MIKE: Gee, that looks swell, Crystal.

MRS. BRADLEY: Put the tray on the table, Mike. Crystal, I'll ask you to do the honors. (CRYSTAL *takes place at tea table.*)

MR. WINTERS: This is really wonderful! A typical family group. Bradley, you are to be congratulated. There's just one thing lacking.

MR. BRADLEY: Name it, and we'll see what we can do, J. W.

MR. WINTERS: An old fashioned Christmas carol. Don't you think we could manage a verse or two of *God Rest You Merry, Gentlemen*?

MR. BRADLEY: I think we could oblige. What do you say, kids? Let's give it a try! (*They start to sing the carol, but before they have proceeded very far, there are loud and persistent howls from the kitchen.*)

MR. BRADLEY: What in the name of saints is that?

MIKE: What, Dad? I didn't hear anything.

MR. BRADLEY: Then you're deaf as a post. Listen. (*More howls.*)

MR. WINTERS: Why, it sounds like a dog . . . quite a young dog, I should say!

MRS. BRADLEY: Oh, dear! It's that wretched puppy!

MR. BRADLEY: A puppy? In our kitchen? Michael, what does this mean?

JUDY: It doesn't mean anything, Dad. It's just a puppy.

MR. BRADLEY: Well, go get him. Get him right away. (JUDY *exits.*)

CRYSTAL: Oh, wait till you see him, Mr. Bradley. He's adorable.

MR. BRADLEY: You've seen him?

CRYSTAL: Oh, yes, and I think he's the most wonderful dog in the world. There! Look at him! (JUDY *brings puppy in.*) Look at his big, red bow!

MR. WINTERS (*Laughing*): Well, bless my soul, Bradley! It looks as if we've stumbled on a surprise. Look, the little fellow wears a tag! (*Reads tag*) Merry Christmas, it says! Merry Christmas! I'll bet my hat, this puppy is your Christmas gift from that wonderful family of yours! (*More laughter.*) Take him, Bradley! Take him! And a wonderful present, I call it. I'd give my whole year's salary to have a family give me a present like that.

JUDY: Here he is, Dad, and Merry Christmas!

MR. BRADLEY (*Holding dog*): Well, I'll be doggonned!

JUDY: Isn't he wonderful, Dad?

VALERIE: Do you like him, Dad?

JUDY: Oh, Daddy, can we keep him?

MR. BRADLEY: But what about Mr. Carlton?

MR. WINTERS: Thunderation! Who is Mr. Carlton?

MR. BRADLEY: Our landlord. There's a clause in the lease about animals.

MR. WINTERS: Who cares? What's a lease to you, Bradley? Starting next year you'll be our new superintendent, and no doubt you will want to make some change in your living quarters. An apartment is no place for three children and a dog!

MR. BRADLEY: Do you mean it, J. W.?

MR. WINTERS: Mean it? Of course, I mean it. You're just the man we need for the job. I don't mind telling you at first I thought you were a trifle hipped on the subject of efficiency and organization. Oh, not that efficiency and organization aren't important within limits, of course. But when I see you tonight, here in this house with your family, I see you have other qualities as well. A man who loves his home, his wife, his children, and has room in his heart for animals . . . that's the kind of man we can use on our staff, Bradley. So congratulations and Merry Christmas.

ALL: Merry Christmas, Dad!

MRS. BRADLEY: Congratulations, dear, and thank you, Mr. Winters. This has made a wonderful Christmas for us all. Now shall we sit down and have our tea?

JUDY: And let me take that puppy, Dad, I'll put him out in the kitchen.

MR. BRADLEY (*Sitting down with dog on lap*): Take him out in the kitchen? You'll do nothing of the sort. I'll have you know the kitchen is not this little fellow's department. From now on, he's an executive in his own right and he shares this easy chair with me. How about it, J. W.?

MR. WINTERS: How about it? It's a case of puppy love, if I ever saw one. You're made for each other! Now let's try another verse of that Christmas carol and see if we can get both of them to join in the chorus. (*All begin to sing as curtain falls.*)

THE END

Silent Night

by Leslie Hollingsworth

Characters

HERR PASTOR JOSEPH MOHR, *pastor of the church at Obendorf*
FRAU MOHR *and* JOSEPH, *their son*
FRANZ XAVIER GRUBER, *choirmaster, a fiery man with an ability to lose himself in his music.*
THE ORGANIST *and his* FOUR DAUGHTERS. *These four should be a quartette who can sing.*

SCENE 1

SETTING: *The pastor's study in the parish house at Obendorf, a small village to the south of Salzburg in Austria.*

AT RISE: *In front of the fire, sunk deep in the chair, his fingers forming a contemplative gothic arch, sits the* HERR PASTOR JOSEPH MOHR. *At the table, leaning argumentatively across it, sits* FRANZ GRUBER, *the choirmaster. He holds the next day's program for the church entertainment in his hand.*

FRANZ: Be satisfied then. The rehearsal went well enough. All of the choir so well knows each song—over and over we have done the music and now without mistake, it will make fine honor for the Christmas Day.

MOHR (*Holding his head*): Ja, Franz, I know, I know.

FRANZ (*Persistent against the faint wistfulness in the* PASTOR'S *voice*): It is not each year that we can have something *new*. And besides (*Coaxingly*) we all know and love the old songs.

39

MOHR: You are right, my friend. (*Sighs.*) What troublesome minds (*Smiles whimsically at himself*) that forever think they must have something new, eh, Herr Gruber? (FRANZ *rises and the* PASTOR *affectionately assists him with his coat.*) I admit I have no right to sigh for a new song to sing this Christmas. (*Continuing as he rises and walks the floor.*) Ja, I know—who better? Every year we have a beautiful concert. And in this village goes every heart to the blessed Jesus out in joy and praise. Such a concert is as praise to heaven. . . .

FRANZ: Beauty is always new. And holiness and power comes from the village throats on Christmas, Herr Pastor. This singing is not like on other nights. In the olden days they have written such beauty that we need now no new songs and hymns. The songs that have lived, they have acquired from every generation new life, new richness. And the choir sings these songs with golden precision! (*Raises thumb and forefinger to show the nicety his training has achieved.*)

MOHR: I love the concerts. My heart aches with the rich stream of song. It is a wonderful custom, and thanks to you, my friend, it is nobly done.

FRANZ: Be content, then.

MOHR: But, Franz, it is not enough, that we take for ourselves, the gifts of the years. We also should speak in song. Without the gift of other hearts, nothing could you sing this Christmas time. And we, too, should give song for voices to come. Christmas is not finished.

FRANZ: Next year, perhaps. I will try for a Christmas song . . . ja?

MOHR (*Walks over and pats his friend on the back. Gently*): You have the concert well in hand. . . . You are content? You take these voices and mould them into glory for me every year! Ah, what singing has meant to this parish. It is a gift from us all. With so fine an organist, and schoolmaster to lead, we should be content with the beauty of the concert, is it not so? (*They cross to the door as the* PASTOR *takes his friend's hand and adds warmly.*) And they sing together with a wonderful sweetness, my friend. (*They shake hands and* FRANZ *looks pleased. He turns to go and is struck with the beauty of the night.*)

FRANZ: Thank you, Herr Pastor. Ach, a snowy night! (*Slowly*) But how peaceful it looks. Like something holy! (*Exits.*) (*The* PASTOR *standing at the window watches him go. Snow falls in large slow flakes. Dusk falls. Stage darkens.*)

MOHR: Peaceful . . . holy . . . like Christmas itself. How beautiful it is. Surely we are closest to our heavenly father at such a time. It *is* a holy time . . . Stille Nacht . . . Heilige Nacht . . . (*He walks back to the table and fingers the paper.*) One more day and it will be Christmas. I wish that we could have given this year's celebration a new song. Something of ourselves should be a gift on every blessed Christmas. (*He is silent a minute.*) What is this Christmas spirit if we do not feed it? We must give, not take. (*He sighs and sits at table.*) Stille Nacht. (*He draws paper to him and idly scratches on it. The room darkens and he goes to the fire for a taper and lights the candle.*) Heilige Nacht! (*He is struck with a thought and there is no sound save the scratch of the pen against the paper as the curtain falls.*)

*   *   *

SCENE 2

SETTING: *The same.*

AT RISE: *It is the next morning. The fire is low and the* PASTOR *is wrapped in an afghan. The candle has burned low.*

The floor is littered with papers. A tray stands on the floor beside the door—the chocolate on it is untouched. The Pastor *is reading over his verses—his cheek rests on his hand. A great stamping outside the door, back. A knock. Enter* Franz *very snowy and bundled to the chin.*

Mohr (*Waving paper and half rising*) : I have it, Franz, I have it.

Franz : Ja, but your good wife tells me that you have stayed all night at your writing. Should we lose you with sickness yet?

Mohr (*Impatiently seizing him by the arm and waving the verses under his eyes*) : Look, all you have to do is write the music. I have yet something new for the Holy Christmas, Franz.

Franz (*Looks perforce—the music is under his nose and he has not been allowed to advance into the room or take off his snowy things*) : My friend, we have only today. Already the program is rehearsed and finished. Could you not let this inspiration go until next year? (*His eyes follow the words and his remarks become less positive.*) Music comes not so quick. No, I could not do it. . . . Ja, wonderful words— Stille Nacht (*Looks at his friend.*) . . . and it was so still . . . Joseph, this is perfect! (*Reads*) "Heilige Nacht" —ja, I know exactly what you mean . . . the snow fell so . . . like music . . . like . . . (*He hums softly to himself. There is now no use. He also has become immersed in the song. He rushes over to the table and impatiently throws off gloves and muffler. He is far away, searching some elusive melody that almost touches the words. Enter* Joseph. *He sees the men bending over the table. He tugs at* Mohr's *coat.*)

Joseph : Papa! Papa! (*Staring at the overcoat on the guest, he forgets his original mission.*) Is Herr Gruber cold? (*No one pays any attention. Remembering his errand.*)

Papa, Mamma says . . . (*His father brushes him off with the abstracted motion he would accord a fly.*) Papa . . . (*He wails.*) And you must eat . . . Mamma says . . .

FRANZ (*Delightedly*): So . . . listen . . . ah . . . (*Hums.*) "Silent Night, Holy Night." (*Familiar tune*) Ja, so goes it . . . calm and peaceful like the great silent snow. The melody must flow with the same silent tread. . . . Ach, I am so mixed up . . . but . . . (*Turning to his friend he says in a different voice.*) We must have music worthy of the words . . . (*He says reverently, slowly emphasizing the sounds of the words themselves.*) simple . . . tender. . . . (*MOHR nods. They bend over the paper again.*)

JOSEPH (*Goes off calling aggrievedly*): Mamma, Mamma . . .

MOHR (*Looking up with delight.*): Lovely! I knew it. (*He hums the melody this time adding the words and going to the second line, "All is calm . . ." FRANZ bends to the paper again but MOHR walks back and forth humming softly. FRAU MOHR enters beaming. She is a nice round little hausfrau, brisk and full of enthusiasm. She is primarily concerned with the comfort of the two men. She is always good-natured, and she is sympathetic with their preoccupation although a little impatient with it. She carries a steaming tray.*)

FRAU MOHR: Well, and wouldn't you take off your coat, Herr Schulemeister? Come, come, you take cold with so much clothes on you. (*She is busily unloading her tray upon the cluttered table.*) Joseph (*She motions him to remove GRUBER's coat.*)—should he take cold he could not sing tomorrow at the festival. So . . . (*She urges the men to the table and tries to press the steaming drink into their hands.*) All night you sit here, Joseph, and when I call you, it's always the same answer, "Ja, in a minute, Mamma." (*She smiles fondly at him.*)

FRANZ (*Setting cup to mouth and as suddenly setting it down.*): I have it! The whole melody comes to me . . . clear . . .

(*Both men rise from the table. The food is untouched. He lifts the paper.* FRAU MOHR *sets her hands on her hips. She surveys the food and then the absorbed men. She sighs and gathers up the dishes.*) See, Joseph! (*He hums halfway through the first verse. The men sing together*:)

> Silent Night, Holy Night
> All is calm, all is bright . . .

(FRAU MOHR, *her dishes on a tray, stops on her way out. She is struck with the song.*)

FRAU MOHR (*Wondering*): Ach, but it is beautiful. . . . (*Exits. The men bend over the table, absorbed. The lights dim. The curtain closes.*)

* * *

SCENE 3

SETTING: *The same, at twilight.*

AT RISE: *The lamps are lighted. The* PASTOR *is stretched out before the fire, asleep, his head sunk on his chest.* FRANZ, *his hair wildly awry, rises from the table with a paper in his hand.*

FRANZ: It is finished. Give me the cup of chocolate.

MOHR (*Awakening with a start*): Ach, ja . . . chocolate, of course. I knew you would do it. (*Crosses to door and calls.*) Mamma! Could we have now a hot drink? (*To his friend*) She comes quickly. (*Clasps* FRANZ's *hand and says with emotion*) Ach, Franz, this Christmas, we truly give. A song written so truly from our hearts, in the beauty and silence of this peaceful snow, is a gift from the village. (*His voice trembles.*) Surely no greater love cometh to the dear Jesus than we pour out to him in this song, through the voices of our young people tomorrow night.

FRANZ (*Tired, but gratified*): I wrote as you and this blessed Christmas time made me feel. I long now to hear it coming mightily forth from the organ. It is so easy that the young people can learn it should they only hear it once. We give it to the organist to learn tonight when he comes tuning the organ. We make some copies, give each singer the words . . . behold a new thing on the program!

FRAU MOHR (*Entering with tray again.*): So . . . now we have time once for eating! All day yet! Tch, tch. . . . Dear to the heart must be such a song! (*She bustles about, giving them food.*)

MOHR: Ach, but this song is a gift to Christmas from our grateful hearts, eh Franz? (*They raise chocolate cups in mild toast to each other. There is a knock. Enter the* ORGANIST.)

ORGANIST: How peaceful you look here. I come to put the organ in shape for tomorrow's program. A wonderful event for the village, this concert, Herr Pastor.

MOHR: And this year . . . a new song for the Christkind.

FRAU MOHR: Franz has just finished the music.

FRANZ: All night the Herr Pastor wrote the words. (*He holds the paper. They crowd around him. They form a pretty tableau in the candlelight which the good* FRAU *holds that they may see the words. They sing the first verse following* FRANZ's *strong voice. Then the entire song.*)

ORGANIST: But this is beautiful! I get to my organ. At once I must try it over. Ach, it is of the heart!

FRANZ: Take it, take it, man. Learn it. Get the melody, and the voices can pick it up easily. (*Exit the* ORGANIST.)

FRAU MOHR (*As she talks* FRANZ *hums the melody in a fine rich bass.*): Such a fine organist. And about the organ, so careful. Always in perfect tune. No wonder they come from far and wide for our Christmas concert.

FRANZ: Now maybe they come to see the four beautiful

daughters who sing so heavenly together. No? (*He chuckles.*)

FRAU MOHR: The organist's daughters? Really, Herr Gruber. (*They laugh pleasantly.*)

MOHR: Ach, but they can make music. I feel it in my heart when they sing. The whole village can follow them.

JOSEPH (*Entering*): Mamma . . . Mamma . . . (*He runs to her and buries his face in her apron. The adults look at each other startled. Wailing*) The organ . . . (ORGANIST *enters in dismay.*)

ORGANIST: Herr Pastor—the organ—it is broken—

FRAU MOHR: Broken! It cannot happen so to us!

FRANZ: Courage! The concert goes forward. Perfectly is my chorus trained. Perfectly they know the program. We go straight on with these concert. Ach, that this should happen to my Christmas concert!

FRAU MOHR (*Puts her arm around the* PASTOR *who has sunk into the chair*): The song . . . *his* song . . . you cannot sing that!

CURTAIN

* * *

SCENE 4

SETTING: *The platform of the village church on Christmas, 1818. The scene begins before the opening of the curtain. Four girls come out front and talk before the curtain. They are the* ORGANIST'S *daughters. Their father is down front, off stage seated at the piano or organ. He is still attempting to make it work.* FIRST DAUGHTER *enters.*

FIRST DAUGHTER: Papa, they are bringing in the chairs. Soon the platform will be in readiness. See, it does not matter that the organ will not play.

SECOND DAUGHTER (*Entering*) : Papa, do not worry. And we have the song. It runs through my head all the time. Ah beautiful.

THIRD AND FOURTH DAUGHTERS (*Running in together*) : The stage is ready. Come up here. Soon the people will be here. Look they are coming. (*Points to back of audience.*)

FIRST DAUGHTER: Ah, the melody. It sang in my ears the whole night through. What a gift from the dear Pastor.

ORGANIST (*Climbing up on the stage*) : Ah, what a catastrophe that the organ should break on this day of days.

THIRD DAUGHTER: And I am glad. Perhaps otherwise you would not have asked us to learn this beautiful song. Already it has brought me pleasure. It lives.

ORGANIST: Ach, the ways of the Lord are inscrutable. (*They press the curtains apart and enter. There is a noise of people settling in chairs. Sound of music. The curtain opens. The singers are seated. The* PASTOR *and* FRANZ *are there. The* ORGANIST *is seated in a corner and his four lovely daughters are seated by him. They are singing, and it is the last of a Christmas hymn.* FRANZ *steps forward and addresses the audience. The chorus behind him listen, too.*)

FRANZ: My good people, the beloved carols have all been sung. I for one did not miss the organ, for your voices were raised in such fine beauty that an immortal organ of a people's grateful love played here tonight. And now we have one more song. It is not on your program, but you will find the words written on a slip of paper which has been passed to each of you. It is a Christmas song written by our beloved Herr Pastor and it comes from his heart. It is a Christmas gift. We cannot play the music, dear friends, but we have an organ of our own making. (*The four girls move center. They are dressed in white and they each hold a slender taper. In the still room they sing softly and in harmony and for the first time publicly:*)

"Silent Night, Holy Night,
All is calm, all is bright," (etc.)
(*The* ORGANIST *hurries forward wiping his eyes.*)
ORGANIST (*To audience*): Sing the next two verses with them.
The music you must already know. (*The audience rises.*
HERR GRUBER *on one side and the* ORGANIST *on the other
lead them. Cast and audience unite in this closing song and
on the last words, the curtain closes.*)

THE END

Santa Goes to Town

by Marjorie Paradis

Characters

MIDGE BENNETT
SPRAT DAVIS
CABBAGE SHAW
UNA FULTON
CLARABELLE PARTRIDGE
HONEY EMERSON
} *pupils at Duncan Hall*

MISS McGILL, *headmistress at Duncan Hall*
KATIE MURPHY, *maid*
TESSIE MURPHY, KATIE'S *daughter*
MISS SHARP, *housekeeper at Duncan Hall*

TIME: *Early afternoon a few days before Christmas*
SETTING: *The dressing room back of the Assembly in Duncan Hall, a boarding school for girls.*
AT RISE: *In the distance comes the faint sound of "Away in a manger . . ."*
UNA, CABBAGE, BELLE and MIDGE *are folding costumes.*

UNA (*Holds up a ballet skirt and points a toe of her scuffy saddle shoe*): I'm not saying it because I was in it, but without the least prejudice, I'm positive "Santa Goes to Town" was the best show ever given by Duncan Hall.

MIDGE: In all its sixty-two years. You have a swell memory. (*General laugh. SPRAT enters.*)

SPRAT: Sorry to be late. (*Sarcastically*) I do hope you girls haven't put away my costume.

UNA: Darling we were about to fight and die for the privilege. I was just saying that our show last night wasn't so punk.

SPRAT: You're telling me? It was a knockout. (UNA *swells with pride.*) Never, never did we have a jollier, robuster, sweller Santa. (UNA *shows her disappointment and goes on packing her dancing costume.*)

MIDGE (*Who has been tucking a Santa Claus costume into a big box, holds up the red cap to which is attached a ruddy false face*): No credit to me. The style in faces is good this year.

UNA (*Imitating a shrill voice*): Be careful. Remember that costume has been hired at great expense to the school. (*Another laugh.*)

BELLE: Poor Miss Sharp. I *can't* help feeling sorry for her.

UNA: Sorry for that old sour-puss? She's the biggest crank on earth.

BELLE: I know, but maybe we'd be cranky, too, if we were nothing but a poor old housekeeper.

UNA: She's not so old, and she's not so poor, but she's plenty cranky. I think she likes people to be unhappy.

CABBAGE: She ought to like me. I'm feeling sad, with the show over.

HONEY (*A pretty girl, enters drearily*): Isn't the day after a letdown!

CABBAGE: That's what I was saying. But you have your carols tonight.

HONEY: Yes—just left the rehearsal. (*Sighs*) Last night was such fun. (*Holds up a bedraggled piece of paper muslin*) Imagine! I wore that and thought I looked divine!

MIDGE: Hold everything, girls. As chairman of the refreshments last night, I think I know how to cut the gloom. If I'm not mistaken, there were some doughnuts... (*Opens closet door, second to right, and takes out a greasy baker's box*) Yes!

SPRAT: Whoopie!

BELLE: I can't say I'm hungry and they're awful for the complexion but—(*Girls help themselves.*)

MIDGE: Let's give the rest to Katie for poor little Tessie. Wasn't it the limit she couldn't stay up and see our show!

UNA: A tragedy, that's what it was. The doctor's a brute making her go to the hospital two days before Christmas.

MIDGE: But if the operation's a success, it'll be the best kind of a Christmas present.

CABBAGE: Katie looks as if she's having the operation.

SPRAT: Bet she wishes she were—mothers are like that.

BELLE: We've got all those nice presents for Tessie. I had to wire for more money from Papa for the doll I bought.

HONEY (*Who is near the door*): Sh-h, here comes Katie.

UNA (*To cover pause*): Yes, girls, I reiterate—that was no ham performance we put on.

KATIE (*A pleasing young maid in uniform. Her eyes are red, her manner depressed. She carries a broom, mop and carpet-sweeper. When she speaks it is with a brogue*): Am I too early to be sweepin' up the place?

MIDGE: We'll be out of here in six jiffies, Katie. (*Hurriedly stuffs red breeches into box.*)

KATIE: Miss Sharp said to tell you, Miss Midge, to be careful of the costume.

MIDGE (*Sighs*): Where have I heard that before?

SPRAT (*Passes doughnut box to* KATIE); Have one. They're not too stale.

KATIE: Thank you, miss.

SPRAT: Could you take the other two to Tessie?

KATIE (*Doubtfully*): The doctor said to be a little careful of her diet. on account of the anesthetic, but . . . I guess a couple of nice doughnuts . . .

MIDGE: Don't look so sad, Katie. This is an operation to end all operations.

KATIE (*Nods*) : That's what the doctor says.

MIDGE: Of course. Next thing you know she'll be doing the jig.

KATIE: The little darlin', I keep hopin' so. It near broke her heart last night not to see Santa Claus.

MIDGE: Me, too. I felt awful about it. (*Faces the other girls*) Oh, girls, why didn't I think! I could have dashed over to Katie's room last night before the show!

BELLE: And taken our presents in the pack.

KATIE: It sure would have been grand. She's that daft about you, Miss Midge.

MIDGE: We could do it now! I could get into the costume and stage a little one-man show for her.

SPRAT: Bully idea!

CABBAGE: Swell.

KATIE: Could you really? Ever since she heard Miss Midge was to be Santa she's been daft to see her.

MIDGE: We've got to be snappy, girls.

KATIE (*Drops broom and dashes, calling back*): I'll run on ahead!

MIDGE (*Pulls out costume and holds up pack*) : Get your presents, girls—Cabbage bring mine, will you—on my bookcase—a scrap book—wrapped in red paper.

SPRAT: And Honey, will you bring mine—the talking doll—I hate to give it up—I'll help Midge dress.

MIDGE: And what ever you do, avoid Sour Puss. (*Exit* UNA, CABBAGE, HONEY, *and* BELLE. MIDGE *with* SPRAT'S *help is getting into the Santa costume.*)

SPRAT: Takes you, Midge. You're the grandest little fix-it-upper. (*A severe looking woman in hat and coat, wearing spectacles, enters and speaks sharply.*)

MISS SHARP: What's this? What's going on here?

MIDGE: Oh, Miss Sharp, we've thought of the most wonderful

plan! Poor little Tessie couldn't get to the show, so I'm taking her our presents dressed up like Santa.

MISS SHARP: No, you're not. Indeed, no!

SPRAT: Why, Miss . . .

MISS SHARP: I thought I impressed on you the necessity of getting that costume back intact. I'm personally responsible for it.

MIDGE: But I'll be careful.

MISS SHARP (*Shakes her head*): Emphatically, no. Take it right off. Really, Midge, I'm surprised and disappointed. The president of the student council shouldn't need checking up.

SPRAT: Miss Sharp, if I agreed to pay for any damages—

MISS SHARP: I'm sorry, Jacqueline, but you don't enter into this transaction at all. I rented the costume and said I would be responsible for its return in good condition. Hurry, Margaret, I'm expecting my nephew any minute and I want to tie this up myself. (MIDGE *slowly gets out of the costume.*)

SPRAT: Oh—oh, I think it's just too—too mean! (*Dashes out of the room crying.*)

MISS SHARP: Where's the list? Here it is. (*Picks up paper and pats box, checking off items.* MIDGE *is hanging up costumes*) Katie is a very lucky girl. Few maids have had so much done for them. The trustees are paying all expenses of the operation. (*Puts cover on box and ties it up*) There. Now can I trust you to return it?

MIDGE (*Politely, but coldly*): Yes, Miss Sharp.

MISS SHARP: Take your little presents to Tessie—she'll enjoy them just as much without the costume. And if I don't see you again—a Merry Christmas.

MIDGE: Thank you, Miss Sharp.

MISS SHARP: Good-bye. (*Exits.* MIDGE *left alone makes a face at her exit, then slowly goes on with her picking up.*)

BELLE (*Hurries in other door with a beautifully dressed doll*):
I just escaped the ogre. She going somewhere—Look, Midge,
isn't this doll an utter dream?

MIDGE: Yes—you showed me when you got it. Belle, she's put
the kibosh on the whole idea. Shot the works when she came
in here and found me dressing.

BELLE: Miss Sharp? (MIDGE *nods*) Oh, isn't that too bad. But
we're giving Tessie such nice things it won't matter so much.

MIDGE: Of course it matters terribly. And the rest of us aren't
handing out our presents unwrapped. It isn't Christmas yet.
Tessie was to look forward to opening them after the operation. I'm awfully disappointed. It's the smallest, meanest
. . . (CABBAGE *and* HONEY *come in with two packages,* UNA
with one. MIDGE *turns to them*) It's all off, girls. She found
out and won't let us. There's the costume. (*Kicks the box.*)

CABBAGE: Honestly?

HONEY: Any wonder we call her Sour Puss!

BELLE: I suppose she has a certain responsibility.

MIDGE: Responsibility my foot. And Katie's gone to tell Tessie!

BELLE: We can give her the doll now as a consolation prize.

CABBAGE: I suppose that would be something.

KATIE (*Comes in beaming*): I got her sittin' up in her wheelchair waitin'.

MIDGE (*Looks helplessly at the other girls*): Oh, Katie . . . we
can't. Miss Sharp . . . it is an expensive costume and she's
responsible . . . not that I would have hurt it . . . but she's
afraid I might.

KATIE: But—but I told her . . . and the eyes on her—like
saucers!

MIDGE: I know. I could cry—I almost am. Sprat has gone off
to weep. But, Katie, we can't do anything about it.

BELLE: I bought this beautiful doll for her, Katie. Suppose I
take it to her and explain—

KATIE (*Shakes her head and wipes her eyes with her apron string*): She'll be that disappointed . . .

BELLE: But when she sees the doll . . .

KATIE: I'm afraid she wouldn't even have the politeness to be thankin' you, Miss Belle. No. I have to tell her, poor little thing. If Miss Sharp had ever been a mother, she wouldn't have been so cruel. (*Exits, wiping her eyes.*)

UNA: If Sharpie was a mother she'd have the Great Stone Face for a child. (*She goes over to the window and looks out.*) There goes Sour Puss. I pity her nephew.

HONEY: I have to leave for carol rehearsal. (*Exits.*)

UNA: Let's all go down to the village with Midge while she returns the precious costume, and drown our grief in an ice cream cone.

CABBAGE: Let's. (*Looks in box*) One apiece.

UNA (*Dramatically*):
"Time's corrosive dewdrop eats
    The giant warrior to a crust . . ."
(*Puts doughnut on her finger like a ring and nibbles it.*)

MISS McGILL (*Headmistress enters. A handsome, cheerful woman*): My, my, how spick and span!

CABBAGE: Miss McGill, we have some presents here for poor little Tessie. Might Midge put on the Santa Claus costume and give them to her? (MIDGE *shakes her head at* CABBAGE.)

MISS McGILL: Why, that's a splendid idea.

MIDGE (*Hesitates, then speaks up with obvious effort*): If we'd only come to you first. Miss Sharp says "no."

MISS McGILL: In that case, of course . . . (*Shakes a finger jokingly at* CABBAGE) Young lady, you know better.

CABBAGE: You're the headmistress.

MISS McGILL: But that doesn't mean going over the head of our housekeeper. Miss Sharp undoubtedly had a very good reason. (*In the distance is heard the carol practice singing*

"Joy to the world, The Lord is come . . .") Listen! It always gives me a thrill!

KATIE (*Dashes in. Sees* MISS MCGILL *and pauses, frightened*): Oh . . . excuse me, Miss McGill.

MISS MCGILL: Anything I can do for you, Katie?

KATIE: No, Miss McGill, I've come after my broom and things. (*Begins picking them up.*)

MISS MCGILL: Tessie goes to the hospital this evening?

KATIE (*Holds back tears with difficulty*): Yes'm.

MISS MCGILL (*Pats her shoulder*): We're all praying for her, Katie. This time the surgeon's sure it'll be a success. I'll be with you during the operation, Katie.

KATIE: Thank you, Miss McGill.

MISS MCGILL: Courage. (*Nods to the girl, touches at her own eyes and goes out.*)

KATIE: If she isn't just the salt of the earth!

MIDGE: She's a knock-out.

UNA: Rather different from some others around here.

KATIE: That's what I came to tell you. I saw Miss Sharp goin' off in a car. And just before she left, she said, "Katie, I've been thinkin' about that Santa Claus business. If you'd wheel Tessie down to the dressin' room, it wouldn't do any harm for Miss Midge to put on the suit for just a few minutes." That's what she said!

UNA: Hurrah! She *has* a heart!

CABBAGE: Well, it is "Joy to the world!" Come on, Midge, make it snappy. (*Yanks at cord on costume box.*)

KATIE: Shall I be fetchin' Tessie?

MIDGE (*Again hauling out the uniform*): Give me a little time. It won't take you a second to get her here.

UNA: Knock on the door three times and wait'll we say "Enter."

KATIE: Sure, I'll do that. (*Exits.*)

CABBAGE: You don't seem as delighted as you were miserable, Midge.

MIDGE (*Kicking off saddle shoes and putting on boots*): Delighted! Of course, I am. Just the same that message of Katie's smelt a little fishy. Miss Sharp never speaks of me as Midge.

UNA: Fish, foul or good red herring, what's the dif? She'll never be any the wiser. Here get into this. (*Holds coat.*)

MIDGE: It isn't up to me to question Katie's truthfulness.

CABBAGE: I'll pack the presents. (*Puts wrapped boxes in bag. To* BELLE) You're determined to hand out your own gift?

BELLE: Well—I'd like to. (*Has seated doll in a conspicuous place.*)

MIDGE: Someone better find Sprat.

BELLE: I'll look. Don't let Tessie in until I get back. (*Exits right door.*)

CABBAGE: Say, I'd better fetch the mocking-bird. She'll want to be in this. (*Exit* CABBAGE *right.*)

MIDGE: I hope Belle can find Sprat.

SPRAT (*Calls from off stage*): Hi, Midge . . .

MIDGE: There she is! (*Dashes out left door shouting*) Good news, Sprat! The best—look!

UNA (*Left alone, picks up doll and begins undressing it*): Hum . . . buttons . . . snaps . . . and hooks and eyes!

BELLE (*Returning*): Sprat isn't in her room.

UNA: No, she just called Midge.

BELLE: For heaven's sake what have you done to the doll?

UNA: Wanted to see if she was wearing underwear.

BELLE: Let me have her. (*She takes the doll,*) Where's everybody?

UNA: Cabbage's gone for Honey, and Midge went to speak to Sprat. (MIDGE *enters*) Isn't Sprat coming?

MIDGE: Later. She got involved in something or other. (*Picks up head piece*) She doesn't want us to wait for her.

UNA: And you thought she was so heartbroken. Fickleness, thy name is woman. (CABBAGE *and* HONEY *return.*)

CABBAGE: Katie come yet?

UNA: Nope. (*Pushes chairs in a semicircle.*) We'll sit here with Katie and the wheelchair in the center. You'd better hide somewhere, Midge, and come out—it's more effective.

MIDGE: I'll be back of the screen.

UNA: And what'll you do when you come out? You ought to have a little line to talk.

CABBAGE: Trust Midge.

MIDGE (*Picks up sleigh bells and bag*): I'll do the best I can.

BELLE: Midge-e—(*Speaks slowly, unwillingly.*)

MIDGE: Uh?

BELLE: I was thinking, Midge, maybe—(*Gets up and hands over the doll*) Here. You give it to her. She might like it better. (HONEY, CABBAGE *and* UNA *applaud.*)

CABBAGE: Good for you.

UNA: Belle, you have a real dramatic instinct. Remember, girls, we don't know anything about the presents. They've come from the North Pole. (*Three knocks on the door*) There they are.

MIDGE: Wait . . . (*Tiptoes to screen and whispers*) All right.

UNA: Who's there?

KATIE: Me and Tess.

UNA: Enter! (*Flings open the door, and* KATIE *wheels in a small girl in an invalid's chair*) Welcome, Tessie.

CABBAGE: Why, Tessie, it's nice to have you with us.

HONEY: We're expecting a very important visitor!

TESSIE: I wanna see Santa Claus! Where's Santa Claus?

UNA: Patience, child. He promised to be here and he never breaks a promise. (*A jingle of bells back of screen.*)

MIDGE (*Comes out and says in a deep voice*): Welcome! Welcome everyone. Well, well, if here isn't little Tessie!

TESSIE: Hello, Miss Midge. I know you. Take off your false face.

MIDGE: Dear, dear, dear, what a thing to say!

KATIE: Ah, now, Tessie, can't you see it's old Santa himself?

TESSIE: It's Miss Midge. There's no Santa Claus. It's only people dressed up.

MIDGE: I'm the spirit of Christmas. A fairy like Peter Pan.

TESSIE: That's what little children believe. I'm big . . . I'm 'most eight.

MIDGE: I'm glad I came to this school. Here's a girl who needs to learn that there *are* fairies! (*Sets down pack*) If I were to give you a big beautiful doll would you think I was a fairy? (*Brings out* BELLE's *gift.*)

TESSIE: Oh-h-h! For me!

KATIE: Never did I see anythin' so grand!

TESSIE (*Hugs doll*): Thanks ever so much, Miss Midge.

MIDGE: Don't thank me. I only fetched it.

TESSIE (*Turns to the girls*): Oh, thanks.

BELLE: You're welcome.

MIDGE (*Shakes her head*): I don't seem to be getting much co-operation in proving I'm a fairy. Little girl, suppose I were to disappear before your very eyes, then would you believe I'm Old St. Nick?

TESSIE (*Pauses, then nods*): But you couldn't.

MIDGE: On the contrary, I believe I could. (*Pointing to door*) What's that door open to?

KATIE: A closet.

MIDGE: No other exit? No other way of getting out?

KATIE: None, Mr. Santa.

MIDGE: Wheel Tessie over and let her see for herself. (KATIE *obeys.*)

HONEY (*To* MIDGE *in a whisper*): What are you planning to do?

MIDGE (*Loud and boastfully*): I'm going to do a disappearing act—disappear and reappear.

TESSIE: Really? (*Looks in the closet*) It's just a closet.

MIDGE: Watch me carefully, ladies. The closer you watch the less you'll see (KATIE *wheels* TESSIE *back to her place in the center.*) I step into the closet . . . (*Crosses to closet*) When I shut the door I'll give a loud cough so you'll know I'm really there—then— But wait and see. (*Closes herself in closet and coughs. Instantly there is a jangle of bells to the left, the door is flung open to the hall on left and there stands Santa. It is* SPRAT *dressed in an identical suit. She struts into the room and copies* MIDGE'S *deep bellow.*)

SPRAT: What did I tell you!

KATIE: Saints be praised! (*There is a stir of surprise among the girls.*)

TESSIE: Do it again!

SPRAT: Anything to oblige. This time, to make it harder, I'll reverse the departure. (*Exits right door, coughs and* MIDGE *steps out of closet.*)

MIDGE: Here I am.

CABBAGE: I'll be jiggered.

TESSIE: Mama, how does he do it?

KATIE: Sure, don't be askin' me. There's lots of wonders in heaven and earth we don't know the half of. (*Kisses* TESSIE *in a burst of feeling and as she straightens she glances out the window. Then she stares, and looks around frightened*) Miss Sharp, comin' back. (*Obviously ill at ease.*) I'm sorry, but we can't be stayin' much longer.

TESSIE: I wanna stay, mama. I wanna stay all night.

MIDGE: Before you go, Tessie, I want you to know what splendid things I heard about you. They say you're a fine brave girl.

TESSIE: But I'm goin' to the hospital tonight and I don't wanna. I wanna stay here with you.

KATIE: Ah, darlin', Santa's got to go see other children . . .

MIDGE: First, though, I want you to be happy. You'd like to run and skip and jump rope, wouldn't you?

TESSIE: Sure, but—

MIDGE: Isn't it worth while going through something that isn't so nice? (KATIE *goes to hall door right and opens it a crack.*)

TESSIE (*Nods and tries not to cry*): Only I've been to the hospital before and I don't wanna go again.

MIDGE: This time it'll be different. Everything's nicer Christmas time. (*Girls gather about her.*)

TESSIE: It's nicer here.

MIDGE: You're going to be brave, aren't you? (TESSIE *nods*) Of course you are. Pull down your vest and bear it like a man. (TESSIE *tries to laugh.*)

CABBAGE: I have an idea . . .

TESSIE: What is it?

CABBAGE: Maybe Santa has something in his pack for you!

HONEY: Something you could open in the hospital.

MIDGE: That I have. A number of big packages.

TESSIE: How many?

MIDGE (*Looks in bag and counts aloud as she takes them out*): One, two, three, four, five!

BELLE: And you already have the beautiful doll. (KATIE *looks worried. Goes to door and listens.*)

MIDGE: How about it, young lady? Think these would help you be brave and happy?

TESSIE: Yes!

MIDGE: Good!

UNA: Fine. That's the idea. (*The presents are laid on* TESSIE'S *knee.* KATIE *comes running back and begins wheeling the chair.*)

KATIE: Saints forgive me—Miss Sharp! I'll lose m' job if she knows. (*Exits.*)

UNA: So-ooo, there is something rotten in the state of Denmark!

MIDGE: Keep her out, girls . . . hurry. (*Exit four girls.* MIDGE *sits down and pulls at boot. Enter* MISS SHARP.)

MISS SHARP: Margaret Bennett! (*Looks at her for a long moment*) What have you to say for yourself?

MIDGE: N-nothing.

MISS SHARP: There's nothing you can say. You realize this is rank disobedience?

MIDGE: Yes, it must seem so.

MISS SHARP: Seem? There's no seem about it. It *is.* You thought I would be away, didn't you? (MIDGE *nods*) This is the most dishonest—in fact the first really dishonest thing I've ever known you to do. You've been in lots of scrapes, I know, but I call this absolutely sneaky.

MIDGE: I haven't hurt the suit.

MISS SHARP: The suit has become a minor matter. This is a question of principle. I shall be obliged to take it up with Miss McGill.

MIDGE: Oh, please don't. I'll apologize to you. I'll . . .

MISS SHARP: Of what use an apology after you've done exactly as you chose, regardless of my strict orders? No, this is a case for Miss McGill. You will wait here, if you please, exactly as you are. (*Walks out with great dignity.*)

MIDGE: Ah-h-h (*Sighs aloud, and walks back and forth.*)

CABBAGE (*Sneaks in*): Where's old Sour Puss?

MIDGE: Gone for Miss McGill.

CABBAGE: I suppose you can't tell on Katie?

MIDGE (*Shakes head*): And don't you girls. It would cost her her job.

CABBAGE: We won't—but it's a punk break. Where's Sprat? She always has good ideas. I'll find her. (*Hurries off, bumping into* HONEY, *who is just coming in*) Honey, where's Sprat?

HONEY: Search me. (*Goes over to* MIDGE) We're awfully

sorry. She was a whirlwind. We couldn't hold her back. We'll all stand with you if it'll help.

MIDGE (*Who has been pacing the room thoughtfully*): It won't. Stay here just a minute, will you. If she returns, say I'll be right back. (*Dashes out the left hand door.*)

HONEY (*Hears choir practicing and joins them*):
"Above thy deep and dreamless sleep
The silent stars go by . . ." (*Sighs.*)

SPRAT (*Enters in Santa costume in a booming voice*): Thank you, my child. You may go now. Look in your stocking Christmas morning. I'll take my medicine alone.

HONEY: You're grand, Midge. It'll come out all right some-how—is there anything I can do?

SPRAT: Find Sprat.

HONEY: I'll do my best. (*Exit.* SPRAT *stands, hands on hips, nonchalantly whistling: "Is it true what they say about Dixie."* MISS SHARP *enters followed by* MISS McGILL.)

MISS SHARP: It's really a pity, Miss McGill, with all you have to do, to take this matter up with you, but it's nothing less than insubordination. (SANTA *stands bowed and humble.*)

MISS McGILL: Yes. (*Sighs*) I'm more than a little surprised myself. You see, Miss Sharp, we went over this a few minutes ago and I supposed the whole matter was settled. Of course the motive was commendable . . .

MISS SHARP: Oh, yes, the motive was all right. I'm sure we all do what we can for poor little Tessie. As a matter of fact, I came back because I had forgotten my gift for the child. But I don't consider there was any excuse for flagrant defiance.

MISS McGILL: Maybe we needn't put it quite as strongly as that, but I'm afraid it is rather serious. (*Puts her hand on* SANTA's *shoulder.*) What have you to say for yourself?

SPRAT (*Head bowed, answers in a choked whisper*): Nothing —only I thought Tessie would like it.

MISS SHARP: That's just going in circles.

MISS MCGILL: Yes, so it is. (*Sighs*) I hate to say there will be no more Christmas festivities for you—but I'll have to. And what I hate worse is chalking down your discredit. Of course you know the trustees take a great interest in scholarship girls and they're going to feel awfully let down.

SPRAT: I don't see why.

MISS SHARP: You don't see why—when they chose you!

MISS MCGILL (*Puts on her oxford glasses and stares through the open door*): Miss Sharp—these are my reading glasses—but look down the hall. Isn't it . . .

MISS SHARP (*Stares in amazement*): It—it certainly *is!* (*Looks at* SANTA) I'm all confused.

MIDGE (*Enters carrying a large box*): I beg your pardon. Is it all right if I take the costume back now?

MISS SHARP: Costume? You mean this? (*Thumbs toward* SANTA)

MIDGE: No. The one the school hired. (*Has set down box*) It's all here, mittens, boots and all.

MISS SHARP: But who . . . who . . .

MISS MCGILL: Well, Santa, suppose you unmask.

SPRAT (*Pulls off head piece and stands, hot and grinning*): I dashed down to the costumers and hired this myself.

MISS MCGILL (*Laughs delightedly*): April fool on us. And a very pleasant joke it is, too. I hope, Sprat, you won't sue the school for a false arrest.

MISS SHARP (*Has pried into the box and admits grudgingly*): Yes, it all seems to be here.

MISS MCGILL: That was quite unnecessary, Miss Sharp. No one ever need check up on Midge. She's the soul of honor. (MIDGE *bites her lip and looks away.*)

MISS SHARP: I'm sorry. I apologize. But I feel so confused. I could swear it was Margaret's voice . . . I must have been wrong.

Miss McGill: You expected it to be hers—that's why you thought it was. I apologize, too, Midge, for all the unhappy thoughts I entertained about you.

Midge: Oh you mustn't apologize to me, Miss McGill. I'm not what you think. Miss Sharp is right. I did wear the suit. We both dressed up as Santa Claus.

Sprat: When I got back here with the costume Midge was already dressed, so we pulled a stunt. We had a signal— Midge hid and coughed and I popped out of a different place.

Midge: And after I was caught Sprat changed places with me.

Miss Sharp: Then we're back where we were in the first place and it was defiant disobedience.

Miss McGill: One thing I don't understand. Sprat went for another costume because Midge would not disobey your instructions, Miss Sharp. (*Turns to* Midge) What made you change your mind?

Midge: I—it was—I knew I wouldn't hurt the costume.

Miss McGill: Not a good reason, Midge.

Una (*Dashes in*): It isn't our fault, Midge. We did our best. She would come. (Katie *enters followed by* Cabbage, Honey *and* Belle.)

Katie: She's not to blame, Miss McGill. Though it costs me my job, good and all as you've been to me, I'm at fault— saints forgive me! I lied.

Miss McGill: Not so fast. Katie.

Katie: It was like this. I promised Tessie that she'd see Santa himself—then I hear Miss Sharp won't have any such nonsense. When a little one's sick, mothers aren't always dependable. I couldn't bear to disappoint the darlin', so in I came and said that Miss Sharp changed her mind.

Miss McGill: And I am sure she would have, had she realized what it meant to Tessie; isn't that so, Miss Sharp?

Miss Sharp: Well, of course I'm human.

Katie: That's how it was, and now even if I lose my place I

won't mind, Tess is that happy. (*Looks at* Miss McGill (*Pleadingly*) Oh, but I would mind losin' my job. It's grand in this here school. Everyone is so good to me. Could you forgive me if I was to get on m' knees . . .

Miss McGill: That's not necessary, Katie. I agree with you. It is a grand school! And I'm proud of your bravery, Katie. Just as proud of you as I am of Midge. (*Gives a hand to each. Choir off sings "Holy night . . .")

Honey (*Joins the song*): "Peaceful night."

All: "All is calm all is bright!" (*Curtain falls.*)

THE END

The Perfect Gift

by H. Graham Du Bois

Characters

DAVID, *a stable-boy*	SOLDIER
RUTH, *the Innkeeper's daughter*	MERCHANT
THE INNKEEPER	THREE SHEPHERDS
LADY	THREE WISE MEN

TIME: *The early morning of Christ's birth.*

SETTING: *The court before the inn at Bethlehem.*

BEFORE RISE: *Voices in the distance, offstage, singing a Christmas hymn. The singing grows louder as the curtain rises.*

AT RISE: DAVID *is kneeling near bench, his back to the audience, his hands folded, in an attitude of devotion, listening to the singing.* RUTH *enters and stands looking in amazement at* DAVID. *At the conclusion of the song* DAVID *rises, sits on bench, and resumes the carving of a wooden figure.* RUTH *approaches bench.*

RUTH: Why were you kneeling like that?

DAVID: I was listening to the song.

RUTH: What song?

DAVID: The song in the stable.

RUTH: There was no song in the stable. What you heard was only that rich woman singing her child to sleep.

DAVID: It was the angels' song I heard.

RUTH: The angels' song? Don't be foolish, David. If there had been a song in the stable, I would have heard it.

67

DAVID: You will hear it soon enough, little girl. All people like you will hear it.

RUTH (*Sighs*): I suppose I shall never understand you, David. (*Sits beside him and points to object he is carving.*) You have been working on that for two days.

DAVID: I have almost finished now.

RUTH: You do carve beautiful things! What are you making?

DAVID: A present for a king.

RUTH: Why, you silly boy! You will never see a king.

DAVID: I have seen him.

RUTH: You have seen a king? Where?

DAVID: Here.

RUTH: There is no king here, stupid. Do you mean that soldier in his gorgeous uniform who came last night and took the large room overlooking the yard? He isn't a king. He is only a captain in Herod's army.

DAVID: I don't mean the soldier.

RUTH: The merchant, then? I suppose his fine clothes and his proud manner deceived you. But I tell you he only buys and sells and makes great sums of money.

DAVID: It's not the merchant I mean.

RUTH: Well, it can't be the other guests at the inn—the lawyer or the physician or the—

DAVID: It is none of them.

RUTH: Don't tease me, David. Speak out: where is he?

DAVID: He is in the stable, lying in the manger.

RUTH: A king in a stable! You do but jest, David. You can't mean that old man who came with his wife last night? They were wretchedly poor. I could tell by their clothes. And he was so weak and tired. I saw his arms tremble when he lifted her down from the donkey. She looked so pale and weary. I thought she would faint before he got her into the stable. But surely you can't have mistaken him for a king.

DAVID: He is the father of a king.

RUTH: But he had no son with him. There was only the man and his wife.

DAVID: He was born last night.

RUTH: Not in the stable? You're a strange lad, David. The old soothsayer in the village told me once that you could see into the future. I noticed you when those poor people came. There was a queer, faraway look in your eyes, and your face shone like a light. You seemed so happy to give them your place in the straw of the stable. Was he really born there?

DAVID (*Proudly*): My wretched quarters are the birthplace of a king.

RUTH: Why do you call the child of these poor people a king? I have never seen a king, but Father has. He was at Herod's court once. And he says that kings have mighty armies. Where are this child's armies?

DAVID: He has no armies. He comes to bring peace into the world.

RUTH: And Father says there were always great princes round the throne, and wise counselors and learned interpreters. This babe has none.

DAVID: He needs no interpreters: he will speak a tongue that all men understand. His is the language of love.

RUTH: Father told me once about the celebrations at court when a royal child is born. There are feasts and music and rich gifts. There was nothing like that here, was there? You sat on this bench most of the night. Did you notice anything unusual?

DAVID: There was a kind of glory in the night, the sudden flaming of a single star that left a path of beauty in the dark. And silence fell upon the sleeping world as soft as snow flakes in a winter dawn; and then above the stable roof I heard the gentle rustle of wings and angel voices raised in songs of praise.

RUTH: You *are* a queer boy, David. But I love to hear you talk. The old soothsayer said you were sort of a prophet and that you spoke with a rare gift.

DAVID: I speak only what is in my heart.

RUTH: Do you remember what you told Father when he refused to let that poor couple have a room? You said that he would regret it all his life. I wonder why he wouldn't take them in.

DAVID: Future ages will ask that question.

RUTH: But why didn't he? Was it because of those guests he's expecting? They must be very great people. He said they were on their way to do homage to a king and he hoped they would stop here. You know, he has had those rooms near the garden cleaned each day, and the cook has been preparing his best dishes. But those rooms are only a small part of the inn. Why did he refuse these poor people?

DAVID: He told them there was no room.

RUTH: But the inn was not full when they came. There were many empty rooms.

DAVID: They had no money.

RUTH: Well, after all, that is reason enough. You can't expect Father to take in people who can't pay.

DAVID: They brought what is beyond money and beyond price.

RUTH: I don't believe that he is a king, David. But he is a little child, and I feel sorry for him. He has no playthings. Do you know what? I'm going to give him something. I wonder what he would like?

DAVID: No matter how much or how little you bring, there is only one gift that will make him happy.

RUTH: Only one gift?

DAVID: Only one perfect gift—yourself.

RUTH: I don't know what you mean, David. I think I shall give him that little bronze statue.

DAVID: Not the little figure of a girl your father brought you from Egypt. Why, you have always prized it above everything else.

RUTH: Yes—I can't explain why—but somehow I feel I want him to have it. (*Faint strains of a Christmas hymn offstage.*)

DAVID (*Stopping work and bowing head in an attitude of listening*): I think you will hear them now. Don't you hear the song?

RUTH: I think I do. I—I can't believe it. Listen! The voices are getting clearer. (*The singing grows louder.*)

RUTH: Tell me: why can I hear the singing now?

DAVID: You have let him in; you have found room for him.

RUTH: I—found room? Where?

DAVID: In your heart. All those who receive him there can hear the song. (*Sound of footsteps and voices approaching.*)

RUTH: Hush! (*Lays hand on his arm.*) You'd better go. Somebody's coming. I think it is the lady who brought the little girl. She is very angry with you.

DAVID: I'll take my gift to the king. (*Exit. RUTH follows him to the portal and stands looking after him. Enter LADY, followed by INNKEEPER.*)

INNKEEPER: But I don't understand you, madam. You had the finest room at my inn—large and quiet and comfortable; you had a warm, soft bed. There is no reason why you should not have slept. No guest has ever complained of that room before.

LADY: It wasn't the room, I tell you. It was my little girl; she cried all night.

INNKEEPER: But you must realize, madam, that is not the fault of the inn.

LADY: It is the fault of that impudent stable-boy.

INNKEEPER: You can't mean David? If he has offended you, I will dismiss him at once. What has he done?

LADY: He has insulted me.

INNKEEPER: I hardly see how that is possible, madam; he is not allowed to enter the inn at night.

LADY: It was here in this court. (*Walks to bench and sits.*) When we came last evening, he was sitting on this bench, carving a doll out of a piece of wood. My little girl was fascinated by it. She watched him until I put her to bed. She wanted it more than she has ever wanted anything. She has dolls from many lands, but she said she would be willing to give them all up for this. And when she couldn't have it, she lay awake all night, weeping. She is a delicate child; my physician said I must not cross her in any way.

INNKEEPER: You should have asked him for it, madam.

LADY: I not only asked him for it, I told him I was willing to buy it.

INNKEEPER: And he refused?

LADY: Yes. He said he was making it for a king.

INNKEEPER: For a king? (*Laughs*) You must forgive him, madam. You see (*Taps his forehead*) there's something lacking here.

LADY: I offered him ten pieces of silver.

INNKEEPER: You were far too generous, madam. One would have been more than enough.

LADY: The boy didn't think so. He only shook his head and told me, "There are some things money can't buy."

INNKEEPER: Maybe he was trying to strike even a better bargain. Sometimes, you know, Madam, these feeble-minded people are shrewd.

LADY: I suspected him of that, and so I raised the amount to fifteen, twenty, and even thirty pieces of silver.

INNKEEPER: Thirty pieces of silver! A preposterous sum, madam. What did he say?

LADY: There was a strange, startled expression in his eyes as if he were looking far into the distance. I saw him shudder. He covered his face with his hands, and then he said, "I can't betray my master." (*Rises.*)

INNKEEPER: His master? Why, I'm his master. Thirty pieces of silver, indeed! That's more than he has had in all his miserable life. I shall see that you have the doll, madam. (*Exit* LADY.) Ruth, where is David?

RUTH: In the stable, Father.

INNKEEPER: With those wretched vagrants, I suppose. I should never have consented to their staying. I'll send them on their way as soon as I have attended to David. Please bring him here, Ruth.

RUTH: Yes, Father. (*She exits.* INNKEEPER *goes to bench, picks up some shavings that* DAVID *has left, walks to portal, and throws them into yard, as* SOLDIER *enters.*)

SOLDIER: Innkeeper, I should like a word with you.

INNKEEPER: At your service, sir.

SOLDIER: I have had very little rest at your inn. (*Goes to bench and sits.*)

INNKEEPER: I am surprised. Very few guests have ever made that complaint. Can you tell me why, sir? Did any noise disturb you?

SOLDIER: There was noise enough. That child in the next room wailed all night. But that wouldn't have kept me awake. I'm a soldier; I'm used to noise. There was too much light. I like a room completely dark.

INNKEEPER: You amaze me, sir. Your room looks out on the stable yard, and beyond that are the hills.

SOLDIER: The light I mean was over the stable. It burned like a great torch so that my room was as bright as day. I suppose it is something you use to guide your guests along the road to the inn.

INNKEEPER: Strange! The servants have been given orders to

use only a small lantern at night, and that only when absolutely necessary.

SOLDIER: It was more powerful than a hundred lanterns, I tell you. It kept me awake all night. I paced the floor.

INNKEEPER: I shall investigate at once, sir. I hope you will delay your journey another day. I assure you that you will not be disturbed tonight.

SOLDIER (*Rising*): I cannot risk another night here. I must have my rest. There are stern days ahead for me—long marches and perhaps great battles. I shall leave as soon as I have had something to eat.

INNKEEPER: I shall see that you are served immediately. (*Exit* SOLDIER, *followed by* INNKEEPER, *as* RUTH *and* DAVID *enter*.)

RUTH: Did you really give him the little wooden doll?

DAVID: Yes. I knelt and offered it to his mother. I told her it was all I had.

RUTH: And what did she say?

DAVID: She said, "His gift is great who gives his all away." I wish you could have seen her face when she spoke. More beautiful than the faces one sometimes sees in dreams. And her voice was sweeter than the songs of birds in early spring.

RUTH (*Looking through portal*): Look, David! There are guests arriving. I believe they are the great people Father has been expecting. They look like princes. Let's go and meet them. (*Exit* RUTH *followed by* DAVID. *Enter* MERCHANT. *He walks about court as if looking for somebody. Goes to portal and looks out, then to bench and sits, as* INNKEEPER *enters*.)

MERCHANT: Ah, there you are! I've been looking for you.

INNKEEPER: Good morning, sir. You are up early.

MERCHANT: I've been up for hours.

INNKEEPER: You mean you haven't had a good night's rest?

MERCHANT: I mean that I have had no rest at all. This is the noisiest inn I ever knew. And it was recommended to me as a quiet place!

INNKEEPER: I hope the other guests didn't disturb you.

MERCHANT: Well, of course, there was a child who cried all night, and that soldier next to me who kept pacing the floor; but I should have made out very well if it hadn't been for the shepherds.

INNKEEPER: Shepherds? There are no shepherds here. This is an exclusive inn, sir; we don't admit people of that class. Why, only last night I turned away a man and woman who were not up to our standards.

MERCHANT: I didn't say they were here. They were on the highway—dozens of them.

INNKEEPER: You surely are mistaken, sir. The shepherds are busy in the fields watching their flocks.

MERCHANT: I tell you there were dozens of them on the highway, shouting and singing and dancing. One might have thought they were celebrating some great occasion. I leaned out of my window and called to them to be quiet, but they paid no attention to me. They were silent only after they had entered the stable.

INNKEEPER: The stable? *My* stable? What were they doing there?

MERCHANT: That's a question for you to answer. Here come some of their companions now. Stragglers, evidently. You might ask them. (*Enter three* SHEPHERDS.)

INNKEEPER (*To* SHEPHERDS): What do you want here? You know that you are not allowed at the inn.

FIRST SHEPHERD: We come to seek the child.

INNKEEPER: What child? There is no child here.

SECOND SHEPHERD: The star led us to this place.

INNKEEPER: The star? Nonsense! There were no stars. The night was dark.

SECOND SHEPHERD: There was the biggest star I've ever seer. It shone like a torch above the inn. It lighted all the hills.

MERCHANT: Were you with those rude fellows that came singing along the highway?

THIRD SHEPHERD: We were, but they outran us. We heard the cry of a little lamb that had been lost in the thicket. It had broken its leg, and we stopped to bind it up. It was while we were doing this that we first heard the music and the song.

INNKEEPER: There's been no music and singing here—except what you knaves brought. . . . What is that you hold in your hands?

FIRST SHEPHERD: Gifts for the king.

INNKEEPER: The king? What king?

SECOND SHEPHERD: This child is a king.

INNKEEPER: You simpletons! There is no king here. If there had been, don't you suppose that I would have known it? Don't you suppose that I would have given him the best room in my inn? But pray tell me, what kind of gifts do you plan to give this king of yours?

FIRST SHEPHERD: I brought this big red apple.

SECOND SHEPHERD: I shall give him a handful of nuts.

THIRD SHEPHERD: I have only a few eggs to bring.

INNKEEPER: Fine gifts indeed for a king!

FIRST SHEPHERD: They were all we had to offer him. (*Soft strains of a Christmas hymn, offstage.*)

SECOND SHEPHERD: There's the music again. (*The singing grows louder. The* SHEPHERDS *kneel.* INNKEEPER *and* MERCHANT *watch them in amazement.*)

THIRD SHEPHERD (*As* SHEPHERDS *rise when singing has ceased*): Beautiful! It came from the stable. The child must be there. (*Looking at* INNKEEPER *in surprise*) Why, didn't you hear it?

INNKEEPER: I heard nothing, except the bleating of the animals in the stable. Get along! Take your gifts to the king and

then go back to your flocks. (*Exit* SHEPHERDS. *To* MER-
CHANT) That's the best way to get rid of them, I suppose.
Once they're convinced that there's nothing unusual here,
these superstitious fools will leave us in peace. . . . If you
will only prolong your stay with us, I can promise that you
will find this inn a very restful place.

MERCHANT: I cannot afford to take chances. I shall seek quarters where there is no danger of having my sleep disturbed.
Quiet, restful nights are essential in my business. It takes a
clear, alert mind to drive bargains. I shall be on my way as
soon as I have packed my belongings. (*Exit* MERCHANT.
Enter RUTH.)

RUTH: Father! Quick! Three men on horseback are in the
yard behind the stable. They wear handsome garments and
they have a dozen servants.

INNKEEPER (*Excitedly*): It must be they—the noble guests I've
been expecting. (*Rubbing his hands happily*) Where is
David? Did you tell him that I wanted to see him?

RUTH: Yes, Father; but he had already given his carving to the
baby.

INNKEEPER: The baby? There is a child, then!

RUTH: The dearest little boy you ever saw, Father. And his
parents are so proud and happy. They say that—

INNKEEPER (*Impatiently interrupting*): Enough of this! Tell
David to attend to the guests' horses; and if there is not space
for them, we must send these vagrants on their way. (*Enter*
DAVID) Here's that blockhead now . . . (*To* RUTH) Inform
these gentlemen that our most luxurious rooms are at their
disposal. (*Exit* RUTH. *To* DAVID) Why aren't you taking
care of the horses?

DAVID: What horses, Master?

INNKEEPER: The horses of those gentlemen who just came, you
idiot!

DAVID: The gentlemen are not staying.

INNKEEPER: Not staying? Where are they now?

DAVID: In the stable, presenting their gifts to the child.

INNKEEPER (*Half to himself*) : There's something strange here! First, those shepherds, and now these great gentlemen bringing gifts. . . . Speak up, boy! What kind of gifts?

DAVID: The most costly, Master—gold and frankincense and myrrh. Gifts that one might bring to a mighty ruler—even to Herod, himself. (*Enter* WISE MEN, *followed by* SHEPHERDS *and* RUTH.)

FIRST WISE MAN: A king was your guest last night.

INNKEEPER: A king?

SECOND WISE MAN: Yes, but you didn't find place for him in your inn.

INNKEEPER: Impossible, sir! There must be some mistake. I didn't go to bed until late last night, and I left orders that I was to be called if any important guest arrived.

FIRST WISE MAN: Two important guests arrived.

INNKEEPER: You mean the soldier and the merchant? I can assure you, sir, they had the—

FIRST WISE MAN: I mean a poor, tired old man and a weak, sick woman.

INNKEEPER: Ah, you're speaking of the two with the donkey. They were not the type of guest we entertain here. I told them there was no room at the inn.

THIRD WISE MAN: You mean no room worthy of a king.

INNKEEPER (*Offended*) : I tell you, sir, men of high estate have been my guests—generals and princes and emperors. Herod himself has stopped here.

SECOND WISE MAN: Then there is no excuse.

INNKEEPER: But I didn't recognize them as royal personages; they looked so poor and miserable. How was I to know?

SECOND WISE MAN (*Pointing to* DAVID) : This poor stable-boy knew. He gave up his bed, and his sacrifice transformed a wretched hovel into a palace wherein a king was proud to dwell. These simple shepherds knew. They left their flocks to bring their offerings, and their devotion made their few humble gifts more precious to him than many rubies.

INNKEEPER: You must believe me, sir, there was no room.

THIRD WISE MAN: Why? Wait! I will tell you why. Because your inn was full of little people seeking little things. There was a woman, her heart so warped by selfishness that she was blind to any but her own; there was a merchant who measured all things in terms of profit and loss; there was a soldier whose only thought was of battle and the enslavement of other men. You let these people crowd him out. And while you slept, smug in the thought that your rooms were occupied, a king was born in your stable.

INNKEEPER: A king—born—in my stable?

FIRST WISE MAN: The King of Kings.

INNKEEPER (*Beginning to comprehend*): The King of Kings? (*In awed whisper*) You mean—

FIRST WISE MAN: Yes, that is what I mean.

INNKEEPER: Is there nothing I can do now? Is it too late?

SECOND WISE MAN: It is never too late.

INNKEEPER: Do you mean that I shall have another chance to feed and shelter him? I turned him from my door. He may never pass this way again.

SECOND WISE MAN: He will pass this way again—many, many times. The poor travel this road. Throw open your doors to them. Feed them, give them shelter, and he will always find room at the inn.

INNKEEPER: I pledge my word, I will. (*Pointing to portal*) Look! It is getting light. (*The stage gradually becomes brighter until at the end it is flooded with light.*)

FIRST WISE MAN: The day is breaking. It is the dawn.

DAVID: The dawn! The dawn of a new day! (*Faint strains of*

music of a Christmas hymn, offstage.) Don't you hear the music, Master?

INNKEEPER (*Listening*) : Faintly.

DAVID: It is only the chorus of a few voices now, but some day it will swell to a mighty symphony that will sweep over the earth. Eager multitudes will hear it then, and men everywhere will learn that the only sure road of peace and love and brotherhood leads to Bethlehem. Along that road all nations will eventually come, and the Prince of Peace will be crowned king of all the world. (*As the singing grows louder, all kneel, their faces toward the stable, and the curtain falls slowly.*)

THE END

The Perambulating Pie

by Mary Thurman Pyle

Characters

MISS SNOWDEN, *Chairman of "The Good Cheer Club"*
FLO
BETTY
FRANK }*pupils from the High School*
WALTER
MRS. ELIZABETH WELLS, *an elderly recluse*
SILAS BENTON, *an elderly man*
MARTHA HAGERTY
JIMMY MARTIN
SAM

TIME: *Early on a Saturday morning, a few days before Christmas.*

SETTING: *A room in the Community House.*

AT RISE: MISS SNOWDEN *is sorting out groceries from some bags and packages which are on a big table.* FRANK *and* WALTER *enter from right carrying large bags of groceries. They place the bags on the table as they speak.*

FRANK: Here's a lot more stuff, Miss Snowden. It was left out front.

MISS SNOWDEN: Thank you, Frank. Thank you, Walter. For only nine-thirty in the morning, we're doing pretty well, don't you think?

WALTER: I'll say! Looks like everybody in this burg is going to get a good Christmas dinner this year.

MISS SNOWDEN: That's what the Good Cheer Club is aiming toward.

FRANK: It's a swell project. Gosh, it would be terrible if anybody in town was hungry at Christmas. That's the time when you're supposed to have plenty of good grub.

MISS SNOWDEN: And not only "grub," Frank. We don't want any of our fellow townspeople to be lonely or feel neglected or left out this Christmas.

FRANK: We sure are glad we can help. What shall we do next?

MISS SNOWDEN: Here are two addresses near here where there are donations of food to be called for. (*She hands* FRANK *a slip of paper.*) And I wish you would take this sign and put it up outside where it will be easily seen. (*She gets a large cardboard sign from the rear of the room. It reads, in large letters with appropriate decorations: The Good Cheer Club says, "Christmas for Everybody." Let's share our blessings!*)

WALTER (*Taking sign*): The High School art class sure did a swell job on this. Come on, Frank. We'll put it where everybody who passes will see it. (BETTY *and* FLO *come in from right, meeting the boys as they start out.*)

BETTY (*To the boys*): Hi-ya, kids. (*The boys respond with* "Hi, Betty," *and* "Hi there, Flo.")

FLO: You're buzzing around pretty early, aren't you—for *you!*

FRANK: *We promised* Miss Snowden we'd be here early.

FLO: Well, so did we—and here we are. (*The boys go off right, carrying the sign. The girls go over to the table.*)

BETTY: Good morning, Miss Snowden. Sorry we're late.

FLO: Guess we overslept just a little.

MISS SNOWDEN (*Smiling*): You're not very late. Hang your wraps in the anteroom and bring in some of the empty cartons you'll find there.

BETTY *and* FLO: O.K. (*They go off left.* MISS SNOWDEN *sits at table and consults her lists. The girls return, each bringing a couple of empty boxes, such as grocery stores use to deliver groceries in.*)

MISS SNOWDEN: Put them on this end of the table and we can begin to fill them from the groceries already donated. I'll put this list here for you to consult. We want each gift box to have the makings of a good Christmas dinner. You can go right ahead and I'll be back in a few minutes. I want to find the janitor.

FLO: All right, Miss Snowden. (MISS SNOWDEN *goes off left. The girls start to work. After a moment or two,* MRS. WELLS *enters from right. She is a severe-looking woman, dressed primly in black. Her face is lined and unhappy. She carries a large pie in a pie tin, carefully wrapped in waxed paper. She speaks to the girls in rather a sharp manner.*)

MRS. WELLS: Good morning. Who's in charge here?

BETTY: Good morning. Miss Snowden is in charge, but we're helping. Have you brought a donation?

MRS. WELLS: I'm Mrs. Horace Wells, and I'd like to speak to Miss Snowden.

FLO (*Surprised*): Oh! I've heard of you! I mean—

MRS. WELLS: You mean what you said—that you've heard of me. No doubt you've heard that I am a recluse—that since my husband died seven years ago, I never go out, never see anybody. Well, you've heard correctly. That's the sort of life I prefer. But I know what the townspeople say about me—that I'm queer. (MISS SNOWDEN *enters from left carrying more empty cartons.*)

MISS SNOWDEN: Good morning.

MRS. WELLS: Are you Miss Snowden—the social worker who thought up this "Good Cheer Club"—and all this food collection?

MISS SNOWDEN: Yes, I'm Mary Snowden. And you—

MRS. WELLS: Elizabeth Wells—Mrs. Horace Wells. I suppose *you've* heard of me, too.

MISS SNOWDEN (*Graciously*): Your husband was one of our most prominent citizens, Mrs. Wells. Of course I've heard of his widow. And I'm very happy to meet you. Have you brought us a donation?

MRS. WELLS: A mince pie. I made it myself, and there'll not be a better one in town at Christmas time or any other time.

MISS SNOWDEN: I'm sure of it. (*She takes pie from* MRS. WELLS *and puts it on the table.*)

MRS. WELLS: I've a special request about who gets it, though.

MISS SNOWDEN: Betty, will you and Flo please check the number of empty cartons?

BETTY: Certainly, Miss Snowden. (*She and* FLO *go out left.* MISS SNOWDEN *places a chair for* MRS. WELLS.)

MRS. WELLS: I read the piece in the paper about your project and how you want to see that no one in town feels lonely or neglected this year. So I decided to bake a mince pie and bring it in. Haven't baked one since my husband died. (*She pauses.*)

MISS SNOWDEN (*Gently*): Yes, Mrs. Wells?

MRS. WELLS: I want you to give this pie to the loneliest person I know—Silas Benton.

MISS SNOWDEN: Oh, yes. Mr. Benton is a retired professor. I don't know him personally, but I have heard he lives alone.

MRS. WELLS: Alone—and neither kith nor kin in the world. My husband and I knew Silas Benton well. He never was a man that "mixed." I've neglected him since my husband died, and I want him to have that pie.

MISS SNOWDEN (*With her friendly smile*): He shall have it, Mrs. Wells.

MRS. WELLS: But he's not to know I sent it, mind you.

MISS SNOWDEN: He won't, I promise you. (MRS. WELLS

rises.) Won't you come to our community sing on Christmas Eve, Mrs. Wells? Here, in the Community House, at six o'clock.

MRS. WELLS: No, I couldn't do that. Well, good-bye.

MISS SNOWDEN: Good-bye, and thanks. (MRS. WELLS *goes off right.* MISS SNOWDEN *selects an empty basket on the table, puts in the pie carefully, and covers it with more paper. The girls re-enter.*)

FLO: Guess we can come back now.

MISS SNOWDEN: Yes. Go on with the boxes. I'm going to see if Walter or Frank has come back. (*She throws a sweater over her shoulders and goes out right, taking basket with pie. The girls continue their work.*)

FLO: I've heard about Mrs. Wells, but I never expected to see her. She *never* goes anywhere.

BETTY: Imagine! I wonder whom she made that pie for?

FLO: I hope Miss Snowden thinks of a way to keep her from being so— well, you know. Being by herself all the time. (SAM *enters left, carrying an armful of Christmas greens. He is a good-natured, rosy-cheeked boy.*)

SAM: Hello.

BETTY: Hello.

FLO: What lovely greens! Holly and everything! Who's it for?

SAM: My dad—he's the caretaker here—he said to bring this to Miss Snowden. He'll be late getting here, but I came early and fired the furnace. Is it plenty warm in here?

FLO: Sure, it's fine. Put the greens down over there. Miss Snowden will be back in a minute.

SAM: Jimmy—he's my pal—we thought maybe we could help around here.

BETTY: I don't see why not. There's plenty to do.

SAM: Jimmy is waiting for me outside. I'll go get him. (*He goes out left.*)

BETTY: I guess he means Jimmy Martin. He has a shoeshine

stand downtown somewhere. My father often gets him to shine his shoes. He's an orphan, my father said.

FLO: How awful—not to have your father or mother living. (MISS SNOWDEN *re-enters with* FRANK, *who carries a large basket loaded with edibles.*)

MISS SNOWDEN: You help in here, Frank, till Walter gets back. I sent him on an errand. (FRANK *begins to unpack the basket he has brought.*)

BETTY: Sam brought this holly, Miss Snowden. Oh, here he is. He can tell you. (SAM *re-enters left, with* JIMMY MARTIN.)

SAM: Hello, Miss Snowden. Dad said he'd be over after awhile. But I fired the furnace, and here are the greens, and I've brought Jimmy to help.

MISS SNOWDEN: Good, Sam—to everything. How are you, Jimmy?

JIMMY: I'm fine, Miss Snowden. Can I help fill the boxes?

MISS SNOWDEN: Yes, indeed. How are you getting along, anyway, since you went to live at Sam's house?

JIMMY: Getting along fine. Sam's folks are swell to me.

SAM: My mom says she's got five of her own, and Jimmy just makes a nice even half-dozen.

JIMMY: It's fun to be in a big family.

FLO: You kids unpack some of these donations.

MISS SNOWDEN: And I'll sort. (WALTER *enters right, followed by* MR. BENTON, *an elderly, white-haired man.* WALTER *carries a bag of groceries, and* MR. BENTON *carries the basket with the pie.*)

MR. BENTON: This is Miss Snowden? Good morning. I'm Silas Benton.

MISS SNOWDEN: I'm glad to meet you, Mr. Benton. Do come and join us.

WALTER: I was on my way to Mr. Benton's, to take him the basket like you told me, and I met him coming here—with this bag of groceries.

MR. BENTON (*Genially*): So we exchanged—since he had a present for me. But I came on anyway, for a word with you. (MISS SNOWDEN *joins* MR. BENTON *at front of room.*)

MISS SNOWDEN: I hope you liked your present.

MR. BENTON: Of course. Everybody likes presents. However, I feel that there are many people in town who could make better use of this handsome mince pie than I can. I received it with a great deal of pleasure and appreciation, you understand, and I assure you the gift has warmed my heart. But one lonely old man shouldn't cut into this pie. I wish to pass it on to someone who can really do it justice.

MISS SNOWDEN (*Smiling*): If you really feel that way about it.

MR. BENTON: There is a nice lad who blacks my boots for me now and then—has a stand on the corner of Market and Third. This boy is alone in the world. Now I have a feeling that he might like mince pie.

MISS SNOWDEN: The boy you mean is right over there now, helping with the baskets. Jimmy, come over here a minute, please. (JIMMY *joins them.*)

MR. BENTON: 'Pon my word! I didn't recognize you among all those young people. You remember me, don't you?

JIMMY: Sure I do, Mr. Benton. Aren't you one of my regular customers? (MISS SNOWDEN *goes back to the table, leaving* JIMMY *with* MR. BENTON.)

MR. BENTON: Jimmy, do you like mince pie?

JIMMY: Yes, sir!

MR. BENTON: Accept this one, with my compliments. (*Hands basket to* JIMMY, *who takes it wonderingly*) And no questions! Take this pie and share it with your new family— make it your donation to the Christmas dinner.

JIMMY: Thank you very much, Mr. Benton.

MR. BENTON: Thank *you,* Jimmy, for many a fine shoeshine. (*To the others*) Good morning to you all.

MISS SNOWDEN: Good morning, Mr. Benton. This donation

of yours will surely help us. (*The young people ad lib their good-byes as* MR. BENTON *goes out right.* MISS SNOWDEN *sees him to the door.*)

JIMMY: Miss Snowden.

MISS SNOWDEN (*Coming back from the door*): Yes, Jimmy?

JIMMY: Mr. Benton sure was swell to give me this pie, but—but—

MISS SNOWDEN: But what? Don't you like mince pie?

JIMMY: Sure I do. But there is somebody I want to give a Christmas present to, and I didn't have anything to give. Do you think it would be all right if I gave this? (*He looks at basket he is holding.*) I wouldn't want to hurt Mr. Benton's feelings.

MISS SNOWDEN: He gave you the pie. Do what you want to with it, Jimmy.

JIMMY: Mrs. Hagerty was awful good to my mother when my father was sick; and after—afterward she helped me a lot, before I went to live at Sam's house. I'd like to give her this for a Christmas present.

MISS SNOWDEN: Martha Hagerty is not only the best laundress and cleaning woman in town, but she has the biggest heart I know of. By all means give her that pie, Jimmy. I think it's a fine idea.

JIMMY: Sam rode me over here on his bike. Maybe he would ride me over to take it to her now.

MISS SNOWDEN: Why not? Sam, go with Jimmy on an important errand.

SAM: O.K. Come on, Jim. (SAM *and* JIMMY *go out left.*)

WALTER: I sure was surprised, Miss Snowden, when Mr. Benton came back with me and brought back that basket you told me to give him. He looked in it, stood right still a minute, then came along with me.

MISS SNOWDEN: Surprising things happen sometimes, Walter.

Sort of chain reactions. (*Looking over the work.*) Suppose you and Frank take a couple of these boxes that are filled and put them out front for the pickup truck.

WALTER: Right! (*He and* FRANK *take two of the cartons and go out.*)

FLO: Isn't it nice to have Jimmy and Sam to help?

BETTY: I feel so sorry for Jimmy. No father and mother—and he's always so shabby—and having to shine shoes.

MISS SNOWDEN: Jimmy's doing all right. Save your sympathy.

BETTY (*Laughing*): I guess he is, at that. (MRS. WELLS *enters right. She carries a small covered jar.*)

MRS. WELLS: I guess you're surprised to see me here again, Miss Snowden.

MISS SNOWDEN: I'm not surprised at anything this morning. Come in and join us.

MRS. WELLS: After I got home, I remembered the hard sauce. Had it all made and in the icebox and came off without it. I always served hard sauce with my mince pies. So I brought it right over.

MISS SNOWDEN: The pie is—er—put away in a safe place, Mrs. Wells. But I'll see that the sauce goes with it. (*She takes the jar from* MRS. WELLS.) Now, why don't you sit down and visit with us for awhile?

MRS. WELLS: I think I will. (*She sits near the table.* WALTER *and* FRANK *re-enter and take two more filled cartons out.* MISS SNOWDEN *goes off and returns at once with two empty cartons. The girls continue sorting and packing.* MRS. WELLS *looks on with growing interest.*)

MISS SNOWDEN: Let's see. (*Checking items on table*) Celery, five bunches; muffin mix, sugar, eight cans cranberry sauce.

MRS. WELLS: I always made my own cranberry sauce, from the fresh berries.

MISS SNOWDEN: It's very good that way.

MRS. WELLS: Where are the turkeys?

MISS SNOWDEN: They're to be delivered direct from the wholesale grocer. He's letting us have them at cost. (JIMMY *and* SAM *re-enter from left.*) Back again boys? We have a visitor—Mrs. Wells. Jimmy and Sam, Mrs. Wells.

MRS. WELLS: Brothers?

MISS SNOWDEN: Well, yes—in a way. Jimmy, you and Sam break up some of that holly into pieces to decorate the boxes. (*The boys begin this.* MR. BENTON *re-enters right.*)

MR. BENTON: Here I am back again, Miss Snowden. I came by to give Jimmy a Christmas card to go with the—

MISS SNOWDEN (*Quickly*): With the present you gave him.

MR. BENTON (*Handing card in envelope to* JIMMY): I bought this card at the corner drugstore and put in a little Christmas message, which you can read later, my boy.

JIMMY: Thank you, sir. (*Feeling a little guilty*) I'll keep this card for a special souvenir.

MISS SNOWDEN: Mrs. Wells, do you know Mr. Benton?

MRS. WELLS: Of course I know him. How are you, Silas?

MR. BENTON (*Who hasn't noticed her before*): 'Pon my word! You here, Elizabeth? This is a surprise, and a very happy one, indeed. (*He shakes hands with* MRS. WELLS.) It's been a long time—too long. (WALTER *enters, accompanied by* MRS. HAGERTY. *She is a comfortably stout woman, with her good heart shining in her face. She carries the basket with the pie.*)

WALTER: Right in here. Miss Snowden, Mrs. Hagerty wants to see you.

MRS. HAGERTY: The top of the morning to you, Miss Snowden.

MISS SNOWDEN: Good morning, Mrs. Hagerty. Come right in. Did I say anything about a chain reaction?

MRS. HAGERTY: What, ma'am?

MISS SNOWDEN: Never mind. What can I do for you? But first, do you know Mrs. Wells?

Mrs. Hagerty: Bless my soul, of course I do. I don't see you as much these days as I'd like to, ma'am. I used to do your day's work regular, and I miss it.

Mrs. Wells: I miss you, too, Martha. But with just one person, there doesn't seem to be much to do around the house.

Miss Snowden: This is Mr. Benton.

Mr. Benton: I am very happy to meet you, Mrs. Hagerty.

Mrs. Hagerty: Likewise, sir.

Miss Snowden: And these young people are my helpers today. (Frank *enters right carrying a paper shopping bag with another donation.*) And I am keeping them all busy.

Mrs. Hagerty: It does my heart good to see them, bless their hearts. Miss Snowden, I meant to have a word with you in private, but come to think of it, I'll say my piece right out. It's about this basket and what's in it.

Miss Snowden: Go right ahead, Mrs. Hagerty. (*Smiling*) The situation is entirely out of my hands.

Mrs. Hagerty: A few minutes ago, Jimmy lad over there brought me a Christmas present—a fine mince pie—given to him by a friend and customer, he said.

Jimmy (*Embarrassed*): Mrs. Hagerty, maybe you'd better not—

Mrs. Hagerty (*Going right on*): You meant it out of the kindness of your heart, Jimmy boy, and I'll remember your present to my dying day. But it's the *thought* that counts—so you'll not be after minding if I keep *that* and pass the pie on to someone else, will you, now?

Jimmy: That's O.K. with me—if that's what you'd like to do.

Mr. Benton (*Chuckles*): Now where in the world did Jimmy get that mince pie, I'd like to know?

Mrs. Wells: A mince pie, did you say?

Mrs. Hagerty: A mince pie, and one of the prettiest I ever saw. The minute I looked at it, I thought of the grand pies you used to bake at Christmas, Mrs. Wells. And I made up my mind that pie would go right up to that big lonely house on the hill—your house!

Mrs. Wells (*Touched*): You thought all that, Martha?

Mrs. Hagerty: That I did. And over I came to ask Miss Snowden if she thought it would be all right if I gave Jimmy's present to someone else. And here I find you, yourself, ma'am. It's the Lord's work, that's what it is.

Mrs. Wells (*Smiling, for the first time*): So you want to give me that pie? Well, I'll take it with pleasure—provided you will join me for a little Christmas dinner and help me eat it. And will you come, too, Silas, for old time's sake? You used to come, when Horace was living, and it's my fault you haven't been since.

Mr. Benton: With pleasure, Elizabeth. With great pleasure.

Mrs. Hagerty: I'll be glad to come and cook that Christmas dinner and serve you—truly, I will.

Mr. Benton: I'll join you at the usual time on Christmas day, Elizabeth. (*To the others*) Good-bye, all. The transactions which have taken place here this morning have been most heartening.

Mrs. Wells (*As if she is responsible for the idea*): We are having a Community sing here on Christmas Eve, at six o'clock. I'll expect to see you here, Silas.

Mr. Benton: Indeed you will, Elizabeth! Well, good-bye again. (*He makes a rather formal little bow and goes off.* Miss Snowden *and the young people ad lib their good-byes.*)

Mrs. Wells: Martha, perhaps you'd be good enough to walk home with me now, if you're not busy. We'll take the pie (*Smiling again*) and I think we had better look over the house and see what needs to be done to put it in proper order.

Mrs. Hagerty: That's after my own heart, ma'am. Good day, Miss Snowden. And Jimmy boy, you understand, don't you—about this pie?

JIMMY (*Grinning*): Sure, Mrs. Hagerty. I understand. (MRS. WELLS *and* MARTHA *start out.* MISS SNOWDEN *picks up the jar of hard sauce and follows them, stopping them at the door.*)

MISS SNOWDEN: Mrs. Wells, wouldn't you like to take this jar of hard sauce, to serve with the mince pie? It was brought in this morning as a donation.

MRS. WELLS (*Solemnly*): Yes, I can use that. Thank you very much.

MRS. HAGERTY: Save you from having to make some, ma'am. You *always* served hard sauce with your mince pies. (*She and* MRS. WELLS *go off right. The young people call good-bye and Merry Christmas.*)

FLO: Miss Snowden, I'll bet your afternoon shift won't have half as much fun as we're having.

MISS SNOWDEN: It's been a very interesting morning.

WALTER: I'll say! (*They are all busy again.* JIMMY *stops for a moment and opens his Christmas card which* MR. BENTON *has given him. He looks at it, and is incredulous.*)

JIMMY: Miss Snowden!

MISS SNOWDEN: Yes, Jimmy? Anything the matter?

JIMMY: It's—this Christmas card Mr. Benton gave me. (*He hands it to* MISS SNOWDEN. *It contains a slip of yellow paper as well as a card.*)

MISS SNOWDEN (*After a moment*): Why, Jimmy! How nice! Mr. Benton has given you a check for fifty dollars, with his "best Christmas wishes."

SAM: What do you know about that! You can buy those new clothes you need.

JIMMY (*Regaining his speech*): And have something left over. Do you think I should take it, Miss Snowden? (*The girls answer before* MISS SNOWDEN *can.*)

BETTY: Of course, keep it, Jimmy.

FLO: If a person gives you a Christmas present, you're supposed to accept it.

MISS SNOWDEN: The girls are right, Jimmy. And remember that courage and a cheerful spirit often bring unexpected rewards.

JIMMY: But it wouldn't have happened if it hadn't been for that pie.

WALTER: I'll say that pie got around.

MISS SNOWDEN: It surely did. But then, *that* couldn't have happened unless all of you who belong to the "Good Cheer Club" had helped. And by the way, suppose we keep the perambulations of that mince pie just among ourselves. How about it? (*The young people all answer together in the affirmative.*)

SAM (*Gathering up pieces of the broken holly*) : Here's the holly for the boxes. (*They are all working away with energy and good cheer as the curtain falls.*)

THE END

The Christmas Snowman

by Mildred Hark and Noel McQueen

Characters

MR. WEATHERBY   TOM
JENKINS   GRACE
SARAH   DICKY
MARY

TIME: *The afternoon before Christmas Eve.*

SETTING: *The library in* MR. WEATHERBY'S *home.*

AT RISE: MR. WEATHERBY, *a crotchety-looking old gentleman, is seated in the large chair leaning forward and scowling at the chess men set before him on a small table. After a moment he moves one of the pieces and leans back with a grunt.*

WEATHERBY: That's got him. (*Then leaning forward and shouting*) Jenkins—Jenkins! (JENKINS, *a butler, enters left.*)

JENKINS: You called, sir?

WEATHERBY: Of course I called. I've been shouting my head off all afternoon. Where have you been? Where's Sarah? Where's my tea?

JENKINS: Sarah is bringing your tea—and we have been for a walk. Mr. Weatherby, sir, there is something we would like to talk to you about.

WEATHERBY: Talk—talk? What is all this? (SARAH, *a housekeeper, enters left with tray containing tea things.*)

SARAH: Your tea, sir. (*She puts tray on a small table, then turns to* WEATHERBY.) We've had such a nice time, sir. We went downtown looking at the windows and the crowds, sir. My, my, everyone is so happy.

WEATHERBY: Crowds—crowds? What are you talking about?

JENKINS: The Christmas shoppers—it's a miracle, sir. With all the pushing and shoving no one gets upset. It's the Christmas spirit.

WEATHERBY: Christmas spirit, humph—lot of nonsense!

SARAH (*Nervously*): You—you may think so, sir, but we've been talking and—and—

WEATHERBY: Well?

SARAH: You ask him, Jenkins.

JENKINS: All right, Sarah. Mr. Weatherby, sir, are we or are we not going to have a Christmas celebration this year?

WEATHERBY: Celebration? What for?

JENKINS: Because it's only right, sir. Perhaps a small tree and something special for dinner and a guest or two.

SARAH: Oh, don't you remember, sir, how it used to be?—with the whole house lighted up. Mrs. Weatherby—bless her—used to make so much of it.

WEATHERBY (*Rising*): No, Sarah, that's enough. (*He goes to table, pours himself a cup of tea and gulps it down.*)

JENKINS: We know you don't like us to speak of Mrs. Weatherby, sir—

SARAH: But we loved her too, sir—and we know she wouldn't like to see you the way you are. Gruff and gloomy and withdrawn from everyone—

WEATHERBY: Why, how dare you speak to me—

JENKINS: Beg pardon, sir, but we have been your faithful servants for over twenty years—Sarah and I came here right after we were married.

SARAH: And we feel we have the right to speak—for your own

good. We've watched you, sir, growing more and more crotchety with the years.

JENKINS: Yes, sir. Why, only yesterday you made such a fuss about the snowman. (*He gestures toward window.*)

WEATHERBY: And why not? (*Pointing out window*) Whose property is this?

SARAH: But, sir, the children meant no harm. You have the biggest lawn in the neighborhood—such a nice stretch of snow. It's natural for the boys and girls who live near to come over. All they did was roll three big balls and set them one on top of another.

WEATHERBY: Yes—and there they stand. Looks ridiculous.

JENKINS: That's because you didn't let them finish, sir. Your shouting frightened them away.

WEATHERBY: Well, they have no right to trespass on other people's property.

SARAH: Perhaps not—but neither have you any right to be such a—such an old grouch.

JENKINS (*Shocked*): Sarah!

SARAH (*To* WEATHERBY): I'm sorry, sir. I didn't mean to say that, but it is hard for us to see you the way you are. Why, I can remember when you were a fine-looking man, smiling and cheerful.

WEATHERBY: Humph.

SARAH: And now—well, I said to Jenkins just the other day— you can tell how much he's changed just by the way he wears his hat.

WEATHERBY: My hat!

SARAH: Yes, sir. You used to wear it jaunty-like but now you set it square on your head like a lid on a box.

JENKINS: What Sarah means is, sir, that we—we don't like to see you so changed. And you don't need to be so shut up and alone. Now, if we could have a festive Christmas—

WEATHERBY: Christmas. So you're on that again?

SARAH: Yes, sir—and why not? Christmas is in the very air. You don't have to go downtown to feel it. Have you been out for your walk, sir?

WEATHERBY: Around the block, as usual.

SARAH: And didn't you notice anything, sir? Why, almost every house has a lighted tree in the window and delivery men are hurrying up steps with packages.

JENKINS: You can hear children laughing and singing carols.

SARAH: And at the big church on the corner, there's a manger scene—oh, sir, didn't you notice any of that?

WEATHERBY: Humph. All I noticed was that it was snowing and I got my feet wet.

JENKINS: Well, sir, Sarah and I have noticed all of these things, and we haven't had a real Christmas in this house for years and we've made up our minds—

WEATHERBY: Christmas—Christmas—all this talk about Christmas spirit. What is Christmas spirit?

SARAH: Peace and good will, sir.

WEATHERBY: Peace and good will for one day in the year. What good does that do?

JENKINS: It helps, sir. It shows people what the world could be like, if everyone had charity in his heart.

WEATHERBY: I don't believe it.

SARAH: But, sir, you do believe it—just a little. You sent a donation to the orphanage.

WEATHERBY: Humph, what else could I do? They sent me a form—how many dinners would I furnish for the orphans. So I wrote down four and sent them a check to cover. If I hadn't they'd still be pestering me. And as for Christmas, that's all I am going to do.

JENKINS: Very well, sir. Then Sarah and I might as well tell you. We're leaving.

WEATHERBY: Leaving? Leaving?

SARAH: Just that, sir. We're going to spend Christmas at our cousin's and then we'll look for a new place.

WEATHERBY (*Shouting*): But—but you can't do that. You listen to me—

JENKINS: No, sir. We have made up our minds.

WEATHERBY: But, Jenkins, wait—(*He paces about, then notices chess board. He lowers his voice.*) Jenkins, whom will you play chess with?

JENKINS: The chess has been very pleasant, sir.

WEATHERBY: But did you see that move I made? What are you going to do next?

JENKINS (*He steps over and studies board for a moment. Then admiringly*): That is a move, sir. It will take some study—now, let me see—(*He reaches for the board as though to touch a piece.*)

SARAH: Jenkins!

JENKINS (*Straightening up*): Yes, Sarah. We are going to leave, sir, and nothing you can say will change our minds. (*He goes to* SARAH, *takes her arm and they start for door left. The doorbell rings off.*)

WEATHERBY: Well, at least answer the door, Jenkins, and whoever it is, tell them to go away.

JENKINS: Very well. (SARAH *and* JENKINS *go out left and* WEATHERBY *slumps down in his chair. Then he leans forward and scowls at the chess board. Suddenly, sweeping his hand across, he knocks the pieces over. There is the sound of a racket and children's voices off.* WEATHERBY *sits forward in his chair and listens.*)

CHILDREN (*Off left*): Hello! Merry Christmas! Merry Christmas!

SARAH (*Off*): Merry Christmas, bless you. But now please— quiet, children. Quiet. You'll have to wait—

WEATHERBY: What's this? What's this? (JENKINS *enters left with a sheet of paper in his hand. He looks amused.*)

JENKINS: Your guests have arrived, sir.

WEATHERBY: Guests? What are you talking about? What's all this hubbub?

JENKINS (*Looking at the paper*): Four children from the orphanage, sir. Mary, Tom, Grace and Dicky, to spend Christmas Eve and Christmas day at the express invitation of —— and there's your signature, sir. (*He hands the paper to* WEATHERBY.)

WEATHERBY: But—but—where'd you get this?

JENKINS: One of the children handed it to me. It appears to be their credentials, sir.

WEATHERBY (*Staring at it*): But—but—but it's ridiculous. I sent them a check—

JENKINS: Yes, sir, but apparently this was also an invitation and you wrote in four.

WEATHERBY: But I thought it was money for four dinners. I didn't read it all.

JENKINS: You should always read the smaller print, sir. But they seem like very nice children.

WEATHERBY (*Putting paper down on chess table*): Nonsense, we'll have to get rid of them—send them back to the orphanage.

JENKINS: But, sir, we can't do that—and we could give them a very Merry Christmas.

WEATHERBY: Merry Christmas. I'll have no Merry Christmas in this house! (MARY, *12,* TOM, *10,* GRACE, *8 and* DICKY, *7, wearing hats and coats, rush in followed by* SARAH *who is now all smiles.*)

CHILDREN: Merry Christmas! Merry Christmas, Mr. Weatherby.

DICKY: Our matron told us your name. She said we were going

THE CHRISTMAS SNOWMAN 101

to spend Christmas with a nice man by the name of Mr. Weatherby.

WEATHERBY: Humph, yes—yes, well—there's been some mistake—

TOM (*Looking about*): You mean we got here too early? Gee, haven't you had a chance to do any decorating yet?

MARY (*Being the oldest, she feels she is in charge.*): Shh, Tom. We've got to introduce ourselves the way Matron said. (*They all march across and shake hands with MR. WEATHERBY while SARAH and JENKINS beam.*)

MARY (*Sticking out her hand*): I'm Mary. It was so nice of you to invite us.

TOM: I'm Tom.

GRACE: I'm Grace.

DICKY: And I'm Dicky. I'm seven years old.

WEATHERBY: Humph, yes—well—well. (*He rises and starts pacing about.*)

SARAH: Oh, isn't it wonderful to hear the young voices in the house? Now, you children had better get your things off—

TOM: Sure, we will. (*They all start taking coats and hats off and putting them here and there.*)

WEATHERBY: Now—now, wait just a minute. (*The children pay no attention and continue.*)

DICKY: I always get so excited at Christmas, I can hardly wait for it to start. My, isn't this a big room?

GRACE: But where's your tree? Haven't you put your tree up yet?

WEATHERBY: Um—well—I—(*Shouting*) Sarah, Jenkins, do something.

SARAH (*All smiles*): Yes, sir. We'll do something.

WEATHERBY: But you don't understand—

SARAH: Don't you worry about a thing. Everything will be taken care of. Come along, Jenkins. Hurry. (*She takes*

JENKINS' *arm and bustles him off left. The children walk about looking at things.* WEATHERBY *paces about distractedly, then goes to phone. He picks it up.*)

WEATHERBY: Hello, give me—oh, I'm sorry, I don't know the number. (*He hangs up and paces again.*)

TOM: What's the matter, Mister? Were you calling to order something for Christmas?

WEATHERBY: No—no—

TOM: Oh, I thought maybe you'd forgotten to order your tree or Christmas decorations.

WEATHERBY: No, I haven't forgotten anything.

TOM: Oh, that's good.

WEATHERBY (*Looking blank*): What's good about it? . . . Now, let me see—where's that paper? Maybe the number's on there. (*Seeing paper on chess table*) Oh, here it is. (*He picks it up.*)

MARY: That's the paper from the orphanage. Oh, I'll bet it's our names you've forgotten, Mr. Weatherby. Well, I'm Mary—he's Tom.

GRACE: And I'm Grace.

DICKY: And I'm Dicky.

WEATHERBY: Yes—yes, I know. Please—(*He puts the paper down and paces about wildly.*)

DICKY: I guess you're nervous, Mister, because you aren't ready for us.

GRACE: If you want any help—we like to decorate for Christmas.

TOM: Sure.

WEATHERBY: No—no—there aren't going to be any decorations.

GRACE: You mean no decorations at all?

MARY: Grace, shhh. (*Trying to be practical and not disappointed*) This is a beautiful room. There are lots of pretty things in it. I guess it doesn't need any more decorations.

GRACE: Mister, aren't you even going to have any strings of **popcorn**?

WEATHERBY: No, I am not.

GRACE: But it's so easy—all you need is a needle and thread and some popcorn. And you've got a big fireplace. You could pop it right there. Have you got a corn popper?

WEATHERBY: No—no—

TOM: Imagine that. A great big house and a great big fireplace and no corn popper.

WEATHERBY (*He stops pacing and looks at* TOM): Is that bad?

TOM: I guess not, sir. It just means—well—I guess everybody can't have everything.

WEATHERBY: Humph.

DICKY (*Running to fireplace*): Boy, this is a big fireplace. I'll bet this is where we'll hang up our stockings tonight.

WEATHERBY: Stockings? What's that?

GRACE: We always do.

DICKY: And in the morning I guess there'll be presents.

MARY: Dicky!

DICKY: Well, what's the matter with that? Matron said we'd probably get some presents—and if we did, to say thank you.

WEATHERBY: Humph. She said that, did she?

MARY: Mr. Weatherby, you'll have to excuse Dicky. He just comes out with things. Matron says she's never known anyone so frank. She says it isn't exactly a bad quality because it shows he's honest—

WEATHERBY: Honest? (*Crossly*) He talks too much. You all talk too much. (*The children are all frightened into dead silence for a moment.* WEATHERBY *glares at them, and then not knowing what to do next, he shouts.*) Well, say something—why don't you say something?

GRACE (*Giggling*): Oh, Mr. Weatherby, you're so funny.

WEATHERBY: Funny, am I?

MARY: I guess we make you nervous, don't we, Mr. Weatherby?

WEATHERBY: Yes, you do.

MARY: You're just like Dicky. You come right out and say so. I suppose that's because you're honest too.

WEATHERBY: Honest? Humph . . . maybe I'd better be honest with you—really honest. There's been a mistake.

MARY: Oh, Mr. Weatherby, please don't worry. If you haven't prepared everything just the way Dicky imagines—it doesn't matter.

DICKY: Gee, no. We like Christmas no matter what. Just as long as there's a Christmas tree—

WEATHERBY: Tree? There's not going to be any tree.

DICKY (*His mouth opened*): No tree?

GRACE: No Christmas tree? My, Mister, you don't know what you're missing.

MARY: Children, please. Remember Matron told us to be polite. We're guests in Mr. Weatherby's home and just because he celebrates Christmas in a different way than we're used to—

WEATHERBY (*Waving his hands*): Never mind—quiet—quiet —all of you! Do something—amuse yourselves—let me think. (*He paces about.*)

MARY (*Nervously*): Yes—yes. Now maybe we can play some games.

WEATHERBY (*Shouting*): There are no games.

TOM (*Noticing chess board*): Here's a game. Checkers.

WEATHERBY: That's not checkers—it's chess.

TOM: Oh. Well, show us how to play.

WEATHERBY: You can't play. It takes years to learn.

TOM: Oh, I guess we won't be here that long.

WEATHERBY (*Still pacing about*): No-o—you won't be.

DICKY (*Pulling some books off shelves right*): I know what I'm going to do. Look at all these books. I'm going to build a house. (*He starts stacking up books on the floor.*)

GRACE (*Starting off left*): Let's play dress up. I saw some funny clothes in the hall. (*She runs off.*)

WEATHERBY (*Staring at* DICKY, *horrified*) : Boy, those are valuable books.

DICKY (*Looking up and smiling*) : No, they're not. They're big rocks and I'm building a castle. (*He sets to work again.*)

TOM (*Taking china cat from mantel*) : Look at this. A china cat.

MARY : Tom, you'd better not touch that.

WEATHERBY : I should say not. Very expensive porcelain. That cat cost a hundred dollars.

TOM : A hundred dollars for this? (*He sets it down again.*) Why, you could get a real live cat for lots less than that. Why, one boy at the orphanage got a cat for nothing.

WEATHERBY : Well, this is not an orphanage—or—or is it? (GRACE *runs in wearing man's long overcoat, carrying a cane and wearing two men's hats on her head, one on top of the other.*)

GRACE : Look at me—look at me. I'm going to parade.

WEATHERBY : Why, you—you're wearing my clothes.

DICKY (*Forgetting books and leaping up*) : Oh, I want to play dress up. (*He takes one of hats from* GRACE'S *head and puts it on. It comes down over his ears.*)

WEATHERBY (*Sputtering*) : Those—those are my hats! (GRACE *starts parading around stage and* DICKY *follows, trampling on the edges of the long coat she wears.*)

DICKY (*Chanting*) : Parade—parade.

MARY (*Worriedly*) : Children—

WEATHERBY (*Wildly*) : Oh-hh! (*Calling*) Jenkins, Sarah— help! (*He starts left.*) Oh, where are those two? (*He goes off. The children all stop.*)

TOM : Gee, I—I guess Mr. Weatherby's mad.

MARY : I don't think he liked your getting his clothes, Grace. In fact, I—I don't think he likes *us*.

GRACE (*Taking off overcoat and hat and laying cane and clothes on chair*) : No, I guess not.

DICKY: Well, I don't like it here very much. There isn't anything to play with.

GRACE: I wish we could go home.

MARY: Maybe we ought to do that.

TOM: But what would Matron say?

MARY: Well, we could explain to Matron that it didn't seem very convenient for Mr. Weatherby to have us.

TOM: Then let's go. I'm for it. Get your coats on, kids. (*They all start putting coats and hats on. DICKY puts his coat on, but forgets he is wearing MR. WEATHERBY's hat. He leaves his own on chair where he had put it when he came in. No one notices.*)

MARY: I don't think we ought to leave without telling him—

TOM: Oh, he doesn't want to see us again.

MARY: Maybe I could write a note. (*Going to telephone table*) Here's some paper.

GRACE: Sure, that's a good idea.

MARY: Let's see—I'll say—(*She is writing.*)

TOM (*Noticing French window, he opens it*): Let's go out this side door. It will be quicker.

MARY (*Still writing*): I'll be there in a minute. (TOM *and* GRACE *go out right. DICKY follows, still wearing* MR. WEATHERBY's *hat.* MARY *is alone. She finishes note quickly, looks for a place to put it. Then takes china cat from mantel, puts it on chess table and leans note up against it. She goes out right shutting the French window behind her. In a moment* WEATHERBY *is heard off left.*)

WEATHERBY (*Off*): Well, I don't care what you've been doing. You've got to come in here and help me. The place is a shambles—(*He enters left followed by* SARAH *and* JENKINS.) See that, my books on the floor—my clothes thrown about—

SARAH: Now—now, we can fix that, and as for Christmas for the children, don't you worry. I've already started some cookies and put in a great big order at the store—a turkey will be here in time.

WEATHERBY: A turkey?

SARAH: And as for a tree, Jenkins is going to chop one down. You've plenty of evergreens in back.

JENKINS: Now, Sarah, just a minute. Mr. Weatherby, sir, I can chop down a tree if you approve—but I wasn't as sure as Sarah that you want all this done.

SARAH: If you don't, sir, then you have a heart of stone. If you won't make a Christmas for those poor little children—then we *will* leave. We'll do as we said. (*Breaking off*) Why, where are they? Where are the little lambs?

WEATHERBY: Lambs?

SARAH: The children. Where are they?

WEATHERBY: I don't know. They'll pop out from somewhere. (*He looks under a chair.*) They were all here a minute ago.

JENKINS: But it's so quiet. (*Seeing note*) Ah, perhaps this would be a clue, sir. It seems to be a note. (*He picks note up, looking at it.*)

WEATHERBY: Well, don't just stand there. What does it say?

JENKINS (*Reading*): "Dear Mr. Weatherby. We guess you don't like us so very well, so we have gone. Merry Christmas!"

WEATHERBY: You mean they—they've gone?

JENKINS: It seems so, sir.

SARAH (*Sadly*): And they said Merry Christmas—(*Then angrily*) Merry Christmas to you—when you've driven them away.

WEATHERBY: Now, just a minute—

SARAH: Of course you did. You probably shouted at them—and scowled at them—and frightened them half to death. You didn't want them here and now they've gone—all by themselves. Poor little mites. They may not go back to the orphanage. They may get lost or run over or—or who knows what? And you'll have only yourself to blame.

WEATHERBY: Now, Sarah, wait—suppose I did shout at them— and scowl—they needn't have run away.

SARAH: What would you expect them to do? Well, this is the end, sir. I'm not going to stay here either—not another minute. Come, Jenkins. (JENKINS *has walked over to French window and is looking out and smiling.*) Jenkins, what are you waiting for?

JENKINS: It seems they haven't run away—not very far anyhow —look! (SARAH *goes to window.*)

SARAH: The children! There they are.

WEATHERBY (*Going to window*): What's that?

SARAH: They must have seen the snowman and stopped. Look, they're finishing it. They've found some stones and made eyes and nose and mouth, and they've put an old hat on his head.

JENKINS: Yes—(*Turning to* WEATHERBY) and isn't it strange, sir? They've made that snowman look a bit like you.

WEATHERBY: Humph, no wonder. It's because he's wearing my hat.

SARAH: Why, it does look like you, sir. The way you used to look. The big smile and the sort of rakish angle on the hat— (*Then remembering, angry again*) But you don't look like that any more, sir. You've got the *heart* of a snowman and that's all.

JENKINS (*Touching her arm*): Sarah, they're starting to leave. We'd better go out and stop them. (*He opens French window.*)

SARAH: Yes—if he won't have them here, at least we can take them back to the orphanage. Oh, the poor darlings. (SARAH *and* JENKINS *start out right.*) Look, they hate to leave their snowman. They're standing around patting him into shape here and there.

JENKINS (*Pointedly at* WEATHERBY): Well, at least they found one friend, if it was only a snowman. (*They go out and shut French window.* WEATHERBY *stands looking out. He smiles a little, then chuckles. Then he goes to chair, picks up his hat and puts it squarely on his head and looks in the mirror over mantel. He turns around with hat on straight, scowling. Then goes to window again and looks out. He takes off his hat and while still looking out the window puts it on again, tipping it at a jaunty angle. He returns to mirror, still scowling, then seeing himself, he turns with a broad smile. He picks up his cane, tucks it under his arm and does a few quick dance steps, then stops suddenly as the French window opens. He takes his hat off quickly, puts down the cane and scowls again.* SARAH *and* JENKINS *enter with* DICKY.) We're going to get our coats, sir. The rest of the children want to wait outside, but Dicky forgot his hat.

DICKY: Yes, I wore yours out by mistake and now we've put it on the snowman. I hope you don't care. (SARAH *and* JENKINS *start left.* DICKY *grabs his hat from chair and starts right.*) I'll wait outside too.

WEATHERBY (*Suddenly shouting*): Just a minute, stay where you are. You, too, Sarah—you, too, Jenkins—don't move. (SARAH *and* JENKINS *turn and* DICKY *stops, frightened.* WEATHERBY *strides to French window, shouting.*) You—children—come in here. Well, don't just stand there—come in here!

SARAH: I'm not going to let you shout at these children any longer.

WEATHERBY (*Turning to* SARAH): And you, be quiet. This is my house and I guess I can run a Christmas celebration the way I want it. (MARY, TOM *and* GRACE *appear in opened French window looking frightened.* WEATHERBY *turns to them.*) Well, children, come in—come in, take off your things. We're going to have Christmas.

GRACE: Christmas?

WEATHERBY: Certainly, Christmas. Christmas, with all the trimmings!

MARY: But, Mr. Weatherby, you mean you—you really want us now, sir?

WEATHERBY: Of course—wouldn't say so if I didn't, would I? Didn't you say I was an honest man—that I came right out with things?

MARY (*Smiling*): Why, I think you do mean it, sir. (*They all take off their coats and hats again.*)

WEATHERBY: Of course—and everything's going to be just the way you want it. We'll have a turkey and a tree.

TOM: But, sir, it's getting late—there isn't much time.

WEATHERBY: Plenty of time. We'll spend this evening getting ready, and tomorrow have a grand day. Why, one of the nicest Christmases I remember was a rush one—my wife and I moved in the house here on Christmas Eve and nothing was ready but we had a lot of fun.

SARAH (*Wiping her eyes*): Oh, sir, I am so happy.

WEATHERBY: Well, then, don't stand there crying. You've got to fix the turkey. And Jenkins, you've got to cut down that tree.

JENKINS (*All smiles*): Yes, sir. (*JENKINS and SARAH rush off left.*)

WEATHERBY: And we're going to have presents too—yes, sir!

DICKY (*Gaining faith again*): Presents? We are? See, Mary, didn't I tell you?

WEATHERBY: You bet. (*He rushes to phone and picks it up.*) Operator, let me have Field's Department Store. The Toy Department. Oh, I don't know the number, operator, but it's Christmas Eve and this is an emergency. Merry Christmas, operator. (*Turning and smiling*) She's getting it for me. (*Into phone*) Hello? Toy department? I'm J. W. Weatherby. That's right. Merry Christmas to you, too. I've got

four children out at my home here and we need presents—lots
of presents. Oh, I don't know—anything you've got. Send
out books, games, dolls, trains, electric trains—(*He turns to
children again*) I haven't played with an electric train in years.
(*Into phone*) Yes, that's right. All sorts of things. And
Christmas tree decorations too. And oh, there's something
else—have you got a popcorner? A popcorner—*popcorner*
—don't you know what a popcorner is?

MARY (*Laughing*): Mr. Weatherby, you mean a corn popper.

WEATHERBY: Oh, yes, a corn popper—a big one—no, wait a
minute—(*Looking around*) send four big ones. Fine—fine.
Yes, yes, as soon as you can make it. Thank you. Good-bye—
Merry Christmas! (*He hangs up.* DICKY *is standing near
him.* WEATHERBY *pokes him in the ribs.*) Young man, you're
going to have popcorn coming out of your ears. (JENKINS
comes in left wearing coat and carrying axe.)

JENKINS: Who wants to help get the Christmas tree? (*He goes
toward French window.*)

TOM and DICKY (*Running right*): I do! I do! (SARAH *enters
left wearing a big apron with flour smeared on it.*)

SARAH: My—my, there are so many things to be done. Who
wants to help cut out cookies?

MARY and GRACE: I do! I do! (*They run left.*)

WEATHERBY (*At center, smiling broadly*): Well—well—is
everybody happy?

ALL: Yes—yes—I should say.

MARY: And do you know, we owe it all to the snowman.

GRACE: Why, of course. If we hadn't stopped to finish him we
would never have come back in again.

TOM (*Looking out right*): And there the poor old snowman
stands—all by himself in the cold.

DICKY: Gee, I wouldn't like to be a snowman, would you, Mr.
Weatherby?

WEATHERBY: Well, that all depends. I know a story about a snowman, Dicky. He lived in a great big house.

DICKY: He did? But if he lived in a house, why didn't he melt?

WEATHERBY: That was the strangest part about him. He just stayed as cold as cold could be. That is until one Christmas Eve when some little children came to visit him, and then he thawed out and melted all over the place.

DICKY: Oh, my, I'll bet that was the end of him and the end of the story too.

WEATHERBY: No, the end of the story was—a merry, merry Christmas for all!

THE END

Naomi-of-the-Inn

by Helen E. Waite and Elbert M. Hoppenstedt

Characters

ELISABETH	LYDIA
SIMON	DORCAS
SALOME	INNKEEPER
THOMAS	JOSEPH
NAOMI, *daughter of the* INNKEEPER	MARY
MARTHA, *her friend*	ANDREW
MATTHEW	TWO SHEPHERDS

SCENE 1

SETTING: *The courtyard and entrance of the Inn at Bethlehem.*

AT RISE: ELISABETH *and* SALOME, *well-dressed travelers, enter from the Inn. They are obviously disgruntled.*

ELISABETH (*Sarcastically*): So this—is Bethlehem's best!

SALOME: Not only her best, but her only Inn. (*She crosses to bench.*) Once it may have been a royal city, but now . . .

ELISABETH: Now it is a place fit only for the most lowly sheep tenders! However, our husbands may be able to gain some special favors from the Innkeeper. Sit here while we wait. (*She gestures toward the bench, and* SALOME *accepts the invitation.*) You and your family made a lengthy journey to attend this gathering of David's kin?

SALOME (*Nodding*): Yea, we came from Joppa.

ELISABETH: And we came from Cana. It was most inconvenient to leave our home at this season.

113

SALOME: Of all the insolent decrees which Caesar has inflicted upon us, this herding us together in the cities of our forefathers, so that we may register in the Emperor's books, is the most wretched, and why we submit. . . . (*She is interrupted by the appearance of* SIMON *and* THOMAS *from the Inn.* ELISABETH *speaks eagerly.*)

ELISABETH: Well, my husband, did you win better quarters from the Innkeeper?

SIMON (*Shaking his head gloomily*): I could gain nothing. The place is a bedlam—every late comer trying to bargain with some early arrival for the best places.

THOMAS: And one might expect to obtain a special favor from Caesar himself as to hope that one of the holders of the best quarters in the Inn will yield it.

ELISABETH (*Half-angry*): Did you say to the Innkeeper that I would not sleep in the place he had allotted to us?

SIMON (*Drily*): I did.

ELISABETH: And what answer did he have?

SIMON: That if you could find a better place he would be glad enough for you to have it.

ELISABETH (*Beating her hands*): This is wretched!

SALOME: But indeed, Bethlehem is filled to the very gates. And must *all* the descendants of our glorious king, David, be crowded into this Inn?

THOMAS: All those who are not fortunate enough to have relations or friends in the city to house them.

ELISABETH (*Tossing her head*): *Our* relations and friends live in finer places than Bethlehem!

SIMON: And because they do live in finer cities, we must abide in this poor Inn. . . . (NAOMI, *the daughter of the* INNKEEPER, *a girl about twelve, appears in the doorway. Behind her is her friend,* MARTHA. NAOMI *holds a water-jar on her head. At sight of her,* ELISABETH *speaks sharply.*)

ELISABETH: Well, girl! Do you go to the well for water?
Make haste to return. My throat burns for a cup of cold
water!

THOMAS: The special cakes which I ordered to be made for my
wife and myself—are they ready? I said they were to be
brought to us in an hour. Go fetch them at once, girl!

ELISABETH: See to it you bring my cup of water before you
do any other errand. Be off to the well, now! (NAOMI *has
remained.*)

NAOMI (*Calmly*): I have come to tell you . . .

ELISABETH: I cannot endure this thirst! Simon, command the
girl to go. . . .

SIMON (*Roughly*): Have you no regard for the comfort of your
guests? Go to the well with all the speed. . . . (*He is
interrupted by the entrance, from left, of* MATTHEW, LYDIA,
and DORCAS, *a child of perhaps seven or eight years.* MAT-
THEW *addresses* NAOMI *and* MARTHA *courteously enough.*)

MATTHEW: Greetings, damsels.

NAOMI: Greetings to you, sir.

LYDIA (*Petulantly*): Do make haste with this business, Matthew! You know how weary I am, and Dorcas will have
another fit of tears if we are not settled soon!

MATTHEW (*To girls*): Do you receive the Inn's guests?—Ah,
yes, I know your face now. I stopped here once before,
for a night, when I went up to Jerusalem last. You are
the Innkeeper's daughter, and they call you Naomi-of-the-
Inn. . . .

LYDIA (*Stamping her foot*): Who cares what anyone calls her?
Why should you waste words with a child, when I am tired
and chilled and hungry? Listen to me, Naomi-of-the-Inn!
Like everyone else who comes to this despised city these
days, we are seeking a place where we may stay until the
people have been numbered for Caesar's pleasure. . . .

ELISABETH (*Interrupting*): The place you find will be poor enough, I promise you.

LYDIA: Why we could not have been registered in our own city. . . . (DORCAS *suddenly crooks her arm over her eyes, and sinks to the step of the Inn, sobbing.* MARTHA *and* NAOMI *glance at her anxiously.* MATTHEW *lifts her up, and* LYDIA *continues scornfully.*) Yes, truly it is enough to make even a child weep, this senseless decree of Rome that each person must be enrolled in the city of his forefathers!

MATTHEW: And so we, who have the honor to be of David's royal line—

LYDIA: David's royal line! And suppose we are! What does it profit us! Another ruler, a conquerer, in far-off Rome, commands us to go hither and yon to please his slightest whim! Where is the Promised One of Israel, of whom the High Priests always talk, and the prophets sang—the Glorious One, who is to lift the oppressors' yoke from our necks and subdue all our foes? He is long in coming!

MATTHEW: He will come at God's appointed hour. (*Places an arm about* DORCAS.) Say no more, Lydia. You are wearied with the journey. (*To* NAOMI.) There is still room for us? I know we come late.

NAOMI (*Doubtfully*): The Inn is well filled, but perhaps my father may find room for you.

LYDIA (*Tossing her head*): I demand a *good* place! (NAOMI *steps through the doorway, followed by* MARTHA.)

NAOMI: If you will enter, my father will show you what room he has.

LYDIA (*Speaking over her shoulder as she crosses the threshold*): It is certain that all the most desirable quarters—if there were any such in this miserable hovel—will be taken, but if you bargain shrewdly enough, you may be able to exchange with some early comer, Matthew!

MATTHEW: You must trust me to do my utmost, Lydia. (*He guides* DORCAS *into the Inn. Having watched them go,* NAOMI *turns toward others.*)

ELISABETH (*Sarcastically*): Perhaps about the ninth hour you will start for the well?

NAOMI: My father bade me come here and tell you that the evening meal was ready. You will find fresh water and everything else waiting for your pleasure.

ELISABETH (*Springing up*): You are tardy with your message, girl!

SIMON: Doubtless the hungry horde within the Inn has devoured everything worth the eating!

THOMAS: Come, Salome, we must make haste, now that the girl has remembered to summon us. (NAOMI *wisely remains silent, and the four enter the Inn. When they are gone, the girls cross to the bench and seat themselves.* NAOMI'S *weariness is evident. Her shoulders sag, and the gesture with which she puts her veil aside is listless.* MARTHA *places both hands over* NAOMI'S *in quick compassion.*)

MARTHA: Are all your days like this one, Naomi? . . . One long stream of jostling, complaining people? When I heard that Uncle Saul had set up an Inn, I thought it would be an exciting thing . . . to see so many people pausing in their travels, to wonder who they were, and what had brought them to Bethlehem, and perhaps see strangers from Crete or Rome, but, I have been following you ever since we arrived at dawn, and never have I heard a traveler speak a gentle word! Tell me, Naomi, are travelers always so impatient?

NAOMI: A few who come are kind. Most often I shut my eyes to the others. But, oh . . . tonight . . . I am very weary of being Naomi-of-the-Inn!

MARTHA: All the day you have been answering the demands of strangers . . . hurrying with water, or carrying meat and

bread, and when the strangers were not clamoring for your
service, you were on errands for your mother, or tending the
door for your father.

NAOMI: It is the decree from Caesar which has caused this
crowd. It does not make them happy to remember that they
are of David's blood, and yet they must obey the law of Caesar.

MARTHA (*Indignantly*): And so, to show how worthy they are
of fine things, they all demand the best spot in the house,
and special service.

NAOMI: My father does not mind. Indeed, he is well pleased
with the day's work. Never has our Inn been so filled. Not
a space left, since the travelers from Capernaum arrived.

MARTHA (*With concern*): No, not so much as an inch even
for *you*.

NAOMI: Truly, Martha, to sleep in the stable is no great hard-
ship. The animals are safe and gentle, and the hay fresh and
clean.

MARTHA: And you will be glad to get away from everyone who
shouts for attention and reviles Bethlehem and everything
in it. How *have* you guarded your tongue and your temper
when everyone reviles Bethlehem and everything within the
city?

NAOMI: Oh, over and over again I have been angry. So many
of the strangers have been scornful of our Inn, calling it
wretched and vile, and not fit to linger in even for a day—
my father's splendid Inn, in which even a High Priest or a
Centurian would fare as well as at any Inn of Jerusalem!
My father has had high praise from many strangers who have
stopped here.

MARTHA: But today. . . .

NAOMI: Yea, most of the guests were wearied with traveling,
irritated by being crowded with so many others, and sore in
spirit because they must obey Caesar's decree. And many of

them seek to seem important by claiming to miss fine things.
But I did bridle my tongue, for I wished to watch all of our
guests. Martha, two days ago Rabbi Joses told me . . .
(*She checks herself suddenly, for* ELISABETH, SIMON, *and
the* INNKEEPER *appear in the doorway.* ELISABETH *almost
darts into the courtyard.*)

ELISABETH (*Angrily*) : I tell you I will not abide in the room
with all those other women! Some other place must be found!

INNKEEPER: If you find it, you are welcome to lodge there,
lady.

SIMON (*Roughly*) : Sir, are you being insolent to my wife?

INNKEEPER (*Folding his arms*) : No. It is no insolence, but
the simple truth. It is my regret my Inn is no larger, but so
it is.

ELISABETH: I tell you, I cannot . . . nay, I will *not* endure
the company of so many! And the crying of that child Dorcas
would surely send me mad! I would sooner sleep in the
street!

SIMON (*To* INNKEEPER) : I would pay you well—

INNKEEPER: So would many others. . . . (MARY *and* JOSEPH,
walking very slowly, enter from right. JOSEPH *supports*
MARY.)

JOSEPH: Here is the Inn. God be praised. Here we may rest.
(*To* INNKEEPER) I know we come late, but we were delayed
upon the road. Will you show us some place . . . any place,
in your Inn where my wife may rest in peace? I am a poor
man, but I will pay you all that I have. . . .

INNKEEPER (*Shaking his head*) : There is no room. Not so
much as an empty corner.

JOSEPH (*In a flat tone*) : No . . . room.

INNKEEPER: None.

JOSEPH (*Unsteadily, as if he had been struck a blow*) : For
myself I ask nothing. But for my wife . . . oh, good sir . . .

MARY: Nay, Joseph, I would not leave you!

INNKEEPER: It is useless to ask. Even my own daughter is turned out of her bed because of the crowd. I have nothing, unless . . . (*He looks at* ELISABETH.) Lady, you were saying you refused to accept the place allotted to you. If you do refuse . . .

ELISABETH (*Scornfully*): Give up the bed and room space for which my husband has paid you his good money? Not I! Doubtless these people can find shelter under some palm tree! (*The* INNKEEPER *is genuinely distressed. He fidgets with his belt and looks down before he turns to* JOSEPH.)

INNKEEPER: I am truly sorry. But there is no other place I know. . . .

NAOMI (*Springing up*): Father! (*Soft eagerness rings in her voice.*) Father! There—there is the stable! They can have that! I will go to sleep in the cave on the hillside. Andrew will be watching his sheep with the other shepherds, and will guard me as well. . . . (*Her father fingers his chin thoughtfully, but* JOSEPH *whirls upon her angrily.*)

JOSEPH: You said a stable? You would lodge my wife in a stable?

NAOMI (*Faltering*): It . . . it is clean and fresh, sir, and the hay is fresh.

INNKEEPER: If it is fit for my daughter, it would be fit for your wife.

MARY (*Touching* JOSEPH's *arm*): The hay . . . would smell sweet, and . . . and it would be soft to rest upon. And we would be alone. Let us go to the stable, Joseph. (JOSEPH *looks first at her, then at the* INNKEEPER, *and makes a gesture of resignation.*)

JOSEPH: Yes, we go to this stable. Lead the way, girl.

NAOMI (*Starting toward left exit*): This way, if you please. (JOSEPH *and* MARY *follow, and* NAOMI *leads from the stage. As they go,* THOMAS *comes from Inn.*)

THOMAS (*To* INNKEEPER): My good sir, something must be done with the child of Lydia and Matthew of Capernaum. Her wails are distracting all the women, and upsetting the children. My wife says the women's quarters are a veritable Tower of Babel, and not to be endured. Even the child's mother would gladly see her taken away . . . is there anyone in the village to whom you could send her for the night?

INNKEEPER (*Shaking his head*): Nay, no one.

ELISABETH: Her wailings are not to be borne, I can assure you of that!

INNKEEPER: I can think of nothing—unless, I send her with my daughter. She has much skill with children. But—would her mother permit her to go?

THOMAS: From my wife's account I think the mother is almost distracted. Send her anyway, so she disturbs no one. (SIMON *and* ELISABETH *chorus approval.* INNKEEPER *stands undecided.*)

INNKEEPER: Well, it will do no harm to approach the parents. I will see what they say. (*He turns, and re-enters the Inn, followed by the others, except* MARTHA, *who still remains seated on the bench. When they are gone, she brings her hands together tightly.*)

MARTHA: Oh, poor, poor Naomi-of-the-Inn!

CURTAIN

*   *   *

SCENE 2

SETTING: *A field upon the hill.*

AT RISE: NAOMI *and* MARTHA *are seated on the ground near the left entrance. They are wrapped in cloaks.*

NAOMI: It was good of you to come with me, Martha.

MARTHA: I could not bear to think of you here alone with that troublesome child. To think of her mother being willing to shift the burden to you! And what a night she has given you! NAOMI (*Sighs*) : It has been hard. But she sleeps now. Let's think of something else. Martha, I believe that wonderful days are close at hand for our poor, conquered country.

MARTHA : Do you think our promised Messiah is about to appear? We are always waiting for him, and always being disappointed. What makes you think his reign is so near?

NAOMI : Rabbi Joses spoke to me about it two days ago, and bade me watch all our guests closely. He thinks the time is at hand, and that our Messiah may appear now, at this very gathering of David's descendants, and lead us from under the oppressor's heel. Remember what the prophet said?—"And thou, Bethlehem, in the land of Judea, are not the least amongst the princes, for out of thee shall come a ruler to rule my people Israel. And his name shall be called wonderful, mighty counselor, everlasting father, and the prince of peace."

MARTHA : It would be glorious—

NAOMI : And since then I have observed every stranger eagerly, hoping that I might have the honor of preparing the place for our Great Redeemer.

MARTHA : And do you think he has taken lodging at the Inn?

NAOMI (*A sudden tired note in her voice*) : I—oh, I don't know. I thought I would know him instantly. That he would be set apart. I—I have seen many commanding men, who spoke with authority, but—oh, I do not know if *he* is there! (*A silence falls.* NAOMI *hides her face in her hands, and* MARTHA *props her chin in her hands. Suddenly the wall opposite them brightens with a soft white light.* MARTHA *watches it for a moment before she speaks.*)

MARTHA : Naomi! Naomi, look! What is this light? (NAOMI *raises head.*)

NAOMI (*Awed*): I—I do not know! It is not the dawn! I've never seen such light before! (*Now the choir begins singing, softly at first, but with swelling voices, "Hark, the Herald Angels Sing." This may be followed by the chorus of "Angels We Have Heard on High," sometimes known as the Westminster Carol. "Gloria in excelsis, Gloria in excelsis, Deo." Then the light gradually fades, and* MARTHA *and* NAOMI *clutch at each other in awe.*)

MARTHA: That music—what was it?

NAOMI: I do not know.

MARTHA: What did it mean?

NAOMI: I do not know—oh, I do not know! (*There is the sound of running feet, and* ANDREW, NAOMI's *brother, followed by* TWO OTHER SHEPHERDS, *enters excitedly.*)

ANDREW: Naomi! Martha! You—did you see—did you know?

NAOMI: We saw a great white light, and we heard wonderful voices singing. Did you see and hear the same?

ANDREW: Oh, there was more! Much more! As we were watching our flocks, the sky opened before us, and an angel from the Lord appeared—

SECOND SHEPHERD: And we were sore afraid!

ANDREW: Yes, we were. And the angel said unto us, "Fear not, for behold I bring you tidings of great joy, which shall be to all men, for unto you is born this day, in the city of David, a Saviour, which is Christ the Lord. And this shall be a sign unto you, ye shall find the babe wrapped in swaddling clothes, and lying in a manger."

NAOMI: A—manger?

THIRD SHEPHERD: And suddenly there was with the angel a multitude of the heavenly host, praising God, and saying, "Glory to God in the Highest, and on earth peace, good will toward men." And when the angels were gone away from us into heaven, we started in haste.

ANDREW: Naomi, you said there was a couple lodged in the stable?

NAOMI: Yes. (*She is plainly bewildered.*)

ANDREW: Then let us hurry down to the stable, and see this thing which the Lord has made known unto us! (SHEPHERDS *hurry off left stage.*)

MARTHA: Oh, Naomi—

NAOMI (*Still bewildered*): Martha, Martha, *tell* me, what does it mean?

MARTHA: It means that Rabbi Joses was right. Our Messiah has appeared in Bethlehem. As a baby. And when you gave up your place in the stable tonight, you—oh, Naomi, don't you see? *You* prepared the place for his coming!

THE END

Angel in the Looking-Glass

by Aileen Fisher

Characters

MISS PINSTER, *a dressmaker*
LUCY, *a young girl*
JIM YOUNG ⎫
ALICE YOUNG ⎰ *a married couple*
AUNT MARTHA, *a stern old lady*
CHARLES ⎫
RALPH ⎰ *her young nephews*
ZORLOVA, *a dancer*

TIME: *A week before Christmas.*
Before the curtain: MISS PINSTER *is fitting* LUCY'S *angel
costume. There is much pinning and adjusting as the two
talk. From time to time* LUCY *looks at herself in a large
full-length mirror placed at one end of the stage.*

LUCY: Are you sure I'll look like a real angel when you get my
costume finished, Miss Pinster?
MISS PINSTER: Yes, of course. Now hold still while I fix this
wing. I had to use cardboard underneath, you know, to
stiffen it.
LUCY: Do they look like real wings?
MISS PINSTER: Quite real, I think.
LUCY: I wish I could fly with them. I wish I could fly and
fly—way up above the town.

MISS PINSTER: Oh, that would be expecting too much. If I could make wings that could fly, I shouldn't have to be a dressmaker, you know.

LUCY: What would you be, Miss Pinster?

MISS PINSTER: Goodness, I have never given it a thought. (*She stands dreamily for a moment with pins and tape measure in hand.*) Oh, I think I should like to have a little shop and sell hand-painted cups and things like that.

LUCY: And red-and-white-striped candy?

MISS PINSTER: Perhaps. Perhaps I could have a little glass case of candy, too. (*She suddenly comes down to earth again.*) But now, my dear, we must see how the halo fits. (MISS PINSTER *picks up the halo.*)

LUCY: Oh, what a beautiful halo! It looks like a real one, all gold and shiny.

MISS PINSTER: I am rather pleased with it myself. I just happened to have some gilt paint on hand, left over from the time I touched up the radiators. (*She adjusts the halo, stands back and nods.*) You look more and more like an angel, Lucy.

LUCY: Do I? (*Then hesitantly*) But . . . I don't always *feel* like one, Miss Pinster. Do you think it's mean of a person to buy another person a Christmas present and then not want to give it away because it's so nice. I mean . . . I know a girl who saved her money to buy her brother a set of pencils with colored leads—twenty different colors in all—and now . . . she wants to keep them for herself.

MISS PINSTER: Well, I wouldn't say she had much of the Christmas spirit, would you? Now, let's see about the sleeves, Lucy. Are they long enough under the wings?

LUCY: But wouldn't it be all right if she gave her brother something else . . . that was cheaper? Oh, you can't imagine what beautiful pencils they are.

Miss Pinster (*Intent on her work*) : Yes, I think the sleeves are all right. My, I haven't made an angel costume in years! (*There is a moment or two of silence, as* Miss Pinster *stands off and looks at the costume.*)

Lucy (*Slowly, thoughtfully*): Do you think if anyone saw me . . . walking down the hall of this apartment building, maybe . . . they would think I *was* an angel?

Miss Pinster: They might! The effect is very good, I think.

Lucy: Would it make any difference to them if they *did* take me for an angel, Miss Pinster?

Miss Pinster: Difference? What do you mean by that?

Lucy: I mean, would it make any difference in the way people acted? I think *I* would act different, if I saw an angel . . . maybe.

Miss Pinster: Perhaps we all would. But, of course, we shall never really know, shall we? Not on this earth, at least. Now turn to the side a little, Lucy. I don't believe the hemline is quite straight. No, it isn't.

Lucy: Do many people live in this apartment building, Miss Pinster?

Miss Pinster: Oh, yes, quite a few. There are twelve apartments in addition to the janitor's. Hold still, now. I must pin up this side a little.

Lucy: Are they nice people?

Miss Pinster: Yes, I think so—as nice as most people are. I have so little time to talk to them, of course. (*She pins at the hem, then stands back to see if it is straight.*)

Lucy: Are you coming to see our Christmas play, Miss Pinster? It's going to be Friday night, in the school auditorium, and it's free.

Miss Pinster: Oh, I should like to come. Then I could see how the costume looks from the audience.

Lucy: I'm the only angel who speaks a part. The others just

sing. I sing too, part of the time. Would you like me to recite my part for you?

MISS PINSTER: Yes, if you wish. Only you must turn around slowly, slowly, so I can be sure to get the hem right.

LUCY (*Turning very slowly*): Well, you see, the three shepherds are there on the stage, wondering about the star. It's not a *real* star on the stage, you know, but it looks like one. Then we angels come in singing. The shepherds are frightened, and they draw away. You know, they don't expect to see angels in the middle of the night. So then I say to them: "Fear not: for, behold, I bring you tidings of great joy, which shall be to all people. For unto you is born this day in the city of David a Saviour, which is Christ the Lord. And this shall be a sign unto you . . ."

MISS PINSTER (*Softly*): "Ye shall find the babe wrapped in swaddling clothes, lying in the manger."

LUCY: How did you know, Miss Pinster?

MISS PINSTER: Oh, I've known that for a long, long time.

LUCY: Well, then the other angels sing, and then I say: "Glory to God in the highest, and on earth peace, good will toward men." And the shepherds aren't afraid any more.

MISS PINSTER: You do it very nicely, Lucy. Now just a few more pins . . . (*The doorbell rings loudly. She looks at her watch.*) Oh, dear, that must be Mrs. Swishton coming for her fitting. She is a few minutes early, but she is always in *such* a hurry. Would you mind waiting a little while, Lucy? (*Doorbell rings again, loudly.*) I can take care of Mrs. Swishton in the other room.

LUCY: I don't mind, Miss Pinster. (MISS PINSTER *hurries out. For a moment* LUCY *stands still. Then she runs over to the mirror.*) Do you know who I am, looking-glass? I'm an angel. But, of course, you're Miss Pinster's mirror, so you knew it already. I wonder . . . if anyone else would know

who *didn't* know already. (*She looks around.*) I could try!
I could slip out the door, and go down the hall of the apartment building, couldn't I, looking-glass? It wouldn't take
long. I could be back before Miss Pinster would miss me at
all. Are my wings all right? Is my halo straight? I don't
think anyone will notice the pins in the hem, do you? (*Tiptoes
across stage*) Good-bye, looking-glass. Don't tell. (LUCY
exits, and the curtain rises.)

SETTING: *The stage is divided into three "apartments": The
YOUNGS' apartment is on one side, ZORLOVA'S on the other,
and AUNT MARTHA'S in the middle. Each apartment is indicated by a small grouping of furniture. As one family talks,
the other two are silent.*

AT RISE: ALICE *and* JIM YOUNG *are talking together in their
apartment.*

ALICE: I'm so glad you agree with me at last, Jim. It's much
more sensible to save the money for a new car than to go to
Mother Young's for Christmas. After all, we've gone every
year since we were married. *Four* times.

JIM: But Mother counts on it. It will be hard to tell her we
aren't coming.

ALICE: Oh, you can make up some excuse—too busy at the office,
or something. Just keep thinking of the new car, and it will
be easy.

JIM: Not so easy, Alice.

ALICE: If you write Mother Young today, she'll be all used to
the idea by Christmas.

JIM: I wonder.

ALICE: Now don't back down. Let's just think about *ourselves*
this year, for a change. Ourselves and the new car. Let's forget about Christmas at Mother Young's.

JIM: I can't help thinking of Mother's face when she gets the
letter. I'm afraid I won't have much peace of mind.

ALICE: Nonsense. (LUCY *enters downstage. She stops in front of the* YOUNGS' *apartment, hesitates, and then pretends to knock.*) I wonder who that can be.

JIM: I'll see. (*He goes to front of stage, pretends to open door, then steps back somewhat startled.*) Well . . .

ALICE (*Curious, going to door*): Why . . . who are you?

LUCY: I'm . . . (*Hesitates*) . . . "Behold I bring you tidings of great joy—peace on earth, good will toward men." (*She turns to go, then calls back.*) Merry Christmas! (*Exits*)

JIM: Well, I'll be . . . what do you make of it, Alice?

ALICE: I don't quite know. It's not one of the children from this building, I'm sure of that. Oh, Jim, it gives me the strangest feeling. There must be some reason why it happened just now . . . just when we were going to write the letter.

JIM: Did you hear: "Peace on earth!" Alice, I think that means peace of mind, too.

ALICE: She looked like one of the angels in the art gallery, didn't she? How strange. Jim, perhaps we can't just sit back and forget about Christmas, after all. Write to Mother Young that we're coming.

JIM (*Happily*): Do you mean it?

ALICE: Yes. You see, it came to me, when the angel was standing there: the new car can wait. But Christmas can't! (*They go in and close the door.*) You can't forget about Christmas. (*At* AUNT MARTHA'S *apartment,* CHARLES *and* RALPH *are talking. They seem to be quite unhappy.*)

RALPH: This is going to be the lonesomest Christmas we ever had. Now we've come to live with Aunt Martha, I bet we won't ever have a real Christmas again.

CHARLES: She doesn't believe in any of the fun of Christmas, like other people.

RALPH: She says Santa Claus is nonsense, and giving presents is foolish, and a Christmas tree is a *heathen* custom. She

thinks you should think about the Christ Child on Christmas
. . . and nothing else!

CHARLES: Do you remember the big tinsel star we always had
at the top of our Christmas tree? And all the colored balls?

RALPH: And the nice Foxy Grandpa?

CHARLES: Aunt Martha would say he was *heathen*. (*There is
a moment's silence.*)

RALPH: We wouldn't dare ask for a Christmas tree, would we?

CHARLES: I should say not. (*Dreamily*) Oh, I wish we could
have a great big Christmas tree, full of presents and lights
and shining things. And I wish we could have someone for
dinner—a big Christmas dinner.

RALPH: Sh! Aunt Martha's coming. (*The boys open books
and read. AUNT MARTHA comes in with her knitting, and
sits down primly. After a moment she looks up over the top
of her glasses and speaks to the boys.*)

AUNT MARTHA: I have been meaning to tell you, boys, that I
am pleased to see you taking such a sensible attitude toward
Christmas. It's just a lot of fiddle-faddle. I am glad that you
aren't begging for one of those heathen Christmas trees.

RALPH *and* CHARLES: Yes, Aunt Martha.

CHARLES (*Timidly*): Would it be heathen to want company
. . . for Christmas dinner? The janitor's boy says he's
never tasted turkey . . . and he's *nine* years old.

AUNT MARTHA: Turkey? Make a fuss over Christmas dinner!
Why, Charles! (*LUCY comes on stage, stops before AUNT
MARTHA'S apartment, hesitates, then pretends to knock.*)
Christmas is all crusted over with foolishness these days.
(*Hears LUCY'S knock*) What was that? Someone must be
at the door. (*AUNT MARTHA goes to the door and pretends
to open it. The boys come up behind her and peer out too.*)
Why . . . why . . . who are you?

LUCY: I'm an . . . (*Hesitates*) . . . "Behold I bring you

tidings of great joy . . . peace on earth, good will toward men." (*She begins to run off, then turns and calls out, "Merry Christmas."*)

AUNT MARTHA: Well, of all things.

RALPH: It was an angel!

CHARLES: I never saw an angel before, did you, Aunt Martha? (AUNT MARTHA *turns back into the room, closes the door, sinks into her chair. Then she speaks slowly and dreamily, as the boys sit down.*)

AUNT MARTHA: I was an angel once . . .

CHARLES *and* RALPH: You were!

AUNT MARTHA: I was an angel once . . . in a Christmas play at the church. It was so long ago I had almost forgotten. I wore a white costume with wings that had real white chicken feathers sewn on. And after the play there was a tall Christmas tree . . .

RALPH (*Surprised*): In the *church!*

AUNT MARTHA: Yes. It almost touched the ceiling. And everyone got presents . . . and we all sang carols. Oh, it was a wonderful Christmas.

RALPH (*Thoughtfully*): Aunt Martha, how can it be heathen to have a Christmas tree, if there was one in church?

AUNT MARTHA (*Giving a start*): What's that? Why . . . why . . . (*Hurriedly she changes the subject.*) Do you know the angel's lines were the very ones I had to speak in the play: "I bring you tidings of great joy . . ." It all comes back to me now. (*Suddenly*) Boys, there must have been some reason that angel knocked on our door just now. She must have come to remind me. I am afraid I had forgotten all about Christmas. About "good will toward men." (*She looks at the boys eagerly.*) Shall we have a Christmas tree, after all? A big one that will reach from the floor to the ceiling, with lights and presents on it?

RALPH *and* CHARLES: Oh, Aunt Martha.

AUNT MARTHA: And shall we have company for Christmas dinner? Goodness, I haven't cooked a turkey in years . . . I wonder if I remember how.

RALPH *and* CHARLES: Oh, Aunt Martha! (*At* ZORLOVA'S *apartment,* ZORLOVA *is sitting at her dressing table, primping. She begins to hum. Suddenly she gets up and tries a new dance step. She does it very well, and knows it! The telephone rings and interrupts her dance. She goes to answer.*)

ZORLOVA: Hello. . . . Yes, this is Zorlova, the dancer. (*She does a few steps as she holds the phone.*) Who? Oh, on the Community Christmas Tree committee. (*Her voice falls and she stops dancing.*) Next week—what night? . . . Well, I might be able to do it, but I'm very busy, you know. How much do you pay, by the way? . . . What! Give up the best part of an evening for nothing! Just to entertain the community? . . . Yes, I realize Christmas is coming. And I realize they haven't had much chance to see good dancing. But a person has to live. . . . No, I never attended a Community Christmas Tree program. Really, I am afraid I'm going to be busy that evening. But if I *should* see my way clear to donating my talent, I'll let you know. Good-bye. (*She shrugs as if to say "What a nuisance."* LUCY *comes along and pretends to knock on the door.* ZORLOVA *looks at the door wonderingly.* LUCY *knocks again.* ZORLOVA *pretends to open the door.*) Oh! Who are you? How did you happen to come?

LUCY: "Behold, I bring you tidings of great joy which shall be to all people. . . ."

ZORLOVA: To all people. . . .

LUCY: "Peace on earth, good will toward men."

ZORLOVA: Oh! (LUCY *begins to run off, then turns and calls back, "Merry Christmas."* ZORLOVA *speaks softly.*) To all people. . . . (*Slowly* ZORLOVA *goes back into her room. She stands silently for a minute, then grabs the telephone book, looks for a number, and picks up the phone.*) 549, please. (*She does a happy tap dance as she waits.*) Hello. Is this the Chairman of the Community Christmas Tree committee? This is Zorlova, the dancer. Forgive me, but I feel quite different now about dancing at the program. A strange thing has happened. I'll be very happy to do it, really, I will. . . . Yes, there *is* something about Christmas, isn't there? (*The curtain falls.* LUCY *enters and tiptoes across stage.*)

LUCY (*Going to mirror*): I'm back, looking-glass. (*Peers at herself*) Oh, I *do* look like an angel. (*She turns this way and that.*) It makes me feel all different inside, it really does. But the other people I saw just now . . . I couldn't tell if they felt different or not. How can you tell how people feel? You can only see their faces . . . you can't see what goes on inside of them! (MISS PINSTER's *voice is heard outside.*)

MISS PINSTER: Good-bye, Mrs. Swishton. Remember, tomorrow at three. And I promise not to keep you waiting. Good-bye. (MISS PINSTER *comes on the stage again and sees* LUCY *at the mirror.*) What are you looking at, Lucy?

LUCY: An angel. I don't look like *me* at all, do I?

MISS PINSTER: Well, not exactly. Come now, just a few more pins in the hem and we'll be through for this afternoon. (*She starts to work on the hem again.*)

LUCY: Something happened while you were away, Miss Pinster.

MISS PINSTER: Oh, is that so?

LUCY: Yes. Something about Christmas.

MISS PINSTER: Really? Where?

LUCY: Right here in this apartment building.

MISS PINSTER: You don't say.

LUCY: Yes. You know that girl I told you about . . . the one

who bought the beautiful box of color-pencils for her brother?
MISS PINSTER: Yes, I remember. Twenty pencils with different colored leads.
LUCY: Well, she's going to give them to him, after all. She isn't going to keep them for herself.
MISS PINSTER: Why, how nice! That's the real Christmas spirit. But how did it happen, Lucy?
LUCY: Well, you see, Miss Pinster, the girl got to feeling different . . . inside . . . because she saw an angel . . . in the looking-glass!

THE END

The Broth of Christkindli

by Eleanore Leuser

Characters

JOHANN	THREE TRAVELERS
MOTHER	FOUR CAROLERS
OLD WOMAN	CHRISTKINDLI, *the Christmas Angel*
WILHELM	

TIME: *The night before Christmas.*

SETTING: *A room in a peasant cottage in Switzerland. A small decorated tree is in one corner, and a pot of broth simmers on the fire.*

AT RISE: MOTHER *is talking to* JOHANN *as she puts on her cloak and packs a small bag.*

MOTHER: I am sorry, Johann, that I have to go out and leave you alone on the night before Christmas. But when there is sickness in the village I must go—and Wilhelm's mother is ill.

JOHANN: I know, Mother. Do not worry. I will light the candle and put it in the window. It will light you home and be a welcome to the Christkindli if she comes.

MOTHER (*Anxiously*): You will keep the broth on the fire, Johann, that she may have some to warm herself on her long cold journey?

JOHANN (*Proudly*): Do not fear, Mother. Never before have

136

I been old enough to watch for the coming of the Christmas Angel. It may be that this will be the very house she will stop at.

MOTHER: Every house in the village is hoping the Christkindli will stop at their door. They say it is but once in a lifetime she becomes visible to human eyes and bestows her blessings.

JOHANN (*Joyously*): Who knows—perhaps tonight, I shall see her.

MOTHER (*Getting ready to leave*): Who knows? (*Pauses as she goes to door*) I think I shall send Wilhelm over to stay with you while I stay with his mother.

JOHANN (*Disturbed*): Oh, no, Mother, not Wilhelm! I would rather be by myself than have Wilhelm come here.

MOTHER: It is not good to be by yourself on Christmas Eve. Wilhelm will, at least, be company for you. Now say no more. I shall send him. Goodbye, my Johann. Watch well for the Christkindli.

JOHANN (*Dolefully*): Goodbye, Mother. I wish you wouldn't send Wilhelm, though.

MOTHER (*Patting him on the head*): Don't be foolish, my son. (*She leaves.* JOHANN *lights candle and puts it in front of window. The door opens and his mother re-enters.*) Johann, I had almost forgotten. The cakes I made for the carolers are in the cupboard. When they come to sing, be sure to give them some. It brings shame to a household if there is nothing to offer the carolers on Christmas Eve.

JOHANN: I will remember, Mother. (*She exits. He goes over to the cupboard, gets out a plate of cakes and puts them by the tree. Then he goes over and stirs the broth, sniffing as he does so.*) Mmm! Never has this broth smelled so good. I hope the Christkindli comes to this house tonight so she may have some. (*A knock sounds at the door.* JOHANN *goes to open it. An* OLD WOMAN *is standing there.*)

OLD WOMAN: Good even to you, my lad. Could a poor body come in this Christmas Eve and warm herself by your fire?

JOHANN (*Opening wide the door*): Good even, good dame, of course you may come in by the fire. (*He takes her over to a chair by the fire.*)

OLD WOMAN (*Looking around*): I see you are ready for the Christmas time. You have the tree of the Christ Child with its message of peace and good will.

JOHANN: Yes—that is the tree of Christkindli. It is all finished but the star on the topmost branch. In all the village we could find no star.

OLD WOMAN: Ah, but it is beautiful even without the star. You see I have no tree—nothing for the festival of Christmas.

JOHANN (*Much disturbed*): Nothing to eat even?

OLD WOMAN (*Shaking her head sadly*): Black bread and water.

JOHANN (*Getting a little bowl*): Here, I will give you some of the Christkindli's broth to take home for your Christmas. It will give you a little cheer. (*He fills bowl.*)

OLD WOMAN (*Taking it*): You are a good lad. May the Christkindli bless you. (*As she goes toward the door with her bowl, WILHELM bursts in rudely, almost knocking her down.*)

WILHELM: Ho there, Johann, here I am. Your mother sent me to stay with you. (*Watching the OLD WOMAN as she goes out the door*) Who is that queer old woman? She is a poor sort of thing.

JOHANN (*Shocked*): Hush, Wilhelm, she might have heard you. She was cold and hungry so I gave her some of the Christkindli's broth.

WILHELM: Oh, so you have some broth, too. I wager every home in the village has some, cooking on the fire, hoping the Christkindli will visit them. A foolish idea! (*Going over and sniffing broth*) The broth smells good, though. I'll take some.

JOHANN (*Horrified*) : Oh, no, you mustn't. No one must eat the broth of the Christmas Angel.

WILHELM : You gave some to that silly old woman, didn't you?

JOHANN : That is different. That was giving her a little of the joy of Christmas for she had none of her own.

WILHELM : Well, for my part, I shall have some myself. I don't believe in those silly tales of Christkindli. (*He proceeds to help himself while* JOHANN *protests. A knock is heard on the door.* THREE TRAVELERS *enter. One is bandaged and ill.*)

1ST TRAVELER : May we come in for a few moments on this cold night and let a sick man rest by your fire?

JOHANN : You are welcome, especially on Christmas Eve. (*The three go over by the fire and the sick man sits down.*)

2ND TRAVELER : Your broth smells good. Could we have a cup for this sick man so that he may be refreshed before we start again on our travels?

JOHANN (*Hesitating*) : It is the broth of Christkindli . . .

WILHELM (*In a loud whisper*) : They want it badly. Sell it to them for gold.

SICK TRAVELER (*Overhearing*) : Yes, I will give you a piece of gold for your broth for I am exhausted and can go no further.

JOHANN : If you are ill I will give you some. (*He gives the sick man a cupful.*) Your friends are cold and weary, also. They too shall have some. But I can take no money. (*He gives the others broth.*)

WILHELM : Johann, you are an idiot not to take good money.

JOHANN (*Proudly*) : Christkindli's broth must never be sold.

1ST TRAVELER (*Putting down cup*) : Thank you, my son. It has warmed me to the depths of my heart.

2ND TRAVELER (*Putting down cup*) : I also thank you. We can go out in the snow warm and cheered.

SICK TRAVELER: The blessings of Christkindli be upon this house.

WILHELM : I say again, Johann, you are very stupid. Look, half your broth is gone. Even if the Christkindli should stop she would have little to sup. Come, we might as well finish it. (*He starts to take a spoonful.*)

JOHANN (*Angrily*) : Wilhelm, I tell you stop. (*He takes the spoon away from* WILHELM. WILHELM *laughs and dances away. He sees the cakes by the Christmas tree.*)

WILHELM (*Taking one and holding it up*): Ah-ha! What are these? They look good.

JOHANN (*Going over to him quickly*) : Wilhelm, don't take them—they are for the carolers. You know each house must have a gift for the carolers when they come on Christmas Eve.

WILHELM (*Stuffing one in his mouth and taking another*) : Try and stop me. Broth for the Christkindli—gifts for the carolers —what a stupid you are, when you could eat them yourself. Why don't you worry about not having a star for the top of your tree. Look how bare it is without one! (JOHANN *looks around and,* WILHELM *stuffs all the cakes in his pocket.*)

JOHANN (*Looking at tree sadly*): Our old one is broken and though we hunted we could find no other. (*He turns and sees what* WILHELM *has done.*) Wilhelm, you have taken all of the cakes. Oh, indeed you must give them back. You must . . . you must. (*He tries to get them from* WILHELM *but* WILHELM *laughs and eludes him pulling them out of his pocket and eating meanwhile. There is a sudden sound of singing in the distance.*)

WILHELM (*Stopping eating to listen*) : There are your carolers. You can tell them your friend Wilhelm enjoyed their cakes mightily. (*He escapes out the door.*)

JOHANN (*Half-crying, half-calling*) : Wilhelm, Wilhelm, bring back just a few. (*He waits and as* WILHELM *does not return he shuts the door and sits down with his head in his hands.*) What shall I do for the carolers? (*The songs of the carolers sound closer and closer until they are right outside. Three knocks are heard.* JOHANN *goes slowly to open the door.* FOUR CAROLERS *dressed in medieval costume enter.* JOHANN *stares surprised.*)

CAROLERS : A good Christmas even to you and all who live within this house.

JOHANN : I thought you would be carolers of this village but you are strangers hereabouts.

1ST CAROLER : We are the carolers of Christkindli.

2ND CAROLER : We came to bring blessings on the house.

3RD CAROLER : The blessings of the Christmas tide.

4TH CAROLER : And peace on earth, good will to men.

JOHANN (*Sadly*) : There is nothing I can give you in exchange for your blessings but the broth of Christkindli. Your cakes were stolen. (*He ladles the last of the broth into the bowls as he speaks and tips the pot into the last bowl to get every drop. The* CAROLERS *sup eagerly.*) If the Christkindli comes she will turn away for I have nothing to offer her. I am sore ashamed but maybe she will understand. (*A tinkle of sleigh bells is heard, then the sound of soft music.* CHRISTKINDLI, *a beautiful angel with a crown on her head and a star in her hand enters. The Carolers bow low before her.* JOHANN *also bows.*) It is Christkindli!

CHRISTKINDLI (*Kindly*) : Yes, I am Christkindli. But do not worry, little Johann. I have already supped your broth.

JOHANN (*Dazed*) : I do not understand.

CHRISTKINDLI : I was the old woman to whom you gave your broth. I was the sick traveler whom you warmed and fed. I sent these carolers of mine to your house knowing full well your cakes were gone. As you gave it to those in need you gave it to me.

JOHANN (*In wonderment*) : Who will believe that this could have happened to me?

CHRISTKINDLI (*Kindly*) : So that all in the village may know and believe that kindness is the spirit of Christmas, I will put this star upon your tree. For Christkindli always comes where there is the spirit of true kindness. (*She puts the star on the topmost branch of the little tree.*) Now, my little Johann, if you never see Christkindli again you will always know she is here and all over the world whenever Christmas comes to spread the spirit of kindness and good will to men. (*The* CAROLERS *start singing softly.* JOHANN *stands looking at the tree and* CHRISTKINDLI *in joy and wonder, as the curtain falls.*)

THE END

Happy Christmas to All

by Jeannette Covert Nolan

Characters

DR. CLEMENT CLARKE MOORE
MRS. MOORE, *his wife*
EMILY, *Mrs. Moore's cousin*
THE MOORE CHILDREN, *two small boys and a girl of eight*

SCENE 1

TIME: *Six o'clock in the evening of December 24, 1822.*
SETTING: *The library of Dr. Moore's comfortable home in Chelsea, New York.*
AT RISE: DR. MOORE *is seated at his desk. He is a handsome man in early middle age. Books are piled in front of him. He turns the pages, and writes, scratching diligently with his quill pen. From outside can be heard the jingle of sleigh-bells and bursts of carols from passing singers. From door at left, MRS. MOORE enters. She is a youthful, pretty woman. She is carrying a tall red candle which she sets on the sill of the rear window.*

MRS. MOORE: Clement?
DR. MOORE (*Without glancing up*): Yes, my dear?
MRS. MOORE: I am sorry to disturb you. But something has occurred. Something rather dreadful. The turkey. I have neglected to buy it. I don't see how I could have done so! It was the confusion, I suppose. So much to think about.

143

Straightening the parlors, readying the spare bedroom for Cousin Emily, preparing the children's gifts and the sweetmeats. (*She pauses.*) Clement, you're not listening! *Clement!*

DR. MOORE (*Glancing guiltily at her*): Eh? Yes, my dear?

MRS. MOORE: I declare, you haven't heard a word I've said!

DR. MOORE: Ah, but I have. You said you were confused, you had neglected the parlors, straightened the sweetmeats and prepared the children's gifts for Emily.

MRS. MOORE (*Exasperated, yet smiling in spite of herself*): Nothing of the kind. You were not listening. I'm talking about the *turkey.*

DR. MOORE: Turkey, eh? What turkey?

MRS. MOORE: The Christmas turkey. For tomorrow.

DR. MOORE (*Nodding*): Ah, yes, of course. I prefer chestnut stuffing, a bit of sage, a hint of garlic—but *just* a hint—and a minimum of spices. I have never fancied a spicy stuffing for roast fowl—

MRS. MOORE (*Advancing, and leaning over the desk*): Clement, do come out of those dusty old books for once. There will be no dressing at all. There is no turkey.

DR. MOORE (*Half-rising, and in shocked voice, as if the gravity of the situation has finally been borne in upon him*): No turkey! For Christmas! My dear, whyever not?

MRS. MOORE: Simply because I've forgotten it—as I've been trying to tell you.

DR. MOORE (*Sinking back into his chair*): But this is terrible! Something must be done about this!

MRS. MOORE: Exactly.

DR. MOORE: Without a turkey, it would scarcely be Christmas!

MRS. MOORE: I agree.

DR. MOORE: The children would be disappointed—

MRS. MOORE: And you, too, Clement. You are very fond of turkey.

Dr. Moore: I am, indeed. (*Thoughtfully*) Well, how can we solve the problem?

Mrs. Moore: Actually, there *is* no problem.

Dr. Moore: Eh? What do you mean?

Mrs. Moore: I mean, you must go to the market and purchase a turkey.

Dr. Moore (*Frowning*): At this hour?

Mrs. Moore: The shops will not have closed.

Dr. Moore (*Shuffling the papers on his desk*): If I were not so—so occupied—

Mrs. Moore: But you will have to put your writing aside, anyway, tonight, won't you?

Dr. Moore: Yes, I daresay. But—

Mrs. Moore: Get your coat and hat, Clement. And hurry.

Dr. Moore (*Obviously reluctant*): It is quite cold, snowing—

Mrs. Moore: But you never mind a little snow.

Dr. Moore (*Gazing at the fire, and seeming to have an inspiration*): I would go, and gladly. But I've lost my *shoes*. (*He stretches forth his feet, on which are felt slippers.*) See, wife? (*Gently, yet with a note of triumph*) You would scarcely expect me to venture outdoors in *these*?

Mrs. Moore (*Laughing at him*): Oh, Clement, Clement, you are only making excuses. You haven't lost your shoes. Where are they?

Dr. Moore (*Solemnly*): I have no idea.

Mrs. Moore (*Circling his chair, and bending down*): I have! They are here. Just where you took them off. Just where you take them off every evening when you come home from your classes. (*She holds up the shoes.*)

Dr. Moore (*Shaking his head*): Astonishing! (*He sighs, and gets to his feet.*) Well, I suppose—(*He reaches for the shoes, steps out of the slippers and puts on the shoes. He is smiling ruefully.*) I have never before bought a turkey, you know.

Mrs. Moore: High time you had the experience! (*She runs out door at left, returning with* Dr. Moore's *overcoat and black stovepipe hat.*) Here you are! And I advise you to wear your muffler. (*She produces black woolen muffler from pocket of coat.*) And your gloves, Clement. (*She helps him don all these wraps, tying the muffler over the hat and knotting it under his chin.*) Now you will be snug. (*She pats him on the back and gives him a little push toward the door in rear wall.*)

Dr. Moore (*Pausing, and looking at her and then at his desk*): I hope no one from the Seminary spies me. None of my students. They might think it comical. Dr. Moore, professor of Hebrew and classical languages at the General Theological Seminary—and strolling about on Christmas Eve with a plucked turkey on his shoulder!

Mrs. Moore: Nonsense!

Dr. Moore: I doubt if my father would have consented to such an indignity. He was a gentleman and a scholar, the Protestant Episcopal bishop of New York.

Mrs. Moore (*Edging him toward the door*): Yes, yes, I know.

Dr. Moore: My father officiated at the inauguration of President George Washington and at the death of Alexander Hamilton. He had a position to maintain, and he always maintained it.

Mrs. Moore (*Impatiently*): Clement, you hesitate merely because you are lazy. Let us just forget about the turkey. Have off your things; go back to your books. There is some salt cod in the house. I shall cook that for our dinner tomorrow.

Dr. Moore (*Horrified*): Salt cod!

Mrs. Moore: And very good, too. I like salt cod. So wholesome.

Dr. Moore (*Shuddering*): My dear! (*He bustles out, slamming door behind him.* Mrs. Moore *smiles, shrugs, hums*

*softly to herself as she straightens a chair or two and then
exits through left door. Stage is empty only a moment, then
a* SMALL BOY *enters through rear door. He carries a covered
basket. He moves to center stage, whistles once, mysteriously.
Immediately a* SECOND SMALL BOY *and a* LITTLE GIRL *appear on threshold of left door.*)

GIRL: Oh, Bud, did you get it? (*She closes door furtively.*)

FIRST BOY: No need to be so careful. I passed Father on the
street. But he didn't recognize me in the darkness.

GIRL (*Crossing to basket, lifting lid and peering in*): What a
sweet, cunning one!

SECOND BOY: Here, let me look. (*He peers into basket.*) Yes,
it's just right. Who gave it to you, Bud?

FIRST BOY: Mrs. De Paul.

GIRL: As usual!

SECOND BOY: What did you tell Mrs. De Paul?

FIRST BOY: That we wanted a fine Christmas present for
Father.

GIRL: As usual! And what did she say?

FIRST BOY: She laughed and said she didn't think Father *could*
be so very surprised.

GIRL: Because we have the same present for him every Christmas!

SECOND BOY: Oh, not *every* Christmas.

GIRL: Every Christmas for the last three years.

SECOND BOY: Well, Father always *is* surprised, though.

GIRL: Perhaps he only acts surprised.

FIRST BOY (*Crestfallen and indignant*): What's the matter?
Are you sorry we planned on this? Is it all a mistake? Shall
I take the present back to Mrs. De Paul?

SECOND BOY: No, no! Why, what else could we get *now?*

FIRST BOY: But if it isn't a surprise—

GIRL (*Less critically, and smiling down into the basket*): Well,

I suppose we mustn't bother. And it *is* so sweet! But—
(*Slowly*)—next year we'll begin very early, and we'll plan
something quite different and original.

FIRST BOY: Sh—sh! Who's coming? Father? (*He snatches
up basket, clamps on lid and hastens through left door, reën-
tering almost instantly, as someone knocks on rear door.*)
No, it isn't Father. (*He flings open door.*) It's—

THE CHILDREN (*In a joyful chorus*): Cousin Emily!

EMILY (*Entering*): So it is. (*She is attractive, her arms laden
with packages.*) Merry Christmas, my darlings!

SECOND BOY: I'll call Mother. (*Scampering to left door, he
shouts*): Mother! Cousin Emily's here.

FIRST BOY (*Politely*): May I relieve you of your burden?

EMILY (*Chuckling*): Thank you, no. My trinkets I shall stow
away, myself. They're secrets.

MRS. MOORE (*Entering and embracing EMILY*): Dear Emily!
Now we shall have the best of holidays.

EMILY (*As FIRST BOY assists her with her wraps*): A charm-
ing welcome!

MRS. MOORE: Children, what's in that basket in the hall?

FIRST BOY: Father's surprise. It's—(*He whispers in EMILY'S
ear.*)

EMILY: What, again? Mrs. De Paul must have an endless
supply. I'd think your yard would be swarming by this
time!

FIRST BOY: No, we keep them only until they grow large. Then
we take them out to the farm.

EMILY: And at the farm you're starting a colony, are you?

SECOND BOY (*Anxiously*): Cousin Emily, we're rather afraid
Father won't be surprised.

EMILY: Oh, certainly he will be! Delighted also. But where is
your father?

MRS. MOORE: At the market.

EMILY: Dr. Moore, the distinguished professor, at market?

MRS. MOORE: He hated to go, but I insisted. And he should be returning any minute. (*Laughing, she glances out window.*) Yes, here he is! (*Enter DR. MOORE, his hat powdered with snow, a turkey over his shoulder. There is a general buzz of greetings.*)

DR. MOORE (*Shaking hands with EMILY*): Emily, behold in me a much abused man.

EMILY: Doing the family marketing?

DR. MOORE: I had to. (*Muttering*) Salt cod!

MRS. MOORE (*Inspecting turkey*): I must say you did well, Clement. A beautiful bird!

FIRST BOY (*Gesturing to his brother and sister*): Shall we?

GIRL: Yes. Father, we have a gift for you. If you and Mother and Cousin Emily will sit down—(*She rushes offstage, comes back with basket, which she deposits in front of DR. MOORE.*)

DR. MOORE: For me? Well, how nice! (*He stoops.*)

GIRL: Wait, though! Father, do you suspect what's in the basket?

DR. MOORE: No. I can't imagine. Fruit? Candies? A holly wreath? (*He taps his forehead, as if in deep thought.*) But I seem to catch a tiny, scratching sound! Can it be something alive?

SECOND BOY (*Excitedly*): Yes! Alive!

DR. MOORE: Can it be—(*He removes lid.*) Well, *well!* A black kitten! Of all the splendid Christmas tokens! *Just* what I've been wishing for!

SECOND BOY: Honestly, Father?

FIRST BOY: We chose a black one, to match your clothes, sir.

GIRL: We gave you one last year, you know. And for several years.

DR. MOORE: The very reason I didn't anticipate receiving one this year.

SECOND BOY: There, do you see! He *is* surprised! (*Still anxiously*) You haven't got tired of black kittens, Father?

DR. MOORE: I *never* get tired of them! (*He sets the kitten on his lap, and strokes it.*)

GIRL: Just the same, *next* year—(*She nods wisely to herself.*)

EMILY: That looks like a superior kitten. May I have a closer acquaintance? (*She takes the kitten from* DR. MOORE, *who rises, fumbles in pocket of his coat, and crosses to his desk.*)

DR. MOORE: And now I have a trifling surprise for you children.

FIRST BOY: Not our presents, sir? We don't get them until tomorrow morning. (*The children all lift eager faces.*)

DR. MOORE: No. This is a little something. (*He pauses, as if embarrassed.*) Well, I wrote something for you.

SECOND BOY (*Flatly*): Oh! Like—the books you're always writing?

DR. MOORE: Not exactly, no. (*He sits, and spreads before him a crumpled bit of paper.*) Verses. Rhymes.

MRS. MOORE (*Amazed*): Rhymes? Why, Clement!

DR. MOORE: I know it's a most extraordinary thing for me to do. But as I was walking along the streets, as I stood in the market—somehow, rhymes suggested themselves to me. About Christmas. So I jotted them down. I haven't yet finished. Would you care to—to—

MRS. MOORE: Oh, do read them, Clement.

DR. MOORE:

" 'Twas the night before Christmas, when all through the house

Not a creature was stirring, not even a mouse;"

(*Beginning timidly, he gains assurance, reading first ten lines of "A Visit from St. Nicholas."*)

GIRL (*Interrupting enthusiastically*): But, Father, this isn't a bit like the things you write! It's—it's good!

MRS. MOORE: Extremely good, Clement!

DR. MOORE (*Beaming over his spectacles*): Oh, it's nothing, really.

EMILY: Nothing? A poem! I shall want a copy, Clement.

DR. MOORE (*Alarmed*): No, no! I should be distressed if anyone ever knew I was so—so foolish. (*He has picked up his pen and is writing rapidly.*) It just spins out in the strangest manner! Well, shall I continue reading?

CHORUS: Yes! Yes, do read!

DR. MOORE:
"Away to the window I flew like a flash,
Tore open the shutters and threw up the sash . . ."
(*As he reads, the lights dim and the curtain falls.*)

* * *

SCENE 2

TIME: *Evening, December 24, 1823.*

SETTING: *The library, as it was in previous scene, except for minor changes which show the passage of a year's time.*

AT RISE: DR. MOORE *is seated in armchair before the fireplace, his slippered feet on footstool. He is reading a newspaper.* MRS. MOORE *sits in another chair, a large bowl in her lap, the contents of which she stirs with a pewter spoon. Occasionally, and rather apprehensively, she looks at* DR. MOORE.

DR. MOORE: Where are the children, my dear?

MRS. MOORE: Upstairs. Very busy with their Christmas tasks.

DR. MOORE: I daresay I shall have the customary offering of a black kitten from Mrs. De Paul's never-failing cattery?

MRS. MOORE: Probably. The youngsters give you kittens because they themselves fairly dote on kittens.

DR. MOORE (*Smiling*): Well, that's an excellent rule for the selection of gifts. And is Emily coming?

MRS. MOORE: I—I think she is.

DR. MOORE: Good! There is never much alteration in our scheme of life, from season to season, is there? I prefer it so. Peace, serenity, nothing to upset routine. And this year the turkey was bought on schedule, and I'll not be forced to parade with it in the public streets.

MRS. MOORE: I'm mixing the stuffing according to your taste.

DR. MOORE: Ah! (*He beams, and resumes his scanning of the newspaper. Suddenly he rattles the pages, stares incredulously.*) Do my eyes deceive me? No! It is! It really is! That ridiculous poem of mine, those silly whimsical verses I wrote last Christmas! About St. Nick! That drivel—it's printed here, in the *Troy Sentinel,* in type, where everybody can see! (*He kicks over the footstool and rises, clutching the newspaper. Much agitated, he paces around the room.*) Oh, this is terrible! A disgrace! And who can have done it? Well, why don't you say something? (*He stops.*) You did it! You sent my verses to the *Sentinel!*

MRS. MOORE: No! No, I didn't!

DR. MOORE: But who else—(*Pausing*)—Emily! Emily, of course!

MRS. MOORE: Clement, I am so sorry—

DR. MOORE: Your Cousin Emily! Knowing how I felt, my own poor opinion of them, Emily deliberately sent them to the paper!

MRS. MOORE: No, Clement. Please be calm. It wasn't like that. Not quite. Emily did make a copy of your poem; she read it to a few friends, and they repeated it to a few of their friends; and soon she had a request from the editor of the *Sentinel* for permission to print it—

DR. MOORE (*Furiously*): A request which she complied with! (*As* MRS. MOORE *nods sadly*) Emily is a meddling woman!

MRS. MOORE: She did not intend to annoy you, Clement.

DR. MOORE: Annoy? She has ruined me! (*He paces, muttering.*)

MRS. MOORE: Oh, no! In her letter last month, Emily told me—

DR. MOORE: So you knew it would be in the paper?

MRS. MOORE: Well, yes, I knew. But I—I hoped you wouldn't notice.

DR. MOORE: Indeed? Everybody will notice. Hundreds of people, thousands. And they will all think that Clement Moore, professor at the Theological Seminary, has turned imbecile!

MRS. MOORE (*Rising, speaking decisively*): I am rather sure they'll not think that. Instead, they'll read the verses with interest and admiration. You should not be ashamed of the poem, Clement. You should be proud. It is lovely, a picture in words. Perhaps it will be reprinted—often. Perhaps it will be read ten years from now—twenty years. You've written all these books. (*She gestures toward the desk.*) Possibly not one of them will live so long or be so popular as the little poem you dashed off just for our own children.

DR. MOORE: I can't believe that! (*Pausing in his pacing, he looks at her.*) Are you—are you *weeping?*

MRS. MOORE (*Dabbing at her eyes*): Only—only a bit. Forgive me.

DR. MOORE: But you mustn't weep at all! Why should you?

MRS. MOORE: Well, our Christmas is—is spoiled—

DR. MOORE (*Remorsefully*): My dear! How badly I'm behaving! (*He goes quickly to her and takes her hand.*) I'm the one to apologize, and I do. (*Slowly.*) The printing, against my wishes, of the poem is merely a minor incident; I have exaggerated its importance. What matters is that we, under this roof, shall be happy together on Christmas Eve.

MRS. MOORE: Oh, Clement—

DR. MOORE: Dry your tears, my dear. (*As she obeys, he is looking into the bowl which is on the desk.*) Is there spice in the stuffing? Not too much, I trust.

Mrs. Moore: Won't you sample it?

Dr. Moore (*Glad that her attention has been distracted*): Yes, I will. (*He dips the pewter spoon into the bowl and nibbles.*) Umm! Delicate and delicious! (*They are smiling at each other as the rear door opens, and* Emily *enters.*) Ah, good evening, Emily!

Emily (*After embracing* Mrs. Moore, *and walking shyly toward* Dr. Moore): Are you angry with me, Clement?

Dr. Moore: No. No, I have been somewhat startled, I admit. But *not* angry. (*He glances at* Mrs. Moore.) Would you say that I displayed anger?

Mrs. Moore (*Stoutly*): Certainly not! (*As she helps* Emily *off with her wraps, voices are heard offstage, and the* Three Children *troop in, left door. They are carrying a covered basket which they deposit at* Dr. Moore's *feet.*)

Children: Surpise! Surprise for Father!

Mrs. Moore: But you haven't greeted Cousin Emily, children.

Children (*In chorus*): How do you do, Cousin Emily! Surprise for Father—

Dr. Moore: Well, well, what can this be? (*Gazing at the basket.*) Candies? Fruit? A holly wreath?

Children: *No, no!*

Dr. Moore: Not a black kitten?

First Boy: No, sir!

Girl: We said it would be a different present this year. It is!

Second Boy (*Dancing about with excitement*): Different! Very different. Oh, you never could guess!

Dr. Moore (*In an aside to* Mrs. Moore): If it isn't a black kitten, then I'm truly mystified. (*He stoops.*) But surely I catch a tiny, scratching sound. Something alive?

Second Boy: Yes, alive!

Dr. Moore (*Lifting basket cover*): 'Pon my soul! A *white* kitten!

CHILDREN: Surprise, surprise!

GIRL: Would you ever have guessed?

DR. MOORE: Never, never. And I've been wishing for a white kitten.

GIRL (*As* CHILDREN *demonstrate elation at their success*): Father, do you remember the poem you read to us last Christmas Eve?

DR. MOORE: Yes, I remember.

GIRL: Such a nice poem. Read it again tonight.

FIRST BOY: But he said it was a "trifle," and maybe he doesn't have the poem any more.

DR. MOORE: As it happens, I've been providentially supplied with a copy of that poem. (*He glances at* EMILY, *who smiles.*)

GIRL: Then you *will* read it, Father?

MRS. MOORE: You get into your nightgowns, children. Father will read to all of us before the fire. (*Exit* CHILDREN *and* MRS. MOORE.)

DR. MOORE (*Wandering to the window*). A beautiful night, Emily. The snow is like a thick, soft veil over the world.

EMILY: Yes. My dear Clement, you see how it's going to be with that poem of yours, don't you? Everyone who encounters it will remember it. *A Visit from St. Nicholas* will make you famous.

DR. MOORE: Oh, no! The rhymes have no literary merit.

EMILY: But they have such appeal!

DR. MOORE: They seemed just to come to me—out of the air.

EMILY: I think I recognize your St. Nick, though. Isn't he Van Kroyt, the butcher here in Chelsea?

DR. MOORE: Perhaps. I bought the turkey in Van Kroyt's shop. I was watching him. (*Looking thoughtful*) "His eyes—how they twinkled! his dimples, how merry!"

EMILY (*Also quoting*): "His cheeks were like roses, his nose like a cherry!" Yes, that's Mr. Van Kroyt. But what prompted you to invent the reindeer?

DR. MOORE: Reindeer? I suppose I *did* invent them.

EMILY: Of course, you did. No one ever before described St. Nick's mode of travel. "Now, Dasher! now, Dancer! now, Prancer and Vixen!"

DR. MOORE: "On, Comet! on, Cupid! on, Donner and Blitzen!" (*He sighs.*) Well, as I've told you, Emily, the circumstances of my composing the poem were odd, to say the least. I can't explain it.

EMILY: Perhaps inspiration can never be explained, Clement. (*Door opens;* MRS. MOORE *enters with* CHILDREN.)

GIRL: Here we are, Father! (*All settle down around the hearth.* DR. MOORE *takes up newspaper and begins to read.*)

DR. MOORE:

" 'Twas the night before Christmas, when all through the house

Not a creature was stirring, not even a mouse—"

(*He continues; lights dim and curtain slowly falls.*)

THE END

Jingle Bells

by Edrie Pendleton

Characters

ELSIE	MOTHER
JACK	FATHER
GINNY	DIANA
DANNY	

TIME: *Christmas Eve.*

SETTING: *The living room of a farmhouse.*

AT RISE: ELSIE, *fourteen years old, is fussing with a light cord from the Christmas tree lights.* GINNY, *nine, is seated in chair left, stringing popcorn from bowl on table near.* Danny, *seven, is holding a glass ball in one hand and grabs some popcorn from bowl with the other and stuffs it into his mouth.*

GINNY: Danny, don't eat the popcorn. There won't be enough for the tree.

DANNY: But I *like* popcorn.

ELSIE: So do I—on the Christmas tree. Oh, it does look nice! Some people may say popcorn trimming is old-fashioned but I think it adds a touch.

GINNY: We always have it. (DANNY *takes another handful of popcorn and* GINNY *playfully slaps his hand.*) But we won't this year, Danny, if you don't stop. (*He grins and hangs ball on Christmas tree.*)

ELSIE: I wish Jack would hurry and get back from the barn so he could help me with these lights.

GINNY: Where's Diana? Couldn't she help you?

ELSIE: Diana probably doesn't like trimming Christmas trees.

DANNY: But everybody does.

ELSIE: Well, don't ask me *what* Diana likes. She's been here over two months now and she hasn't entered into anything.

GINNY: Mother says we shouldn't talk about her, Elsie. After all, she's our cousin and she's visiting us. . . .

ELSIE: I know and I've done my best, but the way she acts . . . so superior to everything! Well, I've made up my mind to one thing . . . I'm not going to let her spoil our Christmas.

GINNY: As though anyone could do that. (FATHER *and* JACK, *who is about twelve, enter left. They are brushing snow off their coats.*)

JACK: Boy, is it snowing! And coming down harder every minute.

FATHER: Children, Jack and I have a Christmas present for you.

ELSIE: But Dad, it's too early for presents. . . .

FATHER (*Laughing*): Not for this one. There are four new kittens out in the haymow.

DANNY: Kittens? Oh, boy! What color are they?

JACK: There's a white, two spotted and an all black.

GINNY: Four baby kittens for Christmas. Why, that's one for each of us.

FATHER: Well, I thought your cousin Diana might like one.

DANNY: I want the black.

FATHER: Maybe you can all draw straws. Where's your mother?

GINNY: She's working on my costume for the play, Dad.

FATHER: What's that? She'd better hurry, hadn't she? Doesn't the play start at eight o'clock?

ELSIE: Yes, and we've got so much to do before we leave. Finish the tree and. . . .

GINNY (*Rising*): Oh, I'm so excited, being in a play on Christmas Eve. (*Dancing around and chanting*) I'm a Christmas angel. I'm a Christmas angel!

JACK (*Pulling her hair teasingly*): Hmm, why they ever picked you for an angel, funny face, I can't imagine. If they knew you the way I do. . . .

ELSIE: Jack, will you help me with these lights?

JACK: Sure. (*Taking off coat and throwing it over chair*) You don't need me any more in the barn, do you, Dad?

FATHER: No. I just want to see that the animals are all good and warm for the night and then close things up tight and I'm done. It's really getting cold out and with this heavy snow. . . .

GINNY: Dad, we'll be able to get to town, won't we?

FATHER: Oh, sure. I think we can get the old bus started.

GINNY: But if it's so cold and the roads get bad. . . .

JACK: It's only a mile to town, Ginny.

FATHER: We'll get to the schoolhouse all right. Why, Ginny, do you think I want to miss seeing you acting like an angel . . . for once? (*He grins at her and goes out left.*)

ELSIE: Dad's so cute. We have more fun around here. Come on, now, Jack, get busy. There's something wrong with the cord. (*She hands him cord.*)

JACK (*Glancing at it*): Nothing to it, Elsie. Just a loose wire. (*He takes out his pocket knife and starts fiddling around with the screw plug. The others continue to trim tree. GINNY adds another string of popcorn. DIANA, a girl about fourteen, enters left. She speaks in a reserved way without much expression, as though holding herself in. She stops and hesitates as she sees them all working on tree.*)

ELSIE: Oh . . . Hello, Diana.

GINNY: Would you like to help us trim the Christmas tree?

DIANA: Why, I—I don't know. I don't think so. (*She crosses to table right.*) I left a book in here.

JACK: Oh, come on. It's fun.

DIANA (*Coming near tree*): Well—all right. (DANNY *hands her a colored ball from box which she tries to fasten to tree.*) How does it work? I can't seem to. . . .

JACK: For gosh sakes. There's a fastener right on it. Just bend it around a little.

GINNY: Doesn't the tree look pretty, Diana?

DIANA: I—I've never seen popcorn used on a Christmas tree before. (*She finally gets the ornament on tree.*)

ELSIE (*Looking at her*): No, I suppose you haven't.

DANNY (*Handing her another ornament*): Here's another one, Diana. Put that right in front somewhere.

DIANA (*She takes the ball and nervously starts to fasten it to tree. It slips out of her fingers and falls and breaks*): Oh. . . . (*The others all stop what they're doing.*)

DANNY: You've broken it!

GINNY: That was my favorite ornament.

ELSIE: We've had that one for years—ever since I was little.

DIANA: Well, I'm sorry. I didn't mean to break it. (DANNY *picks up pieces of broken ornament and sadly puts them in ornament box on floor.*)

DANNY: It was such a pretty one.

DIANA: Perhaps I'd better not help after all. (*She crosses to table and picks up her book.*) I'll go upstairs and read.

GINNY (*Trying to be helpful*): We're almost through anyhow, Diana. We'll be leaving for the play before too long. Don't forget about that.

DIANA (*She is about to go off left*): I don't think I'll go.

GINNY: Not go? But I'm in the play and there's going to be a party afterwards and. . . .

DIANA: Father sent me several new books for Christmas, you know. I think I'll just stay here tonight and read them. (*She goes out.*)

JACK: Can you feature that? Read a book on Christmas Eve!

ELSIE: I guess Diana's just too sophisticated for Christmas.

GINNY: Why does she act so funny? As though she didn't like any of us?

ELSIE: I suppose she thinks we're all a bunch of hicks because we live on a farm near a small town. She doesn't like our town—she doesn't like our school. . . . I'm the same age as she is and you'd think she would warm up to my crowd, but she just looks at them all in that superior sort of way. . . .

JACK: The way she looked at our Christmas tree.

DANNY: She's never seen popcorn on a tree, she says.

ELSIE: I suppose she likes all blue lights and silver ornaments.

GINNY: It sort of spoils everything—having her act so funny.

ELSIE: I just wish she didn't have to be here—that's what I wish. (MOTHER *calls from off left.*)

MOTHER (*Off*): Ginny—oh, Ginny. (MOTHER *enters, carrying a white costume over her arm and a cardboard suitbox. There are shiny beads and sequins sewed on the costume and the sleeves give the effect of wings.*)

GINNY: Mom, you've got my costume finished!

MOTHER: Yes, and I do think it's pretty, if I say so myself. (*Noticing tree*) Oh, the tree looks wonderful!

GINNY (*Taking costume and holding it in front of her, showing the wings*): Mom, you put more shiny stuff on the wings! Look at my wings, everybody. (*Chanting*) I'm a Christmas angel—I'm a Christmas angel.

JACK: Hmm, you know what I said. It will take more than wings to make you an angel, Ginny.

MOTHER: Nonsense, she's going to be perfect. (*Setting suitbox on table*) Ginny, here's a nice clean box to pack it up in.

I suppose we ought to be getting ready to leave before too long.

ELSIE: Dad says it's snowing like anything.

GINNY (*Laying costume across box*): I hope we don't have any trouble getting there. Oh, Mom, wouldn't it be terrible if we couldn't make it?

MOTHER: Now—now, of course we'll get there. Where's Diana? I thought she'd be helping you with the tree.

ELSIE: She didn't want to, Mom, or at least that's the way she acted. And then she broke one of our favorite ornaments. . . .

MOTHER: Now, Elsie, she didn't mean to.

GINNY: And Mom, she's not even going to the Christmas play.

MOTHER: Not going to the play? But I don't understand.

JACK: I guess she thinks it's beneath her dignity—just a school play.

MOTHER: Children, you're being very unkind. I've asked you to be nice to Diana.

ELSIE: Mom, we've tried—we've done everything. But it's just no use.

MOTHER: You know she's living with us this winter because your Uncle Ben wished it. He expressly said he wanted her to have a chance at some real home life.

JACK: Mom, she's just not interested in anything around here.

ELSIE: I simply don't understand her.

MOTHER: Perhaps you haven't tried hard enough. You know how different her life has been from yours. I've told you all that. Her mother died when she was a baby and she's had no one but her father, and your Uncle Ben has had to be away so much on newspaper assignments. Diana's been at boarding school or in an apartment in the city with just a housekeeper. Now she has a chance at a real home. . . .

ELSIE: But Mom, she doesn't like it here. She shows it in everything she does.

MOTHER: If you children would let her share in your fun and your work, too. . . .

GINNY: But she can't *do* anything, Mom. Why, even when I asked her to help me wipe the dishes she broke a cup.

MOTHER: You break dishes, too, sometimes.

GINNY: And she makes her bed so funny.

MOTHER: You could help her.

JACK: And she isn't interested in anything on the farm. Why, when I showed her our prize calf, she was afraid of her. Dad said she'd like one of the new kittens but I doubt it.

DANNY (*Disgustedly*): And she's upstairs now reading a book.

ELSIE: She's just a wet blanket, Mom. Why, she's even spoiling our Christmas.

MOTHER: Children!

ELSIE: I don't care. It isn't half as much fun when you have someone like that around—someone who's critical of everything.

MOTHER (*Really upset*): Children, I'm surprised at you and very displeased. Diana is our guest and it's Christmas Eve, the very time when you ought to be thinking about bringing happiness to others instead of thinking about yourselves.

ELSIE: But, Mom. . . .

MOTHER: No, I don't want another word out of any of you. I'm going up and talk to Diana and ask her to come down. (*She goes out left.*)

JACK: Boy, Mom is really angry.

ELSIE: I—I've never seen her look that way. Why, it just won't be like Christmas with Mom all upset.

GINNY (*Almost crying*): I—I thought we were all going to have such a good time—first the play. . . .

ELSIE (*Putting her arm around* GINNY): Don't cry, Ginny. We'll still enjoy the play. We'll still have a good time. Oh, this is one more thing Diana has done.

DANNY: I'm sorry now I got Diana the best Christmas present. Mom said I ought to get her something nice, and I got the best bracelet the dime store had. I spent fifty cents of my egg money.

ELSIE: Never mind, Danny.

GINNY: She probably won't like any of the things we got.

ELSIE: Well, I'm sorry now I made her those mittens. You should have seen the way she looked at the sweater I knitted for Mom.

GINNY: But Mom will love it. It's beautiful, Elsie.

ELSIE: Diana probably thought it looked homemade. She sent to the city for all her presents. (FATHER *enters left carrying a snow shovel.*)

JACK: Say, Dad, what's up? Are you having trouble?

FATHER: No, not yet. I got the car started all right. But I'm going to shovel out the front driveway a little before we try to get through.

JACK: Is it that bad?

FATHER: Well, the snow's piling up pretty fast. (*He crosses toward right.*)

GINNY: Dad, we've got to get to the play.

FATHER: We'll certainly do our best.

JACK: I'd better help you shovel, Dad.

FATHER: No, you go on and finish your lights. This won't take long. (*He goes out right.*)

GINNY: Oh, dear!

ELSIE: Don't worry, Ginny. We'll make it.

GINNY: I'd better pack up my costume. (*She folds costume carefully and puts it in the box.* DIANA *enters left. She carries an armful of presents wrapped in expensive paper.*)

DIANA: Aunt Stella said perhaps I ought to come downstairs. She said maybe I could help.

ELSIE: Thank you. But we're practically finished with the tree. Jack's fixing the lights. . . .

JACK: In fact, they're all fixed. (*He reaches behind the tree, pushes the plug in and the Christmas tree lights come on.*)

DIANA: Oh! Well, I thought I could bring my presents down anyhow. Put them underneath the tree.

JACK: Oh, not now, Diana.

GINNY: We never do that until later Christmas Eve.

ELSIE: We'll do that when we get home from the play.

DANNY: It's a lot more fun if we do it all together.

DIANA (*Too quietly*): I see.

ELSIE: I suppose you *can* leave them if you want to, Diana, but we just never do. We never put our presents under the tree this early.

DIANA (*Not repressed any longer. Breaking*): And I always do everything wrong, don't I?

ELSIE (*Surprised*): Why, Diana.

DIANA: Of course I do. That's what you all think—that's what you're always saying. And in a way, I don't blame you. You can all do so many things that I haven't been taught to do. Every time I see you making something, I feel so stupid. Even stringing the popcorn—why, I can't even help trim a Christmas tree without breaking the ornaments!

ELSIE: But we didn't think you wanted to help. We thought you didn't like it here.

DIANA: Oh, I've tried to like it here—I wanted to. You all have so much fun together, and I've been so lonesome—but I know you're always criticizing me.

JACK: But, Diana, we didn't mean to. . . .

DIANA: And now that it's Christmas, well, I just don't think I can stand it, knowing none of you likes me. Daddy and I always felt so happy at Christmas—that is, when he could be with me . . . (MOTHER *enters left and stops short as she hears* DIANA.)

ELSIE: Diana, we didn't know how you felt.

DIANA (*Going right on*): Oh, maybe our Christmases were

different from yours but they were fun, too. Daddy and I
would look at the Christmas windows, and on Christmas
Eve he'd bring home a wonderful tree—all decorated—and
we felt warm and close—and now—(*She runs out left crying,
still holding her presents.*)

DANNY (*Sorry for her*): Boy!

MOTHER: Children, what have you done to make Diana cry
like that?

ELSIE: Mom, it's all our fault. We didn't know. We didn't
understand.

JACK: We've been so dumb, Mom.

GINNY: We thought Diana didn't like Christmas, and why,
she loves it as much as we do.

MOTHER: I'm glad you're beginning to understand.

ELSIE: I feel so sorry. I've got to tell her. I wonder if I should
go now.

JACK: I'd wait a minute, Sis. Give her a chance to pull herself
together. Then we'll all tell her.

GINNY: Maybe she'll go to the play with us now. (FATHER
enters right. He is out of breath.)

FATHER: Children, I'm afraid it's no use.

GINNY: Dad!

MOTHER: Tom, you look exhausted.

FATHER: I shoveled a path to the road and then I tried the
car. I got her a little way and now she's stuck. I can't get
her started at all.

GINNY: You mean we can't get to the schoolhouse?

JACK: Maybe if I help you push, Dad. . . .

FATHER: I'm afraid it's hopeless, Son. I know how you children have counted on the play and the party afterwards. . . .

GINNY: But I'm in the play, Dad! I'm the Christmas angel.

DANNY: How can they have the play without Ginny?

MOTHER: Oh, dear! What can we do?

GINNY: Dad, Mary Simpson's in the play too—maybe the Simpsons can get their car started.

JACK: Sure, Dad, and the Simpsons have to go right by here.

FATHER: That's a good idea. I'll call them up.

ELSIE: Mom, while Dad phones, I'll go get Diana.

MOTHER: Yes, Elsie, do that.

(ELSIE *goes out left.* FATHER *goes to phone and is about to pick up the receiver when it rings.*)

MOTHER: My goodness!

FATHER (*Into phone*): Hello? . . . Why, John—John Simpson. I was just going to call you . . . What's that? You can't? Well, I guess that settles it—neither can we . . . Too bad . . . All right, if you have any luck pick us up and if we have any we'll do the same for you. Fine! Goodbye. (*He hangs up.*) The Simpsons are stuck, too. I guess we're just out of luck. (*They all look sad.* ELSIE *rushes in left very upset.*)

ELSIE: Mother—Dad—Diana's gone!

MOTHER: Gone?

OTHERS: What? (*Etc.*)

MOTHER: But she can't be, Elsie!

ELSIE: I tell you she is, Mother, and her heavy coat isn't in the closet. I looked.

MOTHER: But I can't believe she'd go out in this storm. (*Turning to* FATHER.) She was upset, Tom. She and the children had a misunderstanding.

FATHER (*Starting left*): I'll go right out. I don't see how she could have got very far in this snow. She must have gone out the back way—I've been out front all the time.

JACK: I'll come with you, Dad. (*He puts on his coat.*)

MOTHER (*Worriedly*): Oh, Tom!—

FATHER: Now, now, don't worry. We'll find her. She'll be all right. (FATHER *and* JACK *go out left.*)

ELSIE: She's *got* to be all right. Oh, Mom, this is all our fault.

MOTHER: There's no use to keep on blaming yourselves. You children just didn't understand how she felt. I'd better get something hot ready to drink. She'll be cold. (*She goes out.*)

GINNY: But why would Diana rush out like that? Where did she intend to go?

ELSIE: I don't know. Maybe she had some idea she could get to the station—take a train back to the city.

DANNY: But her father's away.

GINNY: Oh, I don't care what happens if only Dad finds her. I don't even care about not being in the play.

DANNY: The play. Gee, I'd almost forgotten about it.

GINNY: I guess they'll just have to do without an angel.

ELSIE: They'll postpone the play, Ginny—they'll have to. The Simpsons can't get there either.

DANNY: But what good's a Christmas play when Christmas is all over?

GINNY: We can still have a nice Christmas Eve if only Dad finds Diana. I'm not even going to think about the play any more.

ELSIE (*Putting arm around* GINNY): Just the same, I know how disappointed you are, Ginny. We all are. (MOTHER *reënters.*)

MOTHER: Well, I've got some hot broth ready. I looked out of the kitchen window but I couldn't see a thing, it's snowing so hard. (*She walks about nervously.*) Oh, I wish they'd come back.

ELSIE: Try not to worry, Mom.

MOTHER: But if anything should happen—Uncle Ben left Diana in our care—

GINNY: What *could* happen?

JACK (*Off left. Calling*): Mother—Mother! Everything's all right.

MOTHER (*Turning left*): Oh!

JACK (*Still off*): We've found her, Mother—here she is! (JACK *enters leading* DIANA *by the hand. She is wearing coat and scarf.*)

MOTHER: Diana! (MOTHER *rushes to her, putting her arms around her. The others crowd around, too.*)

ELSIE: Oh, Diana, we're so glad—

GINNY: We're so glad to see you.

DANNY: I'll say!

DIANA (*Shyly but she is smiling*): Jack's been telling me you would be. He's been trying to explain—

MOTHER (*Feeling her hands*): You must be frozen. Oh, we've been so worried.

DIANA: I'm sorry, Aunt Stella. It was foolish of me to rush out like that. But I'm not a bit cold. I've been in that old shed back of the barn.

ELSIE: That old wagon shed where Dad keeps all the old machinery we never use?

DIANA: Yes. I had no idea where I was going when I started out but I've often gone there before when I felt lonesome.

MOTHER: My goodness! You poor child!

JACK (*Grinning*): Listen—before anyone talks any more—Dad said to tell you all to hurry.

GINNY: Hurry?

JACK: Yes, hurry and get your things on. We're going to the play.

GINNY (*Joyfully*): You mean he got the car started?

JACK: No, but we're going just the same. Diana figured it out.

ELSIE: Diana—but how?

JACK: You know that old sleigh out in the shed—

GINNY: Sleigh?

MOTHER: Why, of course, the old sleigh Grandpa used to use when he lived here. I'd forgotten it was there.

ELSIE: So had I. And besides I'd never have thought—Diana, how in the world did you get the idea?

DIANA: Well, you see I was sitting in the sleigh out there when your dad and Jack found me.

JACK: Dad could see her footprints led to the shed—the snow was covering them up fast but he found them.

DIANA: I suppose one reason I liked to go out there was because of the sleigh. One of the nicest memories I have is of a sleigh ride Daddy took me on when I was small. Sitting there sort of brought it back. Why, there are even some old bells on the sleigh.

ELSIE: So you suggested we use the sleigh tonight?

DIANA: Yes. When Uncle Tom said he couldn't get the car started, I thought why not? Why couldn't we use the sleigh?

ELSIE: Why not, indeed? Diana, you're wonderful!

GINNY: Oh, it's perfectly thrilling. A sleigh ride to the play!

JACK: We're going to pick up the Simpsons, too. Come on now, everybody, hurry and get your coats. Dad's hitching up the horses—I helped him pull the sleigh out of the shed.

GINNY: I'll get our things. (*She runs off left.*)

JACK: Dad says we'd better dress warmly. It's really cold.

ELSIE: Oh, Diana, can you ever forgive us for acting the way we did?

DIANA: Can you ever forgive *me?* I see now that you thought the same things about me that I thought about you.

ELSIE: But we should have known—

DIANA (*Smiling*): I guess when people are a little different, they often misunderstand one another.

MOTHER: Yes. I often think that if people everywhere could really know one another, we wouldn't have any more trouble in the world.

DIANA: That's what Daddy wrote me in his Christmas letter. He's doing a series of articles on different countries, and he said if all the peoples could know what the others are feeling and understand them, perhaps we could really have peace on earth everywhere. But here I read that letter and I didn't apply it to myself at all.

MOTHER: Never mind. Everything's all right now.

GINNY (*Rushing in with a bundle of coats, mittens and scarfs*): Here are the coats— You can find your own. (JACK *and* DIANA *already have coats on.* ELSIE, GINNY *and* DANNY *put on coats and mittens, laughing as they unscramble them.* MOTHER *puts coat on, too.*) And oh, I'd better not forget my angel costume. (*She picks up suitbox.*)

DANNY (*As he puts on his mittens. Happily*): Oh, boy, it's Christmas Eve and we're going on a sleigh ride, and we've got new kittens! Did you know that, Diana?

DIANA: No. Oh, they're so cute—kittens.

DANNY: You can have the black one.

DIANA: I'd love it. I love animals but I haven't been around them much, and I always feel I don't know how to act.

JACK: We'll teach you.

DANNY: I'm glad I got you such a nice Christmas present, Diana. Wait until you see. It's—

ELSIE (*Laughing*): Danny, don't tell! You'll spoil the surprsie. (*Sleigh bells are heard off.*)

JACK: There's Dad with the sleigh!

GINNY: And listen to the sleigh bells.

DIANA (*Happily starting to sing*): "Jingle bells, jingle bells."

ALL (*Singing as they start off*): "Jingle bells, jingle bells, jingle all the way. Oh, what fun it is to ride in a one horse open sleigh!" (MOTHER *tucks a scarf in here and pulls up a coat collar there as they all troop off singing. As much of the song may be sung as is necessary for exit.*)

THE END

The Friday Foursome Packs a Box

by Lindsey Barbee

Characters

DORA

POLLY

SHIRLEY

BEVERLY, *Dora's sister*

ELISE

ANNETTE, *Polly's sister*

SUSAN, *a maid*

TIME: *The present. The day before Christmas.*

SETTING: *Sunroom in the home of* DORA *and* BEVERLY.

AT RISE: POLLY *is standing at the right of the tree and* DORA *is at the left.*

POLLY: That just about finishes the decorating, doesn't it, Dora? (*As she surveys*) Pretty, isn't it?

DORA: It will be prettier when the lights go on.

POLLY: I like the way that the top points up and the sides go branching out, each matching the other.

DORA: Symmetrical is what you're trying to say, darling.

POLLY (*As she touches the tree*): Lights of friendship, star dust of happy days.

DORA: That's rather good. Original?

POLLY: Oh, quite. And I've always thought that every holly wreath should have a spray of forget-me-nots.

DORA: Just why?

POLLY: To remember others along with the Christmas fun.

DORA (*Dramatically*): In my holly wreaths, I'll twine forget-me-nots for you.

172

POLLY: Exactly.

DORA: That's original, too. (*From off left comes the sound of voices, also an occasional laugh.*)

POLLY (*Sitting on hassock*): The Friday Foursome is talking a lot. (*With a glance at the packing box*) Wrapping presents for the Christmas box always excites them.

DORA (*On settee*): I'm bothered about that box.

POLLY: Why bother?

DORA: It's going to the Averys.

POLLY: You and I suggested the Averys.

DORA: Of course. (*Pauses*) I'm wondering if we did the right thing.

POLLY: The Averys are the nicest kind of people.

DORA: Too nice for a charity box.

POLLY: Why do you call it a charity box?

DORA: Because I watched the girls doing up some of the presents, and I've a pretty good idea of what's going in the box.

POLLY: But the Foursomes always pack a good box.

DORA: The boxes have always been for the very poor—the people who are glad to get anything.

POLLY: The Averys are poor.

DORA: But they've always had a sort of—position, we'll say. Mrs. Avery has been left with two growing-up girls and a little girl.

POLLY: Then, more than ever I'm glad that the box will go to them.

DORA: But the Averys have pride. Lots of it. And it would hurt like the dickens to be treated as charity patients.

POLLY: They probably want practical things.

DORA: Maybe so, but a sugar coating would be pretty nice.

POLLY (*Suddenly*): We shouldn't like it a bit.

DORA: Like what?

POLLY: Getting a lot of plain things without anything pretty.

DORA: That's exactly what I mean.

POLLY: Of course we'd be thankful, but it would remind us that we were poor.

DORA: Somewhere or other, somebody or other said he'd rather have a pot of hyacinths to feed his soul than a loaf of bread to feed his body.

POLLY: That's carrying it a little too far I think—but I get the idea. (*Yawns*) Let's have a foursome some day. Our big sisters have a grand time at it.

DORA: I like our twosome.

POLLY: So do I. *Some day* I said. (*Rising and adjusting an ornament on the tree*) This thing is crooked. (*As she steps near the tree, one of the packages around the base is dislodged*) Good gracious! What did I knock?

DORA: Nothing but a stocking box. (*Pauses*) Shirley has chosen gorgeous stockings as her gift to the Foursomes.

POLLY: Annette's giving beads—each string different. They're lovely.

DORA: Elise has slips for her pals. (*Laughs*) Special sale last week.

POLLY: She doesn't need to count the pennies.

DORA: But she does it.

POLLY: What is Beverly giving?

DORA: Compacts. The prettiest I've seen. (SHIRLEY *comes in breezily from left, bearing four packages.*)

SHIRLEY: My contribution is all ready, so I'll dump it in. (*Crosses to box and throws in the packages, each in plain white tissue with equally plain ribbon*) I've an errand down the street, but I'll be right back.

POLLY: What are you giving?

SHIRLEY: Nice warm underwear. Two suits for everybody, even for the little one.

POLLY: She'll just love opening that package.

SHIRLEY (*Cheerfully*): Won't she, though? (*At right*) It's so practical. (*Goes out*)

POLLY: Didn't notice my sarcasm.

DORA: Hasn't a particle of humor. (BEVERLY *comes in from left, carrying four hosiery boxes and a spool of plain red ribbon.*)

BEVERLY: I've run out of white tissue paper. Who wants to hustle to the drug store?

POLLY: I've just bought some wrapping paper and it's out in the hall. You're welcome to it.

BEVERLY: Is it plain?

POLLY: Certainly not. It's the prettiest I could find.

BEVERLY: Then it won't do, for we're packing the charity box.

DORA: It isn't a charity box. (*Crosses to chaise longue.*)

BEVERLY: Dora, you do get such strange notions. Plain, white tissue paper is what I want.

DORA: There's a roll in the kitchen, Polly. (*Sarcastically*) I was saving it to wrap the groceries for our basket for the church.

POLLY: I'll get it.

DORA: Might as well bring our own packages from the hall table.

POLLY: I'll do that. (*Goes out right.*)

BEVERLY (*Crossing to chaise longue*): Why didn't you tell me that you had that white paper?

DORA: Because I thought you were packing that box for human beings.

BEVERLY: You do say the most impossible things, Dora.

DORA: Oh—do I?

BEVERLY: Don't indulge in that little sneering look. It isn't becoming. (POLLY *enters from right with arms full of packages and bearing the roll of white paper.* DORA *meets her, taking some of the packages, all of which are deposited on the small table.*)

POLLY (*Crossing to* BEVERLY) : Here's the paper, Beverly.

BEVERLY (*Taking the paper*) : Thanks a lot. Do you mind help-ing me with these boxes, girls? Here's the ribbon to tie them. (*Hands spool of ribbon as* DORA *and* POLLY *crowd beside her on the chaise longue.*) I have nice, warm stockings for three of them and socks for the little girl. (ELISE *enters hurriedly carrying various packages.*)

ELISE : Well, at last my packages are ready.

DORA : What are you giving?

ELISE : I have a pocket book for the mother—a nice, large one.

DORA : New?

ELISE : Almost new. (*Suddenly and sharply*) Why do you ask that?

DORA : Curiosity.

POLLY : What have you for the older girl?

ELISE : A sweater. Now that it's cleaned and mended it looks as good as new.

DORA : What does the younger girl draw in the shuffle?

ELISE : A nice, gay kimono.

DORA : Did you outgrow it?

ELISE : Completely. (*Suddenly*) Why do you ask that?

DORA : Curiosity.

POLLY : And of course you have something pretty for the baby.

ELISE : Indeed I have. Bright wools and knitting needles.

POLLY : How nice! Left over from your knitted afghan, I suppose.

ELISE : You girls ask such queer and such personal questions. (*Places bundles in box and sits on settee.* ANNETTE, *with packages, hurries in from left.*)

ANNETTE : Those gowns were the dickens to wrap.

POLLY : Gowns? What kind?

ANNETTE : Nice, warm outing flannel ones. Just the thing. (*Places bundles in box and sits by* ELISE. DORA *and* POLLY *take the packages from the table and cross to box. These are beautifully wrapped.*)

DORA (*Displaying her packages*): I have a doll for the little girl—and she'll love it. Polly has a beautiful book for her. (*Pauses*) My own brand new sweater goes to Mary, the oldest girl. Nancy, the second girl, gets a bathrobe—a soft, woolly one—and Mrs. Avery has a pair of nice gloves.

BEVERLY: Dora, what *are* you doing? Such elaborate presents.

ELISE: And so expensive.

DORA: Polly and I feel that we want the Averys to look upon us as friends.

ANNETTE: Practical things would have been more sensible.

POLLY: *Practical* is just what we're trying to avoid.

ELISE: Poor people can't expect anything else.

POLLY: Oh, can't they? (*Sarcastically*) They're human.

ANNETTE: Don't be disagreeable, Polly.

POLLY: I'm giving Mary the bracelet I'd planned to give Dora. (*As* ANNETTE *gasps*) Oh, Dora understands and approves. Nancy gets a pretty bag and I have a book for Mrs. Avery. (*Pauses*) Mother suggested the book. (*Places packages in box.*)

ELISE: I've never heard of anything so absolutely flighty and impractical.

DORA: We just happen to believe that people who are really fine and worthwhile are cheered by a gesture of friendship.

ELISE: You've read that somewhere.

DORA: I have *not!* (*Emphatically*) I know how to express myself.

POLLY: And won't the Averys feel happy tomorrow morning when they find that there are some people who remembered them in the right way.

BEVERLY: I shall tell mother, Dora.

DORA: I've already told her and she approves.

ANNETTE: I suppose that there's nothing we can say.

POLLY (*Smiling*): Nothing. Absolutely nothing. (SUSAN *appears at right.*)

SUSAN: Luncheon is served, Miss Beverly.

BEVERLY: Thank you, Susan. (SUSAN *goes out right*) You won't have much to eat, girls, on the day before Christmas. Just a salad.

ELISE: We'll be back for our gifts, won't we?

BEVERLY: Of course. (*Suddenly*) Where's Shirley? (SHIRLEY *appears at right.*)

SHIRLEY: Right here—and just in time. (*The four go out.*)

BEVERLY (*At the door*): Aren't you two coming?

DORA: No thanks. We've already had a spread in the breakfast room. (BEVERLY *goes out.*)

POLLY: Well—where do we go from here?

DORA: I have an idea.

POLLY: What?

DORA: Instead of Dora, I shall be *Pan*dora.

POLLY: What do you mean?

DORA: Don't you remember the story of Pandora?

POLLY: Why—yes—I think I do. (*Crosses to hassock.*)

DORA: She opened a box and let out all the evils in the world; but along with the evils, she freed a lovely little fairy called Hope.

POLLY (*Sighing*): Sometimes, Dora, it's very hard to follow you.

DORA: There are no particular evils shut up in *my* box, but just a lot of thoughtlessness and maybe, selfishness. (*Emphatically*) Just the same, I don't intend to let them out.

POLLY: Just how are you planning to go about it?

DORA: I shall try an experiment. If it succeeds—well, more converts to Christmas. If it doesn't succeed, we'll go back to just where we started.

POLLY: Naturally, I don't understand one word of what you're saying.

DORA: First of all, get the cards from all those packages under the tree. (POLLY *rises reluctantly as* DORA *seats herself at the desk taking some small cards from a drawer*) I'll take all the blame. (*Writes busily, murmuring to herself*) "Merry Christmas to Mrs. Avery—Merry Christmas to Mary—Merry Christmas to Nancy." (*Turns*) There are nine packages, aren't there?

POLLY: Just nine.

DORA: Bring them here. (*To herself as she writes.*) "Merry Christmas to Mrs. Avery—Merry Christmas to Mary—Merry Christmas to Nancy."

POLLY (*As she brings the packages and cards to* DORA): I'm beginning to understand.

DORA: Grand plan, isn't it? (*Again she writes and murmurs the names.*)

POLLY: The girls will be perfectly furious.

DORA: Then all they have to do is to take back their packages.

POLLY: You haven't the right to do this.

DORA: It's an experiment, I tell you. (*Pauses*) *There!* Slip these cards under the ribbons and be sure that only one gift of a kind goes to a person.

POLLY: Oh, but the girls will be mad. (*Laughs*) The Furious Foursome.

DORA: Let's put everything in the box before they finish luncheon.

POLLY: And before the fireworks begin. (*Together, they place the packages in the box.*)

DORA: Hand me the lid, Poll. (*Places lid on box and sits on it*) And now I'll sit on it. (*Sighs*) I've some busy moments ahead of me. (*There is a sound of talking off right.*)

POLLY: Here they come. (SHIRLEY *enters with* ELISE *and they make their way to the settee, chatting gaily.* ANNETTE *follows with* BEVERLY. POLLY *is in desk chair.*)

ANNETTE: That's the best salad I've ever tasted.

BEVERLY: I call it the cook's Christmas Eve Special.

ANNETTE: It's—heavenly. (*Sits on chaise longue.*)

BEVERLY: Later on, Susan will bring us coffee and Christmas cookies. (*Sits on hassock*) Why are you perched on that box, Dora?

DORA: I'm Pandora.

BEVERLY: And just why?

DORA: Because Pandora had a lot to do with a box years ago.

BEVERLY: As I remember the story, Pandora was so curious that she couldn't obey orders.

DORA: So she opened the box and let out all the little pests and evils and—

POLLY: She also gave Hope a chance to flit around the country.

DORA: So I'm sitting on a lot of things, and when the time comes I'll let out a little fairy called Christmas Spirit.

BEVERLY: You're too silly for words. (ELISE *spies the vacancy at the base of the tree.*)

ELISE: The packages are gone!

DORA: We took them—Polly and I. But I suggested it.

ANNETTE: That's a silly kind of joke.

POLLY: It isn't a joke.

BEVERLY (*Angrily*): Where—did—you—put—them?

DORA: In this box. (*Pauses*) That's one reason that I'm sitting on the lid.

ELISE: I don't see the point, but I suggest that you take them out this very minute.

BEVERLY: How did you *dare* to do this?

DORA (*Calmly*): Mrs. Avery, Mary and Nancy—each of them —will have lovely stockings, a string of pretty beads, a slip and a compact.

BEVERLY: Give us those packages immediately.

DORA: They're all marked with different cards.

POLLY: And all *your* cards are right here on the desk.

ANNETTE: Now that you've had all this play-acting, I suggest that you give us back our property.

DORA: Now listen to me. (*Pauses*) The Averys have been unfortunate—

POLLY: But they're very different from some of the people who are in line for Christmas donations.

DORA: When Polly and I suggested that you send your box to them, we thought that you'd make it *different*—that you'd pretend to be friends or relatives so that their pride wouldn't be hurt.

POLLY: You people don't need those gifts you bought and would think just the same of each other without them.

DORA: What I'm trying to say is just this. (*Pauses*) Unless one forgets herself at Christmas and thinks of someone else there's no such thing as Christmas spirit. (*For a moment there is silence.*)

ANNETTE: I agree, Dora.

BEVERLY (*Impulsively*): I *want* to do it.

ELISE: Well, of course if the others approve, I do, too. But it means that I'll hurry right down to the shops for other gifts.

DORA: Oh, no—never. The moment that any gift is replaced, the whole thing goes to smash.

SHIRLEY: Dora's quite right. Let's think of a *real* Christmas.

DORA: You're dears—all of you. (*Pauses*) Shall I lift the lid and let out Christmas Spirit?

ANNETTE: Christmas Spirit is already here.

BEVERLY (*Suddenly*): Girls, I have an idea. (*Pauses*) Since we have no gifts to distribute, suppose we go into the library and sing a Christmas carol. (*Rises.*)

SHIRLEY (*Rising*): The very thing.

BEVERLY: Then afterwards we can come back here when the tree is lighted and have our coffee and cakes.

ELISE: We'd love it. (BEVERLY, ELISE *and* SHIRLEY *cross to right.*)

ANNETTE: Wait for me. (*Joins the group.*)

BEVERLY (*Turning*): Aren't you two coming?

DORA: Of course we're coming. (*The four go out at right.*)

POLLY: Well—what do you think?

DORA: Four converts to Christmas.

POLLY: It made them *think,* Dora.

DORA: And it made *us* think. (*Happily*) Oh, Polly, it's going to be a very merry Christmas.

POLLY: For us—and for the Averys. (*Laughingly as she holds out her hand*) Come on, Pandora. (DORA *jumps up, gives the box a loving pat, and, with* POLLY, *runs to right and disappears. For a moment, the stage is clear. Then,* SUSAN *enters from right, bearing a large silver tray with silver service. She places it on the small table, lights the Christmas tree, stops to survey it, and then goes out at right. To the strains of a lovely Christmas carol, the curtain falls.*)

THE END

The Best Gift of All

by Mary Smith

Characters

MARY
RUTH
MARTHA

NAOMI
THE ANGEL
OTHER CHILDREN

TIME: *The first Christmas Day.*

SETTING: *One of the roads that leads to Jerusalem.*

AT RISE: *A group of children are seen entering from the left.*

NOTE: *These children may be all boys, or all girls, or boys and girls together. They may be of any and all ages. If all boys are used, the names may be changed. The children carry gifts for the Christ Child.*

RUTH: Aye. This is the road and we must hurry with our gifts.

MARTHA: Last night He was born in a manger in a stable. And today all the people are happy and we come bearing gifts for Him.

MARY: What are you bringing, Ruth? I'm bringing this fine vase. It is made of silver.

RUTH: I'm bringing an armband of gold. Rachel is bringing a jar of new sweet honey.

MARY: And my sister Elisabeth is bringing a fine toy; a lamb carved from wood. What are you bringing, Martha? (MARTHA *is the smallest girl in the crowd. At the question, she hangs her head.*)

RUTH: Yes, Martha, tell us.

183

MARTHA: I am bringing an apple. (*The other children look at each other.*) I polished it and polished it and now see— (*She takes an apple from the fold of her dress.*) How it glows! Like a jewel.

RUTH: You mean—you mean—your gift is an *apple*?

MARTHA: Yes. I helped my mother all day and sang to the baby when he cried and brought my father his sandals when he came in from working in the fields. My mother rewarded me with this apple. It is the prettiest thing I have ever owned, and I am going to give it to the Christ Child.

MARY: Only an apple! Ha! Ha! Ha!

RUTH: That is no gift. Anyone can get an apple. You must bring silver or gold or sweet-smelling perfume. But an apple —Ha! Ha! Ha!

OTHER CHILDREN: She thinks it's a fine gift. (*All laugh.* MARTHA *looks unhappy.*)

MARTHA: I thought it looked so pretty. I did not eat it myself —although I wanted to. I wanted to save it as a gift.

RUTH: You are a very foolish girl. But come. We must hurry. (*All the children hurry off the right side.* MARTHA *stands still looking at the apple.*)

MARY (*Running back*): But hurry, Martha, even if your gift is not so fine, we will tell how you did not keep it for yourself but saved it for a gift. Then your gift may be accepted, too.

MARTHA: I will follow behind you. (MARY *goes off the stage on the right side.* MARTHA *starts to follow slowly. She meets a ragged little girl,* NAOMI, *who is coming on the stage from the right side.* NAOMI *is weeping.*) Why do you cry, little girl?

NAOMI: Because my mother is so poor, and I am so hungry. I have not had anything to eat all day. My little brother is lying in the fields. He, too, is crying because he is hungry. (*She cries again.*)

MARTHA: You must not cry. Today is a day of rejoicing. I am going into the city. There will be a great celebration. Perhaps you will find something to eat there. Come with me.

NAOMI: My brother is too little to walk so far. (*Sees the apple in* MARTHA's *hand.*) Oh how beautiful that is! Like a large ruby. How red and how round. And how good it must taste.

MARTHA: I am taking it to the Christ Child as a gift.

NAOMI: It will be the best of all the gifts.

MARTHA: My mother said that God made it. His sun warmed it into color. And the rain He sent made it sweet to taste. He made this out of a pretty sweet-smelling flower. Smell. (NAOMI *smells the apple.*)

NAOMI: It smells like the wind on a sunny day. How good it must be to eat. But you must hurry. You must bring your fine gift to the city.

MARTHA: The other children laughed at me.

NAOMI: It will be the most beautiful gift of all.

MARTHA: I wish you would come with me.

NAOMI: I cannot. I am so hungry, and my brother is so small.

MARTHA (*Starts to follow after the other children.* NAOMI *sits by the road and starts to cry. Just as* MARTHA *is about to go off the stage, she turns around and sees* NAOMI *crying.* MARTHA *hurries back*): Here, little girl. Take this apple. You are hungry. I cannot see you weep.

NAOMI (*Joyfully*): But the gift—

MARTHA: I will listen to the stories that the other children tell of their gifts—

NAOMI: But this would be the finest gift of all.

MARTHA: There will be many gifts laid in the manger. But you are hungry. You must have this.

NAOMI (*Taking it*): Oh thank you! Thank you! I will give my brother half and he will stop crying and be happy again. (NAOMI *skips off happily with the apple.* MARTHA *sinks*

down on the side of the road and starts to cry. A beautiful
ANGEL *in a white robe appears.*)

ANGEL: Why do you weep, my child?

MARTHA: I gave my gift to a hungry child. And now I have no gift for the Christ Child. (*She cries harder. The* ANGEL *places her hand on* MARTHA'S *head.*)

ANGEL: Do not weep. God has seen your gift to the hungry child. Because you thought of another and not of yourself, your gift is twice as precious as all the gold and silver and sweet-smelling perfume. When you gave it to the hungry child it was as though you had given something precious to the Christ Child. So be comforted. Your gift was the best of all. (MARTHA *looks up with a smile, as the curtain falls.*)

THE END

Everywhere Christmas

by Alice Very

Characters

TED
GINNY } *American children*

OLD MAN (*Santa Claus*)
TOM THUMB
JACK HORNER
MARY CONTRARY
JACK
JILL } *English children*

KLASS
KAREN } *Dutch children*

PIERRE
PIERRETTE } *French children*

MYRA, *a Greek girl*
GIUSEPPE, *an Italian boy*

HAENSEL
GRETEL } *German children*

REUBEN
RACHEL } *Jewish children*

CARL
CHRISTINA } *Swedish children*

MOKI, *a Hawaiian boy*
EAGLE FEATHER, *American Indian*
PEDRO, *Mexican boy*
WAITS
ELVES *and* FAIRIES
GINGERBREAD CHILDREN

SETTING: *An American living room.*
AT RISE: *The door at right opens and* TED *and* GINNY *peep in, look about cautiously, and enter. They are in night clothes.*

TED:

I want to see Santa.
Why doesn't he come?
I wish he would hurry
And bring me my drum.

187

GINNY:

My stocking is empty.
I very much fear
Old Santa's forgotten
He meant to come here.
(*A knock at the door is heard.*)

TED: There's a knock at the door!

GINNY: Now who can that be?

TED: It may be a present!

GINNY: Perhaps it's for me! (*They open the door, and an* OLD
MAN, *dressed in shabby clothes, enters.*)

OLD MAN:

Christmas is coming
And the geese are getting fat.
Please put a penny
In the old man's hat. (*Holds out hat.*)

TED:

Come in, won't you please, sir;
It's chilly out there.

GINNY:

Sit down for a moment
And rest in this chair.
(*The* OLD MAN *seats himself in the easy chair.* TED *and*
GINNY *take bank from mantelpiece.*)

TED (*Aside*): Go, look in the bank.

GINNY (*Aside*): There's only one penny.

TED (*Aside*):

Let's give it to him,
For he hasn't got any.
(*They put the penny in the* OLD MAN'S *hat.*)

OLD MAN:

I thank you, dear children,
My blessing on you,

And whatever you wish
May your wishes come true!

TED:

We want to see Santa.
We've waited so long—

GINNY:

We're afraid he's forgotten,
Or something is wrong.

OLD MAN:

Now how can old Santa
Have time to see you
When everywhere children
Are wanting him too?

TED:

I should think he'd have helpers
To work for him.

OLD MAN: Right!

All over the world
They're busy tonight.
There's hardly a country—
I'm sure this is true—
Where Santa Claus' helpers
Aren't working for you.

(*Sound of sleighbells outside, growing louder.*)

GINNY: Oh, listen!

TED: It's sleighbells!

GINNY: They're coming this way!

TED: Perhaps it is Santa!

GINNY: It sounds like his sleigh! (*Enter* TOM THUMB, JACK
HORNER, *with a plum pudding,* MARY CONTRARY, *with holly,
ivy, and mistletoe, and* JACK *and* JILL, *with a Yule log.*)

TOM THUMB:

My name is Tom Thumb.

From England I've come,
With Mary Contrary,
With elf and with fairy.

JACK HORNER:

And little Jack Horner,
With pudding and plum.

MARY CONTRARY:

I've brought you some holly
To make Christmas jolly,
And white mistletoe
On the doorway must go
To welcome the friend
And keep out the foe.

(*Hangs mistletoe over door, left.*)

JACK:

The Yule log we're bringing
To keep you from cold.

(JACK *and* JILL *put log in fireplace.*)

JILL:

While out in the snow
The merry Waits go
With carols they're singing
That never grow old.

TED:

Oh, let them come in
And sing for us here!

GINNY:

Their music and din
Will add to our cheer.

(WAITS *enter with lantern and musical instruments.*)

ENGLISH CHILDREN *and* WAITS (*Sing*): "The Holly and the Ivy." (*etc.*)

TOM THUMB:

With feasting and frolicking,

Dancing and singing,
With jolly red noses
And sleighbells a-ringing,
With the green ivy leaf
And the red holly berry,
You can see why in England
Our Christmas is merry.

TED: But you haven't a stocking;
You haven't a tree.

GINNY:
Without Christmas presents
How queer it must be!

MARY CONTRARY:
Oh, yes, we have stockings,
And Christmas trees too,
But our little Dutch cousins
Have brought those to you.

(*Enter* KLASS *and* KAREN *in Dutch costume and wooden shoes.*)

KLASS:
Klip-klop,
Hippity-hop,
Wooden shoes
Never stop.

KAREN:
Only Christmas night they go,
Standing neatly in a row,
For San Nicolaas to see
And leave a penny there for me.

(KLASS *and* KAREN *place shoes by fireplace. Enter* PIERRE *and* PIERRETTE, *also in wooden shoes, which they place beside fireplace.*)

PIERRE:
We have wooden shoes as well

That we leave for Père Noël.

KAREN: San Ni'claas!

PIERRETTE: No, Père Noël!

KAREN: Which is right?

PIERRETTE: Now who can tell? (*Enter* MYRA.)

MYRA:
Saint Nicolas,
The stories say,
Came from Greece,
So far away.
In every land
That you can send,
He's always been
The children's friend.

PIERRE:
Santa Claus
Or Père Noël,
English, French,
It's just as well.

KLASS:
Greek or Dutch,
He's just the same,
Though he has
A different name.
(*Enter* GIUSEPPE *with a large urn.*)

GIUSEPPE:
Our presents come out of
A wonderful jar.
The children come running
From near and from far.
There are presents for all
And we each have a turn
To pull out a gift
From the wonderful urn.

TED:

Shoes and jars
May play their part.
Give me stockings
For a start.

GINNY:

But the thing
I love to see
Is a lighted
Christmas tree.

(*Enter* HAENSEL, *with a Christmas tree, and* GRETEL, *with*
GINGERBREAD CHILDREN.)

HAENSEL:

We're Haensel and Gretel.
We've brought you a tree;
The tallest and greenest
You ever did see.

GRETEL:

With gingerbread children
And cookies and cake,
That only a good witch
Would know how to bake.

(HAENSEL, GRETEL, GINGERBREAD CHILDREN, *and* WAITS
*sing "O Christmas Tree!" The children put up the Christ-
mas tree.*)

TED:

But now we need trimmings
And bright colored lights

GINNY:

To shine like the stars
On cold winter nights.

(*Enter* REUBEN *and* RACHEL, *with Christmas tree lights.*)

REUBEN:

We're Reuben and Rachel

From far Palestine.
We've brought you our candles
To make the tree shine.
(*They put lights on the tree.*)
RACHEL:
Now up with the Christmas tree,
Up with the star,
Shine for all children
Wherever they are!
(*Enter* CARL *and* CHRISTINA, *with a sheaf of grain on a pole.*)
CARL:
Don't forget a
Crumb or seed
May a little
Birdy feed.
CHRISTINA:
The snowbird and
The chickadee
Will like our Swedish
Christmas tree.
(*They set up the birds' tree opposite the Christmas tree.*
Enter MOKI *and* EAGLE FEATHER.)
MOKI:
My name is Moki,
From the newest state;
In warm Hawaii
We celebrate
Christmas as our favorite day.
We make our wreaths of tropical plants
And eat sweet fruits
And sing and dance.

EAGLE FEATHER:
  The Indian boys
  Are welcoming Christmas
  With plenty of noise.
  They laugh and they shout
  As they dance in a ring,
  And "Hoya! Hoyanna!"
  The Indians sing.
  (INDIAN CHILDREN *may dance here.*)
PEDRO (*Entering with a* piñata) :
  Don't forget there are other
  Americans, too.
  I'll tell you what children
  In Mexico do.

  We don't hang up stockings
  For Santa; instead
  We have a *piñata*
  Hung up overhead.

  We hit it with sticks
  And bang it about
  Until the bag breaks
  And the presents fall out.
  (*The* OLD MAN, *meanwhile, has been taking packages from his bundle and putting them in stockings. Now he takes off his ragged clothes, showing a red Santa Claus suit.*)
TED: Santa, dear Santa!
GINNY: It really is you!
SANTA CLAUS:
  Didn't I tell you
  Your wish would come true?
  (TED *and* GINNY *hug* SANTA CLAUS.)

Now it's time
To ride away
In our jolly
Reindeer sleigh
Listen while
The sleighbells ring
And all together
Join and sing.
For Christmas comes
To you, to share
With all my children
Everywhere.

ALL (*Sing*) : "Everywhere, everywhere, Christmas tonight."

THE END

The Littlest Fir

by Ella Stratton Colbo

Characters

THE LITTLEST FIR	FATHER
FIRST TALL FIR	FIRST CHILD
SECOND TALL FIR	SECOND CHILD
MOTHER	

TIME: *The Christmas season.*

SETTING: *Outside of home showing front door with the* LITTLEST FIR *between two tall* FIRS *near door.*

AT RISE: LITTLEST FIR *is in front of home between two taller* FIRS. *For a short time a sound of muffled sobbing is heard.*

1ST TALL FIR:
Hark! I keep hearing the strangest sound,
Like somebody crying, there on the ground.
Be still, and tell me what *you* hear.
The Littlest Fir is unhappy, I fear.
(*Sound of sobbing continues.*)

2ND TALL FIR (*Urgently*):
Why, he really *is* crying!
Oh, my! Oh, my!
Bend down, bend down
And ask him why!

1ST TALL FIR (*Leaning slightly toward* LITTLEST FIR):
What is troubling you, little friend?

I'd come down to see, but I cannot bend.
2ND TALL FIR:
    Yes, tell us what's hurting you, my dear.
    We can't come down to hold your hand,
    But we *can* hear, and *we'll understand.*
LITTLEST FIR (*Unhappily*):
    Oh, I've tried to grow, and I don't know how.
    My top doesn't come to your lowest bough.
    I'm all alone, and I feel so queer,
    Why, even the breeze doesn't know I'm here.
1ST TALL FIR (*Consolingly*):
    There are many ways that being small
    Is better by far than being tall.
2ND TALL FIR:
    Sometimes when the breeze gets *very* rough
    We're afraid we won't be strong enough!
LITTLEST FIR:
    But I want to be tall and straight like you.
    I want to be tall, and busy too,
    Where the birds build nests,
    And the squirrels play,
    And the stars seem so close at the end of day.
    Really and truly, it's hard to be
    Such a little, tiny, *useless* tree!
1ST TALL FIR:
    Tiny and *useless!* Why that's not true!
    We often speak of the good you do.
2ND TALL FIR:
    Remember those boys with a bee-bee gun,
    Who shot at a squirrel, just for fun?
    He was frightened and hurt, and he couldn't climb,
    But *you* covered and hid him, just in time.
1ST TALL FIR:
    Those big boys searched in our branches tall,

But they never noticed *you* so small.
You saved his life, oh Littlest Fir.
You saved his life, I'm very sure!

LITTLEST FIR (*Thoughtfully*):
And he chattered his thanks
When he scampered away.
I *was* glad I was small
That Autumn day!

2ND TALL FIR:
And *I* like to think of that wild Spring night
When the Robin family got such a fright.
Thunder and lightning filled the sky,
And a birdling was blown from their nest so high.

1ST TALL FIR:
He might have died in the rain and storm,
But with your small branches, so soft and warm,
You reached right out and broke his fall.
He was only scared, not hurt at all.

LITTLEST FIR (*Happily*):
He often stops, as he's flying by,
To sing me a "thank you," sweet and shy.
I see what you mean,
And maybe you're right.
I *was* glad I was little
That wild Spring night!
(*Sound of Christmas carols being sung in distance.*)

2ND TALL FIR:
Hush!
Do I hear our folks coming down the street,
Talking and laughing and singing?
They have boxes and bundles piled in their arms—
What *do* you suppose they're bringing?

1ST TALL FIR:
Didn't you know? *They're* for Christmas Day.

People buy presents and give them away.
It's the season of love, and peace on earth,
When they celebrate the Christ Child's birth.
(*Enter* MOTHER, FATHER *and two* CHILDREN, *carrying many
packages and singing last few lines of a Christmas carol.
Continue walking toward house. Stop singing.*)

1ST CHILD:

Oh, here we are,
At our very own door,
But I'd like to go back
And shop some more!

MOTHER:

Well, *my* feet are tired,
And I, for one,
Am glad we're *home*
With our shopping *done!*

FATHER:

Yes, home looks mighty good to me—
(*Stops suddenly in front of* LITTLEST FIR)
And do you know what *I* think—
That Littlest Fir's just right to be
Fixed up for an out-door Christmas tree.
I'll get the lights, if you all agree.

2ND CHILD:

Daddy, we've never done that before—
Had a Christmas tree by our own front door!
I'd *like* to share our Christmas fun,
Oh, *please,* let's trim the Littlest One.

1ST CHILD:

All who pass, as they come and go,
Will look at our lighted tree and know
That happy hearts keep Christmas here—
That it's shining out for the Christ Child dear.

MOTHER:
> First bring your things in the house, and then
> You can all hurry right back out again.
> But you'll *have to hurry,* or dusk will fall.
> When dinner's ready, you'll hear me call.

FATHER:
> We *will* have to work fast,
> Before long it will be
> Too dark to trim our out-door tree.
> (*All hurry inside house.*)

1ST TALL FIR:
> Did you hear what they said?
> Won't it be fun!
> They're going to *trim* the Littlest One!

LITTLEST FIR (*Waving about wildly*):
> I'm *so excited,* I can't stand still!
> *Do* you suppose they *really* will?

2ND TALL FIR:
> Hush! Here they are!
> Now you'll soon see
> How it feels to be trimmed—
> A Christmas tree!
> (FATHER *and* CHILDREN *re-appear from the house.* FATHER
> *is carrying a string of Christmas tree lights.*)

FATHER (*Beginning to place lights on tree*):
> We'll be through in a minute—
> This tree's *just right,*
> So easy to reach and fasten each light.

1ST CHILD (*Patting the branches of the* LITTLEST FIR):
> If I weren't a child
> I'd choose to be
> A dear little, green little
> Christmas tree!

FATHER:

> There! It's finished—
> Now who'd like to go
> And turn the switch
> That will make it glow?

2ND CHILD:

> I'll go! I'll go!
> Let me! Let me!
> I want to be first
> To light the tree!
> (*Starts to run inside.*)

1ST CHILD:

> Yes, light it quickly!
> We'll wait to see
> What a beautiful sight
> Our fir will be.
> (*Lights flash on.* 1ST CHILD *comes racing back and all stand admiring the lighted tree.*)

MOTHER (*Calls from inside house*): Dinner is ready now, you three!

> You'll have to leave your Christmas tree!

FATHER:

> Come, we'll leave it here by itself to glow,
> We mustn't keep Mother waiting, you know.

BOTH CHILDREN:

> Good night, Little Fir! You're a beautiful sight!
> And you'll shine for the Christ Child, Christmas night.
> (*All go inside house.*)

LITTLEST FIR (*Joyfully*):

> Oh, look at me, look at me,
> Covered with light!
> I'm *glad* I'm little
> This Winter night!

BOTH TALL FIRS:
    Oh, look at him, look at him,
    Covered with light!
    He's *glad* he's little
    This Winter night!

THE END

Mrs. Santa's Christmas Gift

by *Deborah Newman*

Characters

MRS. SANTA CLAUS
SANTA CLAUS
TEN ELVES

TIME: *Christmas Eve.*

SETTING: *Santa's workshop. Part of the stage is littered with bits of wood, paper, ribbon and greens.*

AT RISE: MRS. SANTA *is placing packages wrapped with Christmas paper under a decorated tree in one corner. She steps back to admire the effect.*

MRS. SANTA: There now! I've taken from my shelves
The gifts I've made for all the elves.
I think this year the gifts are best,
But my, I feel I need a rest. (*Yawns*)
Yet there is work I have to do;
I never seem to get all through:
This room to clean—letters to file—
I really can't rest for a while. (*Picks up paper, then stops*)
Ah, well, perhaps some day there'll be
Long hours of spare time for me! (MRS. SANTA *picks up another piece of paper and exits wearily at right as the* ELVES *come dancing in at left.*)

1ST ELF (*Dancing around stage*): Hooray! I hardly can believe
That at last it's Christmas Eve!

2ND ELF: Hooray, hooray, our work is done;
From now on we can have some fun.

3RD ELF: The gifts we've made are on their way—
They'll give great joy on Christmas Day.

4TH ELF: And soon we will be free to go
And romp and play all day in snow.

5TH ELF: A holiday to ski and skate
'Til next July. What fun! But wait— (*Thinks*)

6TH ELF: Why, what's wrong? What did we forget?
I thought that everything was set.

7TH ELF (*Counts on fingers*) : The presents done, and Santa's
too,
I think he'll like our gift, don't you?

8TH ELF: A watch with chain of golden braid
That tells when presents should be made—
Of course he'll like it—that we know.
Let's wind it up and watch it go!

5TH ELF (*Jumping up and down*) :
Oh, now I know! We're in a spot,
I just can't see how we forgot!

9TH ELF (*A plump one*) : Forgot? Don't tell me it was sweets!
Oh, dear, I want my Christmas treats.

10TH ELF: You eat too much. You're getting fat.
We've candy canes—it isn't that.

5TH ELF: It's more important—can't you guess?
Oh dear, this is an awful mess!
It's really terrible because
We've left out Mrs. Santa Claus!

1ST ELF: No gift? No gift? How could that be?

2ND ELF: There are *our* presents 'neath the tree. (*Points to
tree*)

3RD ELF: She made them sitting up at night—
And we forgot! It isn't right.

4TH ELF: She always does so much for us:
  When I was sick she made a fuss.
5TH ELF: Perhaps there's something we can make?
  A platter good for holding cake?
9TH ELF: For holding *cake?* Oh, good, let's try!
6TH ELF: We couldn't until next July
  When Santa gets supplies again.
  We can't make *anything* 'til then.
7TH ELF: Not anything? (*Looks around. Sadly*) I guess
    you're right,
  And here it is so late at night.
8TH ELF: And Santa's coming back real soon;
  The reindeer speed when it's full moon.
10TH ELF (*Looking at clock on wall*): He'll be here quicker
    than a wink,
  So come on, elves, we've got to *think.*
  (*All of the* ELVES *sit down on the floor and think.* 5TH ELF
  *picks up a piece of wood and paper and looks at it. Then he
  jumps up.*)
5TH ELF: We needn't worry any more!
  I should have thought of this before.
ALL (*Jumping up*): You've thought of something? Good for
    you!
  Please tell us quickly what to do.
5TH ELF: Now, listen, and don't miss a word.
  Keep quiet, please, so I'll be heard.
  (ELVES *gather around* 5TH ELF *and listen intently.*)
  You know that making toys is fun,
  But when the cleaning up is done
  We elves have left and gone away
  To have our winter holiday.
  While Mrs. Santa must stay here
  And work all day throughout the year.

She has to make this workshop clean—
(*Looks around*)
A bigger mess I've never seen!
1st ELF: But if we stopped to clean up too,
Our Christmas work would not get through.
5th ELF: I know, but tell me, why should she
Clean up for us? I just can't see.
2nd ELF: Why, we could do it quick enough.
For ten of us that's not much stuff.
3rd ELF: And we could get her files all fixed
So children's letters won't be mixed.
4th ELF: We know what's liked by girls and boys
So we could order wood for toys.
6th ELF: I want to write down on her list!
7th ELF: I'll help, and no one will be missed.
8th ELF: I think that we should scrub the walls
And clean and paint the reindeer stalls.
9th ELF: I know of a delicious treat:
I'm going to cook things to eat!
10th ELF: I think this idea's really good.
5th ELF: I'm so glad you all understood.
Now, get some paper—I will write
Down all the things we've thought tonight.
(*They get a long sheet of paper, and all sit down while* 5th
ELF *writes.*)
Wash. . . .
1st ELF (*Crowding near*): And clean. . . .
2nd ELF: And paint. . . .
9th ELF (*Rubbing stomach*): And cook!
5th ELF (*Holding up paper*): Why, that's enough to fill a book.
(*The sound of bells is heard outside.* 5th ELF *jumps up and
rolls up paper.*)
It's done. Let's tie it with a bow;

Until it's time she mustn't know.

(*The* ELVES *get red ribbon and tie up the paper. They finish just as* SANTA *and* MRS. SANTA *enter.*)

SANTA (*Laughing*): Oh, ho, my elves, you up to pranks?
I just dropped in to give you thanks.
I've left something at every house
And was as quiet as a mouse.

MRS. SANTA: Did you miss anyone this year?

SANTA: Why, no, I don't think so, my dear.
But let me tell you what I saw. . . .

MRS. SANTA: Now, Santa, you must stop before
You keep us up all night with tales
Of forests tall and singing whales.
Our elves should go beneath the tree
To find their gifts from you and me.

SANTA: Of course. A name is on each one—
A Christmas gift for work well done.
(ELVES *go beneath tree and get packages.* 1ST ELF *comes forward with large box.*)

1ST ELF: I'll say thanks now for all my friends;
Your kindness to us never ends.
Now *this* gift is for Santa dear
With Christmas wishes of good cheer.
(*Gives gift to* SANTA *who opens it and takes out a large watch with a long gold chain*)

SANTA: Why, bless your hearts and thank you, elves,
You really have outdone yourselves.
A watch that tells me when to make
Each little gift that I must take
To children at this time next year.

2ND ELF: It works! Just put it to your ear!
(SANTA *puts the watch to his ear and nods happily.*)

5TH ELF (*Stepping forward with roll of paper*):

And now for Mrs. Santa, too—
We hope this present pleases you.
(*Gives paper to* MRS. SANTA *who unrolls it and reads.* SANTA
peers over her shoulder.)
MRS. SANTA: Dear elves, this gift means much to me.
I never have spare time, you see.
Now I'll have all the time I need
To knit and sew and write and read.
You really were so smart to guess!
I thank you for your thoughtfulness.
3RD ELF: Let's start in working right away
For Mrs. Santa's holiday.
(*Starts to pick up things on the floor.* Other ELVES *join
him.*)
MRS. SANTA: Just one more thing I want to do:
Here are the cakes I baked for you.
(*Goes to cupboard and gets tray of cakes.* All eat.)
SANTA: Merry Christmas, merry, merry. . . .
MRS. SANTA: Oh! I am so happy—very!
ALL (*To audience*): And to you all, good Christmas cheer,
And wishes for a glad New Year.

THE END

The Unhappy Santa

by Natalie Simonds

Characters

JANE, *aged 9*
BILLY, *aged 11*
SANTA CLAUS

SETTING: *The Tracy home on Christmas Eve.*
AT RISE: SANTA *is sitting beneath the gaily-trimmed tree,
weeping; his sack is on the floor beside him.* JANE *and* BILLY
*enter right in their pajamas and stop short when they see
him.*

JANE: Why, look, Billy. It's Santa Claus! But he's crying.
I never heard of Santa Claus crying.
BILLY: That's perfectly ridiculous. Santa Claus never cries.
He's always happy and jolly.
JANE: Well, he certainly is crying now! What do you suppose
is the matter?
BILLY: He might be sick. . . .
JANE: Or hurt.
BILLY: Maybe he broke his leg coming down the chimney.
JANE: Let's see what the trouble is. We can't just stand here
and let him cry—especially on Christmas Eve. (*They ap-
proach* SANTA *slowly.*)
JANE (*Tapping him on the shoulder gently*): Excuse me.
You're Santa Claus, aren't you?

210

SANTA (*Looks up startled; then gruffly*): Of course I am! Don't I look like Santa Claus?

JANE: Well yes, only . . .

SANTA: Only what?

JANE: Only we thought you never cried.

SANTA (*Crossly*): I guess I can cry if I want to.

JANE: Of course you can. (*Brightly*) Sometimes it's good to cry. Mother says so.

BILLY: Did you hurt yourself?

SANTA: No, I didn't. Is that the only reason *you* cry?

BILLY: Well, no . . . but why *were* you crying?

SANTA (*Slowly*): Promise you won't tell anyone . . .

JANE *and* BILLY (*Quickly*): We promise!

SANTA: Honest?

JANE *and* BILLY: Honest.

SANTA: I was feeling sorry for myself. Here it is Christmas Eve, I go around giving everyone what they want, wearing myself out jumping from housetop to housetop—but does anyone think to give poor old Santa anything . . . NO! Jane, you wanted a doll carriage. There it is. (*JANE spies the carriage under the tree and runs to it.*)

JANE (*Delighted*): Oh Santa, you *did* bring it! It's beautiful.

SANTA: And Billy, you asked for a train. There it is.

BILLY (*Gazing at the train, wide-eyed*): Oh boy! What a pip! (*He goes over to it and starts examining it—picking it up, turning it over to look at the mechanism, etc.*)

SANTA (*Sadly*): You've both got what you want. And you're happy. I've given all the other children in the neighborhood what they asked for and they're happy. (*Bursting into tears again*) Everybody's happy but me. (*At this fresh outburst JANE and BILLY stop playing with their toys and look remorseful.*)

BILLY: Oh, Santa, don't cry. Please don't.

SANTA (*Through his tears*): Year after year. Through snow and hail and rain. Dashing around just to please people. And not so much as a thank you do I get.

JANE (*Slowly*): I never thought of it that way.

BILLY: Neither did I. (*They are silent for a minute, then BILLY catches JANE's eye.*)

BILLY: If you'll 'scuse me . . . I forgot something (*Running from the room and calling over his shoulder*) . . . be right back.

JANE (*Quickly*): Me too. (*She runs after BILLY. SANTA sits on the floor, picks up one package after another, puts it down; then rests his chin on his hands and looks dejectedly at the floor.*)

SANTA: A fine Christmas Eve. That's all I can say. (*BILLY enters right, a package held behind him.*)

BILLY: Close your eyes, Santa. It's a surprise!

SANTA (*Incredulous, yet delighted*): A surprise? For me?

BILLY: Yup! Now close your eyes. Or I won't give it to you.

SANTA (*Clapping his hands over his eyes*): All right. I won't peek. (*BILLY puts the box in SANTA's lap.*)

BILLY: O.K. Now you can look. (*SANTA takes his hands from his eyes.*)

SANTA: May I open it now?

BILLY: You really shouldn't open it till Christmas, but seeing it's *your* holiday I guess it'll be all right. (*SANTA opens the box excitedly and takes out a pair of brightly colored socks.*)

SANTA (*Smiling broadly*): Say! Those are some fancy socks! And warm, too. They'll sure come in handy on cold nights at the Pole.

BILLY (*Pleased*): Do you really like them?

SANTA: I'll say I do. Thanks a lot, Billy. (*JANE enters right also holding a box behind her back. She goes up to SANTA and hands the parcel to him.*)

JANE: Merry Christmas, Santa!

SANTA (*Delighted*): Is this for me, Janey?

JANE: Nobody else!

SANTA (*Chuckling*): I'm certainly glad I encouraged this Christmas business. (*Opens the package and takes out a scarf.*) Boy, this is lovely, Janey. I don't know what to say. This is my lucky night, all right.

JANE: I'm glad you like it.

SANTA: Like it! Gosh—and do I need one! You know, this beard doesn't keep my neck as warm as you think. (*Laughing*) Must have got moths in it. Mrs. Santa kept wanting to spray it, and I said I wasn't going to have her chasing me around the Pole like a confounded fly. (*Looking at his watch*) Goodness, but it's getting late! I've got to be on my way. Still have some calls to make. (*Picks up his knapsack and throws it over his shoulder.*) You children had better get to bed before your mother hears you. Thanks again. And if I can do anything for you, just drop me a line. You know the address. (*He waves good-bye and exits through the chimney.*)

JANE and BILLY (*Facing chimney and waving*): Good-bye, Santa. Thanks for everything.

JANE: We'd better go to bed. (*Looking longingly at the doll carriage*) I hope it won't be long till morning.

BILLY (*His eyes on the train*): I hope so too. (*Reluctantly they start toward right.*)

JANE: Santa certainly was pleased, wasn't he?

BILLY: Gosh, yes.

JANE: I'm glad we found him crying. It would be awful if Santa didn't have a merry Christmas after all the time he spent making others happy.

BILLY: We'll have to get up early and get Dad something else. We can take the money out of our piggy-bank. (*Chuckling*)

Y'know, Janey, that's a funny one—giving Santa Claus presents. It's like playing Santa Claus yourself.

JANE (*Laughing as she exits*): Yes . . . well, Merry Christmas, Mr. Claus.

BILLY (*Bowing her out*) : Merry Christmas, Miss Claus. (*Their laughter can be heard offstage as the curtain falls.*)

THE END

The Christmas Train

by Helen L. Howard

Characters

THE ENGINE	OTHER TOYS
RAGGEDY ANDY	HORSE
RAGGEDY ANN	BOAT
DOLL	TRUCK
BEAR	AIRPLANE
JACK-IN-THE-BOX	

SETTING: *A railroad track.*

TIME: *The day before Christmas.*

AT RISE: *The* ENGINE *of the Christmas Express comes chugging on to the stage followed by the toys pulling back on the shoulders of the one in front. The first toy in line is pulling on the* ENGINE. *The* ENGINE *wears a sign CHRISTMAS EXPRESS. As he nears the center of the stage he goes more slowly until he stops.* RAGGEDY ANDY *and* RAGGEDY ANN *leave the line and come to see what the trouble is.*

ANDY: What's the matter, Engine? Why did you stop?

ENGINE (*Panting for breath*):
Up this hill I cannot run.
You Christmas Toys must weigh a ton!

ANN: But we'll be late for Christmas! It's nearly Christmas Eve now!

ENGINE: Without some help I cannot pull this heavy load over the hill, Raggedy Ann.

ANN: But what will the children on the other side of the hill do without their toys for Christmas?

DOLL: I'm sure that my new mother will be awfully upset if I don't make it by Christmas.

BEAR: To say nothing of the little boy who ordered me!

ANN: And what will Santa Claus do if we aren't there to meet him when he comes with his reindeer tonight?

ANDY: Oh, dear! I never thought of that.

ENGINE: I'm sorry, but I'll have to have some help to pull you Christmas toys over the hill!

ANDY: I guess it's up to us, Ann, to get someone to help the Engine. We'll try to flag down someone who will help Engine.

ANN: I'll take the river on this side, and you take the highway on that, Andy.

ANDY: Here comes a horse down the highway. I'll ask him to help Engine. (HORSE *trots in across down stage.*) Oh, Horse! Do stop a moment. We need some help.

HORSE (*Canters to a stop*): What can I do?

ANDY: Will you help Engine pull this load of toys to the top of the hill? We must get to the other side of this hill or the children over there won't have toys for Christmas.

HORSE: I'm afraid I can't. My hoofs weren't made to go on rails, you know. Sorry.

ANDY: That's right. You couldn't go up this track. Well, thank you for stopping. Merry Christmas.

HORSE: Merry Christmas. (*Trots off.*)

ANN (*Excitedly*): Here comes a boat down the river. Maybe it will help Engine. (BOAT *enters.*) Oh, Boat, will you help Engine pull this load of toys to the top of the hill? Santa Claus is to meet us on the other side and we don't want to disappoint him.

BOAT: I wish I could help but I can't go up hill, you know.

I have to have locks to do that. Sorry. Merry Christmas. (*Goes off as* Toys *call "Merry Christmas."*)

ANDY: Now there's a truck coming along the highway. Trucks are strong. Maybe it can help you, Engine. (*Flags down* TRUCK *as it crosses down stage.*) Please, Truck, will you help the Christmas Express? Our Engine cannot pull all of us up this hill.

TRUCK: I'm sorry, my wheels won't stay on the rails. They are just not in the groove, you might say. I must get home in time for Christmas Eve. Merry Christmas. (*Exit*)

ANDY: Thanks for stopping, anyway, Truck. Merry Christmas.

ANN: There's an airplane. I'll call to him. (AIRPLANE *goes whizzing by far up stage.* ANN *and* ANDY *both call but he doesn't hear them.*)

BEAR: It's no use. He doesn't hear you. If only we had wings so we could fly across the hill.

DOLL: Oh, dear! This is terrible. My new mother will be so disappointed. (*All of the* TOYS, *except the* JACK-IN-THE-BOX, *begin to wail.*)

JACK (*Jumps out of his box*): Here now! Stop all of this noise! Let me think! I know! Why don't we all get off and push?

ANDY: The very thing!

ANN: Why didn't we think of that?

ENGINE: If you all help I'm sure we can pull the Christmas Express to the top of the hill.

TOYS: We will! We will! (TOYS *begin to push forward on shoulders of one in front and against the* ENGINE's *back.*)

ENGINE (*Begins to move slowly across stage*): Mer-ry-Christ-mas! Mer-ry Christ-mas! (*All of the* TOYS *begin to say "Mer-ry-Christ-mas" with the* ENGINE *slowly and then as if gaining a little momentum.*)

JACK: Hurrah! Engine's at the top! It's remarkable what

can be done when everybody cooperates. Hop on, everybody, as the train goes to the other side in time for Christmas. (*As the train goes down the hill, off stage, the* CHARACTERS *all say "Mer-ry-Christ-mas" in unison. They keep gaining momentum as the curtains close.*)

THE END

Candy Canes

by Claribel Spamer

Characters

SANTA CLAUS   DOROTHY, *a little girl*
BEPPO, *an elf*   GRANDFATHER
CLIP, *another elf*

SCENE 1

SETTING: *A wood.*

AT RISE: SANTA *enters followed by* BEPPO. SANTA *is carrying a bag which he opens and from which he takes out a letter. He sits on the stump and reads it.*

SANTA (*Quoting*): "And Santa dear, please give me something brand new. I have a doll already. I have skates—" (*Looking up and scratching his head*) My word, this child has everything!

BEPPO (*Annoyed*): Skip her then. Her folks are rich. They'll give her things.

SANTA (*Thoughtfully*): No, I never skip anyone. If I could just invent something new. (CLIP *enters and gives* SANTA *another letter*) What? Still another? (*Opens it and reads*) "Dear Santa, I would like more than anything else to have some candy—some very special candy, because I don't get sweets very often." Poor little girl! She has so few toys too. Her daddy hasn't much money.

219

CLIP (*Cheerfully*): We've lots of chocolates, peppermints, and lemon drops this year. Beppo and I made an extra thousand.

SANTA (*Rubbing his chin*): I'd like to think of something even better. (*Getting up*) But I must go back to my doll-making. (*Sighs*) I love my work, but it certainly is getting to be a problem, with so many children nowadays.

BEPPO (*Sympathetically*): Poor Santa! (*Trying to cheer him*) But we finished painting the wagons, Santa!

CLIP: Can we do anything about the candy?

BEPPO: Or make something for the rich girl?

SANTA (*Hopefully*): Yes, maybe you can! Try to invent something new for Christmas, something to eat, something sweet. Then I can give it to both girls and other children too. I can treat them all alike. (*Exits, but drops a red mitten as he does so.*)

CLIP (*Whistling*): Phew! We asked for it that time!

BEPPO (*Cutting a caper*):
Something new and something sweet,
Something children like to eat.
That's a riddle, I confess,
Which I am at a loss to guess.

CLIP: Sh! Someone's coming! (*They hide between two trees. DOROTHY and GRANDFATHER enter. GRANDFATHER is leaning on DOROTHY'S arm.*)

DOROTHY: Sit down here and rest, Grandfather. (*Helps him to sit on the stump.*)

GRANDFATHER (*Rubbing his back*): My, but I'm tired! If we could only find my cane.

DOROTHY: Are you sure you lost it here?

GRANDFATHER: Well after I took my snooze in a grove of trees, I could find it nowhere, but I can't remember if this was the grove or not.

DOROTHY (*Sitting beside him*): Oh dear. (*Sees SANTA'S mitten on the ground*) Look, a red mitten! (*Picks it up*) With a white cuff! Santa's!

GRANDFATHER (*Looking at it*): What did you ask him for, Dorothy?

DOROTHY (*Smiling*): That's a secret. But it's something nice. Are you rested now?

GRANDFATHER (*Getting up stiffly*): Yes, I think so. Let's go on. (DOROTHY *places the mitten and note on the stump. They exit, and* BEPPO *and* CLIP *come out from hiding.* BEPPO *picks up the note and reads it.*)

BEPPO: Clip, listen. Can you beat this? (*Reads*) "Dear Santa. Don't give me any toys or sweets this year. All I want is a good strong cane."

CLIP: For her grandfather! Poor little kid.

BEPPO: She deserves twice as many toys as most kids. Let's go make the cane.

CLIP: And not do the job Santa asked of us?

BEPPO: That's right. I almost forgot. (*Snaps fingers*) Say! I've an idea.

CLIP (*Excited*): What is it? (SANTA *reenters, unnoticed by the elves. He looks for his mitten. Sees it, and picks it and the note up. Reads the note.*)

BEPPO: We'll not only make a cane for Dorothy's grandfather; we'll make her one too—of candy! Peppermint candy! All striped red and white!

CLIP (*Slapping* BEPPO *on the shoulder*): Wonderful! And that is something brand new for the rich girl—

BEPPO: And a very special sweet for the poor little girl—

SANTA (*Enthusiastically*): And for all children. I can hang them on their Christmas trees too. Beppo, you are a genius.

BEPPO (*Beaming*): Thanks, Santa.

CLIP (*Dreamily*): We'll make big canes and little ones, fat ones and thin ones—

SANTA (*Starting offstage*) : Come on, then. (BEPPO *and* CLIP *start to follow him.*)

BEPPO (*As he exits*) : And maybe we can make three little extra ones, just for Clip and you and me, Santa.

SANTA (*Laughing*) : Why not? Three *big* extra ones.

THE END

The Spirit of Christmas

by Robert St. Clair

Characters

MEG MARCH, *the oldest sister.*
JO, *the tomboy.*
AMY, *the affected one.*
BETH, *the meek one.*
MARMEE, *the beloved mother.*
HANNAH, *the housekeeper.*
MRS. HUMMEL, *an ill neighbor.*

THEME MUSIC: *"Long, Long Ago" up and under.*

ANNOUNCER: Almost every man, woman and child has at some time in their lives read that classic of American literature, "Little Women." Today we are presenting an episode in the lives of the lovable March family, who knew the true meaning of Christmas and the joy of giving. Four devoted sisters are sitting in front of the fireplace in a Civil War home in a small New England city. One is Jo, the tomboy; the other is Meg, the oldest; the third and fourth are Amy, the youngest, and Beth, the meek. They are waiting for their mother to come home.

THEME MUSIC: *Up and out.*

JO (*Whistling: "When Johnny Comes Marching Home."*)
AMY (*Petulantly*): Why do you always have to whistle when you knit, Jo? It sounds like a boy.

Jo (*Cheerfully*): That's why I do it, Amy.

AMY: Now you're being rude, and I detest rude, unladylike girls.

Jo: And I hate affected, niminy-piminy chits! I wish I were a boy, so I could go and fight with papa in the war, and wouldn't have to stay at home and knit like a poky old woman!

AMY: Listen to her, Meg!

MEG: Don't peck at one another, girls. You are almost as old as I am, Jo, and should learn how to behave better. And as for you, Amy, you put on altogether too many grand airs for a child of thirteen.

AMY: Oh, don't be so elderly, Meg. Just because you're the oldest you don't have to be so doctatorial.

Jo: You mean, dictatorial, don't you, Amy? (*They all laugh.*)

BETH: If Jo is a tomboy, Amy affected and Meg is bossy, what am I?

MEG (*Warmly*): You are our patient, lovable little Beth and nothing else.

Jo: On that subject I guess we all agree.

SOUND: *Clock striking six.*

MEG: It's six o'clock!

Jo: Almost time for mother to be home.

BETH (*Fade*): I'll sweep up the hearth and put her slippers down to warm.

MEG (*Fade*): I'd best light the lamp. It's getting dark.

SOUND: *Rattle of lamp chimney.*

AMY: And I'll start toasting the bread for tea.

Jo: The day before Christmas. (*Sighs*) It won't seem like Christmas if we can't give each other presents.

AMY: I don't think it's fair for some girls to have so much and us not have anything at all. Move over, Jo, so I can hold the toasting fork in the blaze.

BETH: And *you* move over, Amy, so I can sweep the hearth.

SOUND: *Sweeping.*

BETH (*Over sound effect*): We have mother and father and each other, you know.

JO: We haven't father, Beth, and shan't have until the war ends.

MEG (*Fades in*): The reason mother suggested that we don't exchange presents this year was because she thought we ought not to spend money for pleasure when our men are suffering so in the army.

JO: I know, Meg, but we've each got a dollar and the army won't be helped much by our giving that. I agree not to expect anything from you girls or mother, but I'm going to buy a book for myself. I love to read.

BETH: And write. You're a wonderful authoress, Jo. I planned to spend my dollar on some new music.

AMY: And I shall get a box of drawing pencils with mine. How can I draw well without the proper materials?

BETH: Just look at mother's slippers, girls. They're quite worn out.

JO: She ought to have a new pair.

BETH (*Thoughtfully*): I believe I'll buy her some with my dollar.

AMY: No, Beth. I shall.

MEG: Now, Amy, I'm the oldest—

JO: And I'm the man of the family while papa's away. *I* shall buy the slippers because he told me to take special care of her while he was gone.

BETH: Let's each buy her something then and not get anything for ourselves.

MEG: All right, Beth. I shall give her a pair of gloves.

BETH: And I'll buy handkerchiefs. Amy?

AMY: I shall buy her a bottle of cologne. That won't cost so much, so I'll still have enough left over to get my pencils.

MEG: How shall we give the things?

JO: Put them on the table in the center of the room and bring her in to open them. We'll go shopping tomorrow morning, Meg, and— Look, Amy! You're burning the toast!

AMY: Oh! Oh!

SOUND: *Door opens off mike.*

MARMEE (*Off mike*): Well, girls, I'm home.

GIRLS (*Ad lib*): Marmee! We've been waiting for you. What kept you so long?

MARMEE (*Fades in*): We've been getting the Christmas boxes off to the soldiers. Has anyone called, Beth? How's your cold, Meg? Jo, you look tired to death. Come and kiss me, Amy. (*The girls ad lib short, appropriate answers to the above questions.*)

MEG: Let me take your cloak and bonnet.

JO: Sit down by the fire, Marmee, and let me put your slippers on.

BETH (*Fades*): I'll arrange the tea-table.

MARMEE: Thank you, girls. It is nice to sit down. Oh, don't take my bag, Meg. I've a treat in there for you.

SOUND: *Slight rattle of dishes off mike.*

JO: I know what it is; a letter from father! Hooray! Hooray! Hooray!

AMY (*Reprovingly*): Jo!

MARMEE: Gather around me, children, and I'll read an especial message he sent to his daughters.

SOUND: *Paper rattles.*

MEG (*Fades in*): I think it's splendid of father to go as a chaplain when he was too old to be drafted.

JO: I wish I could go as drummer boy, or a nurse, so I could be near and help him.

AMY (*Sighs*): It must be very disagreeable to sleep in a tent, eat all sorts of bad-tasting food and drink out of a tin mug.

MARMEE: Well, here's what he says. "Give them my love and a kiss. Tell them I think of them by day, pray for them at night, and find my best comfort in their affection at all times."

AMY (*Sighs*): Poor father.

MARMEE (*Reading*): "A year seems a long time to wait before I see them again, but remind them that while we wait we must all work so that these difficult days need not be wasted. When I come back I know that I will be fonder and prouder than ever of my—little women." (*Sighs.*)

SOUND: *Slight rattle of paper.*

MEG (*Softly*): I will work, even though I hate it.

AMY: I'm going to try not to be vain any more.

JO: And I shall try to be what he calls me—a little woman—and not be so rough and wild.

MARMEE: Girls, do you remember when you were little things and liked to play Pilgrim's Progress?

JO: Oh, what fun it was, especially going through the middle of the house where the hobgoblins were supposed to be.

MEG: I liked the part where we let the bundles fall off our backs and tumble downstairs.

BETH: My favorite part was when we came out on the roof, which we called the Celestial City.

AMY: I don't remember it much except that I was afraid of the cellar, but liked the cake and milk you gave us on the roof. If I wasn't too old for such things I'd like to play it again.

MARMEE: We are never too old for this, my dear, because it is a play we are playing all the time in one way or another. We all have our burdens, the road is before us, and the longing for goodness and happiness is the guide that leads us through our troubles to the peace that is the *true* Celestial City. Now, my pilgrims, suppose we play it again—in earnest this time—and see how far we can go before father comes home?

AMY: Really, Marmee? Where are our burdens?

MARMEE: Each of you told what your burden was just now, except Beth. I rather think she hasn't got any.

BETH: Oh, yes I have, Marmee. I envy girls with nice pianos, and I would so like to get over being afraid of people.

MEG: It's just another name for being good, girls.

JO: We ought to have our list of directions though, like Christian had in the book. What shall we do about that, Marmee?

MARMEE (*Quietly*): Look under your pillows on Christmas morning, and—you will find your guide books.

MUSIC: *Up and out.*

SOUND: *Clock striking seven off mike.*

JO (*Yawns*): Ho-hum. Seven o'clock. Time to get up. Meg. Oh, Meg.

MEG (*Yawns*): Ho-hum. (*Sleepily*) Merry Christmas, Jo.

JO: Same to you. Move over, will you, so I can look under my pillow?

MEG: Oh, yes! Our guide books!

SOUND: Jo *patting pillow.*

JO (*Excitedly*): Look, Meg! It's a book! The story of Jesus.

MEG: Here's mine! Bound in green.

JO (*Reading*): "To Jo, my tomboy, who, I am sure, will become a very good pilgrim indeed." How perfectly jolly!

MEG: She's written in mine—(*Reads*) "To Meg, who in spite of her small vanities, has a sweet and pious nature that influences all who know her." Dear Marmee.

BETH (*Off mike*): Amy! Amy, look under your pillow—quickly!

JO: That's Beth. They're awake. (*Calls along with* MEG) Merry Christmas, Beth. Merry Christmas, Amy.

BETH (*Fades in, excitedly*): Look, girls! Jo, Meg, look at my book!

JO: See ours, Beth?

BETH: Bound in red and green. Mine's dove-colored.

AMY (*Fades in, excitedly*) : Aren't they precious, girls? Mine's blue.

JO: Blue to match your eyes, Amy.

MEG: Now listen, children, mother wants us to read and mind these books, and we must begin at once. I shall keep mine on the table here beside the bed and read a little every morning as I wake, for I know it will do me good and help me through the day.

JO: Come, Amy, let's read some now. I'll help you with the hard words.

AMY: Oh, no, Jo. I'm going to hurry and get dressed. (*Fades*) I'ye got something terociously important to do.

JO (*Laughs*) : The child means terrifically.

MEG: Weren't we stupid to think we weren't going to have a nice Christmas this year?

BETH (*Quietly*) : I knew we had father and mother and each other, and I couldn't wish for anything better.

JO: Beth, you're a dear.

MEG: Read a little out loud, will you, Jo? While I'm dressing.

SOUND: *Muffled rattle of pots and pans off mike.*

BETH: We don't have to go downstairs until eight. Hannah just came into the kitchen—I can hear her rattling the pots and pans.

JO: All right. At eight we'll go down to thank Marmee and wish her joy. (*Reads and fades.*) "Suffer little children to come unto Me, for of such is the kingdom of heaven—"

SOUND: *Slight pause. Clock striking eight. Rattle of pots and pans. Door opens off mike.*

HANNAH: (*Fades in, singing an old-fashioned hymn off-key.*)

MEG *and* JO (*Fade in*) : Merry Christmas, Hannah. Merry Christmas.

HANNAH: An' the same to you, dear girls.

MEG: Where's mother?

HANNAH: Goodness only knows, Miz Meg. Some poor creature came a'-beggin' an' your maw went straight off to see what was needed. Honest-to-goshen, Miz Jo, there never was such a woman for givin' away vittles an' drink, clothes an' firin'.

MEG: She'll be back soon, so fry the cakes, Hannah, while— (*Fades*) Jo and I go into the parlour and wait for her.

SOUND: *Door closes.*

HANNAH: (*Sings and fades.*)

JO (*Fades in*): It was a good idea to hide the presents in the basket under the sofa, wasn't it, Meg? Oh, there's Beth. (*Fades*) Are the presents all there, Beth?

BETH (*Fades in*): Yes, Jo, they're all here.

MEG (*Fades in*): Put the paper around the slippers, Jo, while I get the little notes we wrote—(*Fades*)—to go with the presents.

SOUND: *Paper rattle.*

JO: How thoughtful of you, Beth, to arrange the vase of geraniums as a centerpiece for us to put the presents around.

MEG (*Fading in*): Too bad we can't have holly and mistletoe. It won't be a very splendid show, I'm afraid, but a lot of love will be done up in our small bundles.

BETH (*Fading in*): Here are my handkerchiefs.

JO: And there are the slippers. I'll watch through the window for her to come. (*Fades on last few words.*)

SOUND: *Door opens and closes off mike.*

AMY (*Fading in*): Here's my bottle of cologne, girls—all wrapped. Doesn't the flower I put on top of it look pretty though?

MEG: Yes it does, Amy.

JO (*Off mike*): Here she comes, girls! She's coming through the gate! (*Fades in, excitedly.*) Play your most rousing march, Beth, and Amy, you open the door. All ready, girls?

GIRLS (*Off mike. Ad lib*): Yes, Jo! All ready. Isn't it exciting though?

JO: All right. Three cheers for Christmas. Hooray!

ALL: Hooray! Hooray!

SOUND: *Piano, rousing march. Door opens and closes.*

GIRLS (*Off mike*): Merry Christmas, Marmee! Many of them. Thank you for the books.

SOUND: *Music stops.*

MARMEE (*Fading in*): Girls! Oh, my girls! What on earth—?

MEG (*Stiffly*): Mrs. March, it gives me great pleasure to take your coat and bonnet and direct your glance to this table where a great surprise awaits you.

MARMEE: For me? Oh, my girls—my dear girls. I thought we agreed not to—

JO: We bought them with our dollars, Marmee.

AMY: Open mine first, will you?

SOUND: *Paper rattle.*

MARMEE: Goodness, this is such a surprise. I—Cologne! Such a handsome bottle too. Amy, how sweet.

JO: Now mine.

SOUND: *Paper rattle.*

MARMEE: Jo, this looks suprisingly like—I knew it! Slippers. How thoughtful of you.

JO: Sit down, Marmee, and let's see if they fit.

MARMEE (*Sighs as though sitting*): I'm overcome.

MEG: Now open mine, Marmee.

SOUND: *Paper rattle.*

MARMEE: You're making me very happy, girls. I feel like crying for joy. Gloves! Just what I needed. Thank you, Meg. What a lovely color, too.

JO: Look, girls, the slippers do fit, and don't they look fine on her feet?

BETH: My present isn't very much, Marmee, but—

MARMEE: I know it will be lovely, Beth.

SOUND: *Paper rattle.*

MARMEE: Handkerchiefs! Marked by yourself, too. You sweet child. Was ever a mother so blessed?

MEG: Now read the notes, Marmee.

MARMEE (*Reading*): "To the best mother in all the world. Meg. To Marmee from Amy with a heart full of love and— (*Spells*) A-P-P-R-I-P-I-O-N."

AMY: That's "appreciation." I didn't quite know how to spell it.

MARMEE: It's lovely, dear. (*Reads*) "To Mother, the lighthouse in our domestic sea—whose soul is a shining beacon that will forever be our guiding light in times of doubt and trouble. Jo" What a pretty sentiment, Jo.

BETH: Jo can always think of the loveliest things to write.

MARMEE (*Reads*): "To Marmee with love—Beth." Oh, my dears.

JO (*Clears her throat*): Now—now let's celebrate with a hearty breakfast.

GIRLS: Yes. Let's do.

MARMEE (*Gently*): Just one moment, girls. Listen. Not far from here there lies a poor sick woman with a little newborn baby. Several other children are huddled into one bed to keep from freezing, for they have no wood to make a fire. There is nothing to eat over there, and the oldest boy came over here early this morning to tell me that they were suffering hunger and cold. My girls, will you give them your breakfast as a Christmas present?

JO (*Slight pause*): I—I'm glad we waited for you, Marmee.

BETH: May I go along and help carry the things?

AMY: I shall take the cream—

MEG (*Fades*): I'll tell Hannah to fry all the buckwheats.

MARMEE: I thought you'd do it. You shall all go and help me, so get your things on at once. When we come back we'll have bread and milk for breakfast and make it up at dinner time. It isn't far so we ought to be there long before nine.

MUSIC: *Up and out for change of scene.*

MRS. HUMMEL (*Fades in, weakly*): Ah, Mrs. March, it is like good angels have come to me in my hour of need.

JO: Funny sort of angels, Mrs. Hummel, in hoods and bonnets.

SOUND: *Children laugh off mike.*

MRS. HUMMEL: Listen to the children. It is the first time I have heard them laugh in weeks.

MEG: Just look at the darlings eat, Marmee.

MARMEE: It does one's heart good to see them, doesn't it, Meg?

HANNAH (*Fades in, matter-of-factly*): Well, I've made a fire an' stopped up the broken window panes with old hats an' my own cloak, no less.

MARMEE: Thank you, Hannah. Well, we've done everything we can, I guess. Now we must go.

MRS. HUMMEL: God bless you, Mrs. March. You and your angel children have given me and mine a Christmas we shall long remember.

JO: Open the door, Meg. (*Fades*) Merry Christmas, children.

CHILDREN (*Off mike*): Merry Christmas. Merry Christmas.

SOUND: *Door opens and closes. Winter street noises, and fade in off mike.*

MEG (*Fades in*): Well, that is certainly loving our neighbors better than ourselves, and I—I like it.

MARMEE: I think there are not in all the city four merrier people than my hungry girls who gave away their Christmas breakfasts.

HANNAH: Bless the dear girls. They have the true Christian spirit.

BETH: I feel like I'm really being what mother wants us to be—a little pilgrim.

AMY (*Sighs*): And now we're on our way home to our bread and milk!

JO: Christopher Columbus, but it's cold!

AMY: Jo! Such slang! You talk like a dreadful boy.

JO: I wish I were a boy, Amy. Then wouldn't I make things hum!

THEME MUSIC: *Up and out.*

THE END

Vision of the Silver Bell

by Winston Weathers

MUSIC: *Up and under.*

NARRATOR: As usual, Christmas Eve finds the Mason family eagerly awaiting Christmas Day. The evergreen tree has been decorated and all the presents have been placed under it. Mrs. Mason has just finished brewing a pot of spiced tea and the family is seated in front of the glowing embers of the fireplace. The silence is broken by Mr. Mason who picks up a little brown box beneath the Christmas tree and starts to open it . . .

MR. MASON: Don't get the wrong impression, children. I'm not opening any of the gifts. This little box has been in the Mason family for over 150 years and its contents have been in the family exactly 200 years tonight.

DAVID: What is it, Father?

MR. MASON: Just a moment and you shall see.

ALICE: It must be a family heirloom if it's that old! Anything over fifty years old is supposed to be an antique!

GRANDMOTHER: I'm not an antique!

ALICE: Oh, I wasn't talking about people, Grandmother!

MR. MASON: Here it is.

DAVID: Why, it's a little silver bell!

MRS. MASON: A very unique silver bell.

DAVID: It looks just like any other bell to me.

MR. MASON: And so it did to your great-great-great-grandfather on Christmas Eve, 1750.

ALICE: 1750! That was before the Revolution!

MRS. MASON: George Washington was just 13 years old and the English were fighting the French and Indian Wars.

DAVID: Were there Masons way back then?

GRANDMOTHER: David, my boy, the Masons are a very old family. They settled in Massachusetts in the year 1703.

MR. MASON: In fact, on Christmas Eve, 1750 . . . the Mason family that sat around the fireplace was, I imagine, a great deal like our own. There was John Mason and his wife, Alice . . .

ALICE: Is that where I got my name?

MRS. MASON: Yes, dear.

MR. MASON: And there was Grandmother Mason . . . the very first Mason woman to come to America . . . and there was little David . . . and Anna. As the story was told to me . . . (*Fades*) It was Christmas Eve, 1750, and the Masons had been busy preparing for the holiday . . .

MUSIC: *Up and out.*

ALICE: David, keep your fingers out of the molasses! You won't get a single cookie tomorrow if you keep bothering me.

DAVID: Yes, Mother.

ALICE: Run and look out the window and see if you can see your father. He should be here soon.

DAVID: Is he bringing a Christmas tree?

ALICE: I think so. He went into the hills to cut one.

ANNA (*Fading in*): Mother . . . Grandmother would like her tea, now. She says it's quite chilly.

ALICE: There it is, still hanging over the fire. . . . Watch yourself or you'll get burnt.

ANNA: Yes, Mother. Do you want me to light the candles in the parlor? We'll need light to decorate the Christmas tree by!

ALICE: Not yet, Anna. Our supply of candles is running short and until your father can get into Boston to get some more we must use them sparingly.

ANNA: When do you think Father will go to Boston? I wonder if he would let me go with him!

DAVID: I want to go too! I want to see the soldiers marching in their red coats. I wish I were a soldier!

ALICE: Your father won't go to Boston until spring. The carriage couldn't get through now.

ANNA (*Off*): It's starting to snow again, Mother.

ALICE: I wish John would get back before dark. The way the wind sounds you'd think we might have a blizzard.

ANNA (*Off*): I'll be right back. I have to take Grandmother her tea or she'll grunt at me.

ALICE: Poke the fire will you, David? It is growing colder. And did you fill the wood box? I told you to an hour ago.

DAVID: Yes, I filled it.

SOUND: *Door opens, wind outside, shuts.*

ALICE: Oh, John. I'm glad you're back. I was beginning to worry.

JOHN: It's going to be a blizzard tonight, Alice.

DAVID: And he brought a Christmas tree! Anna! Anna! Come here.

ALICE: Sit down and have your supper, John. The rest of us have eaten. The tea is still hot and here are some baked potatoes . . .

ANNA (*Fading in*): Where is it, David? Oh, hello, Father. Oh, my goodness! It's bigger than the one we had last year! Get the cranberries and popcorn, David . . . Mother . . . can we decorate it now . . . we'll be very careful . . .

ALICE: All right . . . but take it into the parlor . . . and don't disturb Grandmother.

DAVID: We won't . . . (*Fading*) Come on, Anna . . . I'll drag the tree . . . you get the decorations . . .

JOHN (*Whispering*): Are they out of hearing?

ALICE: Yes. They're too busy to hear anything!

JOHN: Well, I got them. The messenger brought them to me down at the village this afternoon . . . all the way from Boston. A china doll for Anna, and a drum for David.

ALICE: Wonderful! They'll be thrilled!

JOHN: I left the presents out in the barn . . . I'll go get them later on tonight when the children are asleep.

ALICE: I've knitted your mother a shawl . . . It's about all I knew to give her . . .

JOHN: She'll like it very much. . . . Did you get the gingerbread made for the children tomorrow?

ALICE: Can't you smell it? It was done an hour ago . . . I made some molasses cookies, too . . .

JOHN: The children will like that.

ALICE: And you, too!

JOHN: That I will. You ought to see the drum . . . it's a bright red . . .

ALICE: And the doll . . . I can just see it . . . with rosy little cheeks . . .

JOHN: Shh! Here they come.

DAVID (*Fading in*): Mother . . . there's someone knocking at the door . . . I was afraid to answer it. . . . Maybe you'd better go.

JOHN: I'll go, Alice.

ALICE: I can't imagine who it could be. It's dark now . . . and with a storm coming up.

JOHN: Everyone else is celebrating Christmas Eve in his own home.

SOUND: *Unlatching door, opens, wind outside.*

JOHN: Yes . . . what do you want . . .

MAN (*Off*): May . . . may we come in . . . my wife . . . she's . .

ALICE: Let them come in.

JOHN: Come on in.

SOUND: *Door shuts.*

MAN: Thank you. We were on our way to Boston.

JOHN: Boston! In this kind of weather?

MAN: We started several days ago. My wife's parents live there . . . and . . . and my wife is going to have a child . . .

JOHN: Oh . . . I see . . .

ALICE: Sit down in this chair . . . and warm yourself . . .

WOMAN: Thank . . . you . . . I . . . hope we're not . . . bothering you . . .

ALICE: Not at all!

MAN: We wanted to be in Boston for Christmas and to have the child there . . . but when this storm came up . . . and I'm afraid we can't make it. . . . We could stay in your barn if . . .

JOHN: In the barn! Goodness no! We have room for you.

ALICE: Certainly. David and Anna can sleep in front of the fireplace . . . they like to anyway.

ANNA: Yes, we do.

ALICE: We'll put your wife up in the children's room. She needs a good bed. . . .

MAN: She's very weak . . .

JOHN: You can stay up there and watch over her . . . David, bring us some candles!

DAVID: Yes, Father.

ALICE: Here, my dear . . . let me help you.

WOMAN: Thank you . . . you're very kind . . .

ALICE: Your clothes are all wet, too . . . I'll get some dry ones. . . . It was a bad night to be out . . .

WOMAN (*Fading*): We should never have started . . . but we so wanted to be in Boston.

ALICE (*Fading*): Watch your step . . . lean on my shoulder . . .

DAVID· Here are the candles, Father.

JOHN: Take them up to your mother. Light them first, though.

MAN: You are very kind, sir. My wife, Mary, and I will never forget your hospitality.

JOHN: You're quite welcome. If you need us in the night . . . if the . . . child . . . well . . . be sure . . . and call.

MAN: Yes, I will . . . but here. I have a little silver bell. If my wife needs you . . . I'll ring the little bell.

JOHN: All right. If you ring, we'll come.

MAN: I'll go now . . .

JOHN: Don't you want something to eat?

MAN: Not now . . . I'd better be with Mary.

JOHN: All right. Run along. Give my wife any instructions you think necessary . . . but I can tell you . . . she's an experienced hand . . . David and Anna you know . . .

MAN (*Fading*): Good night.

JOHN: Good night.

MUSIC: *Up and out.*

ALICE (*Whispering*): John . . . John!

JOHN (*Disturbed*): Huh . . . what do you want, Alice?

ALICE: What time is it?

JOHN: I don't know . . . I'm sleepy . . .

ALICE: I thought I heard something.

JOHN: Dreaming . . .

ALICE: No I wasn't, John . . . Do you suppose the children are all right?

JOHN: Yes . . . I'm sure they're . . . all right . . .

ALICE: But, John . . . I heard something . . .

JOHN: Alice, you're just . . . dreaming now let me go . . .

ALICE: Listen . . .

SOUND: *Bell rings . . . silence . . . bell rings . . . silence . . . bell rings.*

JOHN: Oh, heavens! It's them . . .

ALICE: Who?

JOHN: Upstairs . . . He said he'd ring a bell if his wife . . .

ALICE: You don't mean . . .

JOHN: Yes, I do.

ALICE: Where's my robe. . . . Goodness! We'd better hurry, John . . .

JOHN (*Fading out*): Come on, Alice . . . you know more about this than I do . . .

ALICE (*Fading out*): I'm coming, John. . . . Go and get her husband out of the room. . . .

JOHN (*Fading in*): All right, Alice . . . but hurry up . . .

SOUND: *Opening door.*

ALICE (*Fading in*): All right, John. . . . Now you run and put on a kettle of water. . . . What is it, John?

JOHN: Look, Alice. . . . There in the room . . . it's empty!

ALICE: But, John . . . they were here just a few hours ago. . . .

JOHN: The bed hasn't even been slept in!

ALICE: But there's the bell . . . there on the table . . . a little silver bell . . .

JOHN: But they're not here . . . and there's no sign of their ever having been here.

ALICE: Maybe it was a dream . . . maybe we just dreamed . . .

JOHN: No. It wasn't a dream . . . for there is the silver bell. And we both saw them . . . and so did the children . . .

ALICE: Maybe they left . . . maybe they ran away . . .

JOHN: If they had done that they would have wakened the children sleeping downstairs . . . and where could they have gone . . . not out into this storm!

ALICE: What does it mean, John? We both saw this man . . . she called him Joseph . . .

JOHN: And he called her . . . Mary . . .

ALICE: But John! It couldn't be . . .

JOHN: No, Alice . . . it was all a dream . . . all . . . except for the silver bell . . .

MUSIC: *Up and out.*

MR. MASON: And the story goes that though they looked and looked no trace was ever found of the man and woman . . . but the silver bell has remained in the family.

DAVID: Golly! Gee! It's like a fairy story!

MRS. MASON: But there's more still, David.

GRANDMOTHER: The best part in fact.

MR. MASON: Yes, Mother . . . the best part.

ALICE: What is it?

MR. MASON: One hundred years later in 1850 the bell was in the possession of Charles Mason . . . after it had been handed down to the eldest son for four generations. The story was being told as it ofttimes is in the Mason family on Christmas Eve . . . and the bell was under the Christmas tree . . . when suddenly midnight came and the bell . . . without any help from anyone . . . rang three times . . .

DAVID: I don't believe it!

MRS. MASON: Well, that's the way the story goes.

ALICE: But how could the little bell ring all by itself?

GRANDMOTHER: When I was a little girl your age, I remember hearing my Aunt Jessica, who was present at the Christmas Eve incident in 1850, tell about it . . . and she swore on the Bible that that little silver bell rang all by itself . . . three times . . .

MR. MASON: And so Charles Mason theorized that the little bell would ring every one hundred years.

MRS. MASON: And tonight is one hundred years later . . . 1950 . . . Christmas Eve.

ALICE: And it's going to ring tonight! Golly! I don't believe it either!

GRANDMOTHER: We're going to see.

DAVID: It's almost midnight now. . . . My watch says . . . 11:57.

MR. MASON: I'll hang the little bell there on the branch of the tree . . . Now we'll all stand away from it . . .

DAVID: I . . . I . . . this is just like a story . . .

MRS. MASON: We must all be quiet. . . . The little bell rang in 1750 . . . in 1850 . . . Maybe it will ring tonight . . .

MR. MASON: It's midnight. . . . Be still everyone. . . .

SOUND: *Silence . . . bell rings . . . silence . . . bell rings . . . silence . . . bell rings . . . silence.*

GRANDMOTHER: It did ring! I saw and heard it myself!

DAVID: Goll—ee!

MRS. MASON: Then the story is true. Someone did come to John Mason's home way back in 1750.

ALICE: And left a bell that rang a hundred years later . . . and will ring every hundred years on Christmas Eve . . .

MR. MASON: It's almost like a vision . . . the vision of the silver bell . . .

MRS. MASON: I wonder who those strange people were who left the bell with the Masons?

MR. MASON: I guess we'll never know.

MUSIC: *Up and under.*

NARRATOR: And that is the story of the silver bell. Every hundred years in the silence of the midnight . . . on Christmas Eve . . . when the embers are burning low and soft . . . and the scent of evergreen fills the Masons' home . . . when the spirit of the Yuletide abides . . . the Vision of the Silver Bell appears . . . and there are heard three vibrant beckonings . . . still calling good people to the aid of their fellow man . . .

MUSIC: *Up and out.*

THE END

The Elves and the Shoemaker

by Eleanora Bowling Kane

MUSIC: *"Fairy Tale-ish"—behind* NARRATOR
NARRATOR:
> Once upon a time . . .
> A long while ago . . .
> In a quaint little town
> Where *we* could *never* go
> On a twisting, curving path
> That called itself a *"street"*
> Stood a gabled little cottage
> A shoemaker's retreat.
> But the grimy little window
> Held *not a pair* of shoes—
> You could not have told its business
> Had not a *sign*
> Proclaimed the news.
> Sighing in the cold wind,
> Creaking from the dews
> A swaying, groaning, battered sign—
> One faded word—said—*SHOES*.

LITTLE GIRL:
> But the *window* is *so* empty
> And I *did* want *sandals red*—

BOY:
> And I'd set *my heart* on slippers
> To wear upstairs to bed.

YOUNG GIRL:
 I want to dance at Christmas
 When the mayor gives a ball—
MATURE WOMAN:
 And *I* need some sturdy walkers
 For shopping on the mall.
LITTLE GIRL (*Disconsolately*):
 But the window is *so* empty—
ALL: *There's nothing there at all!*
MUSIC: *Up and segue into something plaintive.*
SHOEMAKER (*Slowly, sadly*):
 They turn from my window, good wife, with tears standing
  in their eyes—
 And *my* disappointment is as deep. I am sad.
 Christmas is nearly here—a time for fun—surprise—
 And I, so poor, cannot do *my* part to make them glad.
WIFE (*Stoutly*): You are the best shoemaker in the land.
SHOEMAKER: But I cannot—out of *air*—fashion a *shoe.*
WIFE: There's enough leather, husband, for *one* pair.
SHOEMAKER:
 Such harsh, coarse stuff
 'Tis hardly worth a try.
 If only I could buy the *best* hides—
 Shoes made from *this* coarse stuff—*no one* would buy.
WIFE:
 Ah, well—do not despair
 Put your best work on this one last pair.
MUSIC: *Up and into:*
SOUND: SHOEMAKER'S *hammer tapping.*
NARRATOR:
 And he settles down to working
 With a heart that will not sing
 But he taps a merry rondeau

You can hear his hammer ring.
Till the ugly things are finished.
He has worked hard with a will,
Yet they are coarse and clumsy
Despite his cunning skill.

SOUND: *Out.*

SHOEMAKER:
When the material's so poor to begin with—
What chance has a mere man to create beauty?
(No one will buy these.)
Now, I am weary; I must sleep.
(*Yawning*) 'Tis hard work making silk purses from sows'
ears.

MUSIC: *Segue into lullaby.*

SOUND: *Clock strikes twelve.*

NARRATOR:
Now the clock is striking midnight—
And *you* know as well as I—
That the *strangest things* can happen
When the witching hour is nigh
(*Mysteriously*) And the strangest things *are* happening—
But I shan't tell *you* the news
You will have to wait till morning
When the *cobbler* sees the shoes.

MUSIC: *Up and into—Music for morning—"Peer Gynt."*

SHOEMAKER:
Wife! Wife! Come here at once.
Things have been happening while I slept.

WIFE (*Coming up*): Did you finish the shoes last night, dear?

SHOEMAKER:
Aye, finish them I did—
Such coarse and ugly things—
Fashioned from those stiff and clumsy hides—

I placed them on the bench beside the fire—
And went to bed.
Then, when I came in here
This morning, all was changed.
Look!

WIFE (*Amazed*): The most *enchanting* pair of *red sandals!*

SHOEMAKER:
Of the softest, most flexible leather.
They will fit like gloves
On a child's dainty foot.

WIFE: But who could have done such a thing?
Where are the shoes *you* made?

SHOEMAKER:
I cannot tell
My poor head's still a-whirl.

SOUND: *Bell jingles as shop door opens.*

SHOEMAKER: Now who is this? Oh, little Greta. Come in, my child.

LITTLE GIRL:
I'm sorry, good shoemaker,
If I trouble you
But I thought I'd have one last try—
Christmas is coming, you know—
And I would *love* to buy—
(*Catches sight of shoes and squeals happily*)
Oh, you *did* make them
The *darling red sandals*
Oh, the darlings, the darlings—

WIFE:
Why, they just fit you.
It's a miracle indeed.

LITTLE GIRL (*Happily*):
And mother gave me five gold pieces to spend for Christmas—

Here, good cobbler.

(*Fading*) I must hurry to show mother my *darling red shoes.*

SOUND: *Bell jingles as door shuts.*

MUSIC: *Up and into neutral background.*

NARRATOR:

Now he's jingling, jingling, jingling the money in the till
And he's tingling, tingling, tingling with a happy, surging
thrill.

There is money for *their dinner—*

There is money for—*more shoes!*

MUSIC: *Alone for a moment then—fade in sounds of busy
market place—horses and wagons—vendors crying.*

VENDORS:

Buy my ribbons! Ribbons for milady's hair—
Silken hose for milord—velvet daublets and breeches—only
the best—buy here— Steel blades from Damascus—keen and
sharp— Buy a steel sword from Damascus. (*Out of this
confusion emerges the voice of the* TANNER *clear and distinct.*)

TANNER:

Leather! Fine leather
Soft as velvet—
Buy the finest here,
Leather! Fine leather.

SHOEMAKER:

At last! The market place confuses me
There is so much to hear and see.
I must get to that fellow.
(*Calls*) Tanner! Oh, Master Tanner!

TANNER (*Fading in*): Why 'tis the poor cobbler. But what
are *you* doing *here?* The *old hides* are as usual in the *tan-
nery,* sir. You'll have to go back there.

SHOEMAKER (*Proudly*): Today I want the best.

TANNER: Leather from Cordova!

SHOEMAKER: Soft as velvet.

TANNER: The finest in the world.

SHOEMAKER: Enough for *one pair of shoes.*

TANNER:
And when the poor cobbler buys the finest leather—
Sir—that's news.

MUSIC: *Alone—then down as background.*

SHOEMAKER (*Proudly*):
And when the poor cobbler buys the finest leather—
Wife, that's news.

WIFE (*Laughing*): And such *good* news— But husband, to-night—don't make shoes.

SHOEMAKER (*Puzzled*): Don't—make—shoes?

WIFE:
No— I'd suggest you cut them out—most carefully
And leave the leather—
We shall sleep—
Then we shall see *what* we shall see!

MUSIC: *Into mysterious music and clock striking twelve.*

NARRATOR:
And once again queer things transpire
Around the cobbler's dying fire—
Oh— *I* can see. I know it all.
But *you* must wait
Till the cobbler's call.

SHOEMAKER: Wife! Wife! Just look at that!

WIFE: A handsome pair of slippers—

SHOEMAKER: Velvet and ermine with golden ties.

WIFE: It's enough to make saucers of a boy's eyes.

SOUND: *Bell jangles and door opens.*

LITTLE BOY (*Coming in eagerly*):
Oh, Master Cobbler, pray excuse—
I'm not looking for just *everyday* shoes.
I want slippers with fur and gold
To keep me warm against the cold.

WIFE: Maybe *these* are what you desire.

BOY (*Excitedly*):
But they are— The very thing—
Ah, Master Cobbler,
Now you shall hear the gold pieces ring. (*Sound of clinking
of gold pieces.*)
Twenty of them for *ermine* and *gold*.

SHOEMAKER (*Dazedly*): It's a *magic* pair of shoes I've sold.

MUSIC: *Up and then down.*

NARRATOR:
And his heart is singing madly
For the leather that he buys
Is enough to fashion two pairs
And he cuts them out and cries—
"Once again, good wife, we'll leave them—
And mayhaps, a new surprise."

MUSIC: *Up and down behind* NARRATOR.

NARRATOR (*Quietly*):
And when the soft light stole across the skies,
It's rosy fingers touched the sleeping eyes
And bade them wake and see—
For in the night once more *somebody's* hands
Had toiled so busily.

WIFE: Husband, look!
The loveliest yet are these.

SHOEMAKER: A sturdy, well-made pair—with golden buckles at
the toes.

WIFE:
And, oh my dear, just look at these— I pinch myself— They
can't be real.

SHOEMAKER:
The softest golden kid.
With brilliants blazing from the toe to heel.

WIFE: In these a maid could dance the night away.

SHOEMAKER:

But they are worth a fortune.

Who in this town, such price could pay?

SOUND: *Bell jangles as door opens.*

YOUNG GIRL (*Fading in*):

Oh, I know—'tis probably a fruitless quest—

Yet in the evening I shall be the Mayor's guest.

His son is tall. His dancing is divine,

And, oh my friend—*the finest dancing slippers in the world*—

Just *must* be mine!

MATURE WOMAN (*Laughs good-naturedly*):

Ah, well—such is youth.

Now all that I require

Is good workmanship

And fine lasting qualities.

That's my desire.

SHOEMAKER: And here's just what you wish, good dame.

WOMAN (*Delighted*):

Indeed they are.

Cobbler, o'er all the town

I'll sing your fame.

YOUNG GIRL:

And oh, just see—

He must have made

These just for me.

(*She becomes poetic and ecstatic*)

Tonight my shoes shall be ablaze

And twinkle from my skirt hem

As I dance

Like fallen stars.

WOMAN: Good cobbler, these are works of art.

YOUNG GIRL: I shall dance my way to a young man's heart.

You must accept our gratitude.
Here—fifty pieces of gold—
And some more shoes
When you have time.
(*Fading*)
Good-day, sir, and a happy Christmas season.
SOUND: *Bell jangles as door shuts.*
SHOEMAKER: Fifty pieces of gold!
WIFE: You can buy more leather!
SHOEMAKER: And food—and protection from the cold.
WIFE: Husband! Does it not strike you the time has come—
SHOEMAKER: For us to know who toils so busily.
WIFE:
Tonight we'll set the leather out again—
But we shall *watch* and *wait*—and see.
MUSIC: *Up and into.*
SOUND: *Clock striking twelve.*
NARRATOR:
And again there are strange doings
In the cobbler's humble store
Queer shadows flitting here and there
A creaking of the floor.
The tinkle of clear laughter,
An elfin hammer blow.
The ruddy firelight bathes the scene
In supernatural glow (*Drop voice*)
So the cobbler can see clearly
Two—frisky—little *elves.*
MUSIC: *Up and down.*
1ST ELF (*Light, silvery voice*): *You* will *stitch.*
2ND ELF: And *I* will *tap.*
1ST ELF: See my *needle fly.*
2ND ELF: Hear *my hammer rap.*

1st ELF: Silver my thread.
2nd ELF: My nails are gold.
1st ELF: The shoemaker is hungry
2nd ELF: And poor and cold.
ELVES (*Together*):
  Stitch, tap, sew, rap—
  Cut with a shining blade.
  Stitch, tap, sew, rap—
  The finest shoes that are made.
WIFE (*Soft*):
  Husband—do look at the poor little creatures
  They have no clothes.
SHOEMAKER: And working themselves to death providing
  for us.
WIFE: Husband, I have an idea.
  Tomorrow is Christmas Eve
  Let us return their kindness.
SHOEMAKER (*Thoughtfully*): We could make them warm
  clothing—two little sets.
WIFE: A gift for Christmas. They couldn't object.
MUSIC: *Up and into Christmas music.*
NARRATOR:
  They sewed all day till their poor hands were sore,
  And when the black shadows crowded up to the door,
  They laid the clothes on the cobbler shop floor
  And crept away till time to explore.
MUSIC: *Alone for a moment—then down as background.*
NARRATOR:
  And then came the elves—
  With shouts of glee
  They donned the tiny suits
  And capered merrily
  (ELVES *laugh gaily in background.*)

About the room
Their laughter rang like silver bells—
And suddenly—the *Christmas* bells
(*Christmas bells in background.*)
Gave tongue, and, oh, the beauty of their song—
The love of neighbor—
The righting of the wrong.
And then the tiny creatures
Perching on the sill
Before *they* left
Spoke also of *good will*—

1ST ELF: You, oh cobbler, have lived a good life.
2ND ELF: Good luck we leave to you and your wife.
1ST ELF: A cozy home and a kettle to boil
2ND ELF: And money to buy the hides for your toil.
BOTH:
We leave you now.
This is good bye
But our blessing goes with you
For ever and aye.

MUSIC: *Up and background.*
NARRATOR:
And then—suddenly—they had disappeared—
The cobbler and his wife opened the window
Feeling heartened and cheered
While the music of the Christmas bell
Swelled and soared and wove its own spell,
Repeating in measured cadence again and again
"Peace! Peace! Good will to men."
(*Music and bells—up and out.*)

THE END

A Christmas Carol

by *Charles Dickens*

Adapted for stage by WALTER HACKETT

Characters

EBENEZER SCROOGE	MRS. CRATCHIT
BOB CRATCHIT	PETER
FRED	DICK
SOLICITOR	TOM
MARLEY'S GHOST	MARTHA
THREE SPIRITS	TINY TIM
EBENEZER, *the boy*	PEG
FAN	TWO BUSINESSMEN
EBENEZER, *the young man*	YOUNG BOY
FESSIWIG	CRIER
BELLE	CHORUS OF BOYS

SCENE 1

TIME: *Late afternoon before Christmas, 1844.*

SETTING: *The counting house of Ebenezer Scrooge in London.*

AT RISE: SCROOGE *is seated at his desk upstage left, poring over some papers. Upstage right, perched on his stool and hunched over his high desk is* BOB CRATCHIT, *making entries in a ledger. The late afternoon sun filters through one window. A church bell can be heard striking five times in the distance.*

CRIER (*After the last stroke, offstage*): Five o' the clock in the City of London, on this day before Christmas, and all is well!

255

(*Neither* CRATCHIT *nor* SCROOGE *look up. There is a pause.* CRATCHIT *shivers and pulls his scarf tighter around his neck. He looks almost furtively at* SCROOGE, *then he goes up to wood box and picks up a very small piece of wood.*)

SCROOGE (*Without looking up*) : Cratchit!

CRATCHIT: But, sir, it's very cold.

SCROOGE: Put that wood back.

CRATCHIT: Very good, sir. (*He drops the wood back into the box. He goes to his stool and climbs it.*)

SCROOGE: Directly after Christmas, I shall put a lock on the wood box. Understand?

CRATCHIT: Yes, Mr. Scrooge. It's only that it's a bitter day and I have a bit of a cold, sir.

SCROOGE: That is no excuse for you to rob my wood box. Besides, we all work better in air that is a bit brisk.

CRATCHIT: Yes, sir. (*They continue their work. After a pause, from outside can be heard a chorus of boys' voices singing* "God Rest Ye Merry Gentlemen." *After a few seconds* SCROOGE *rises and goes up to window and throws it open.*)

SCROOGE: Stop that noise! Do you hear? Stop it at once!

1ST BOY: Merry Christmas, sir.

SCROOGE: Be off with the lot of you.

2ND BOY: No need to wish 'im a Merry Christmas. That's old Scrooge, it is. (*With an exclamation of disgust,* SCROOGE *slams down the window and crosses to his desk. There is another pause, the door bursts open, and* FRED, SCROOGE'S *nephew, enters.*)

FRED: A Merry Christmas, uncle. God save you!

SCROOGE: Bah! Humbug!

FRED (*As he crosses to desk*) : Christmas a humbug, uncle! You don't mean that, I'm sure.

SCROOGE: I do. Merry Christmas! What right have you to be merry? You're poor enough.

FRED: What right have you to be dismal? You're rich enough.

SCROOGE: Bah! Humbug!

FRED: Don't be cross.

SCROOGE: What else can I be when I live in such a world of fools. Merry Christmas! What's Christmas time to you but a time for paying bills without money; a time for finding yourself a year older, and not an hour richer; a time for balancing your books and finding 'em dead against you. If I had my way, every idiot who goes about with "Merry Christmas" on his lips would be boiled with his own pudding, and buried with a stake of holly through his heart.

FRED: Now, see here, uncle.

SCROOGE: Nephew, keep Christmas in your own way, and let me keep it in mine.

FRED: Keep it! But you don't keep it.

SCROOGE: Let me leave it alone, then.

FRED: I've always thought of Christmas as a good time; a fine, charitable, pleasant time, when men and women open their shut-up hearts freely. And, therefore, though Christmas has never put a scrap of silver in my pocket, I believe it has done me good. So I say, God bless it!

CRATCHIT (*Applauds*): Well spoken, Mr. Fred.

SCROOGE (*Turns toward* CRATCHIT): Let me hear another sound from you and you'll keep Christmas by losing your situation. (*To* FRED) You're quite a powerful speaker, sir. I wonder you don't go into Parliament.

FRED: Don't be angry. I came here to ask you to come and dine with Peg and me tomorrow.

SCROOGE: I'm not interested.

FRED: But I want nothing from you, only your company.

SCROOGE: No!

FRED: But why? You've never met my wife.

SCROOGE: Why did you get married?

FRED: Because I fell in love.

SCROOGE (*Growls*): Because you fell in love. (*He picks up some papers.*) Good afternoon. (*He reads the paper in front of him.*)

FRED: Why can't we be friends?

SCROOGE: Good afternoon!

FRED: I'm sorry, but I'm not going to allow you to chase away the Christmas spirit I feel in my heart. A Merry Christmas, uncle. (SCROOGE *grunts.*) And a Happy New Year. (*As he turns and exits*) Merry Christmas, Bob.

CRATCHIT (*Fearfully*): The same to you, Mr. Fred. (FRED *exits.* CRATCHIT *works away on his ledger and* SCROOGE *returns to his reading. After a pause, there is a knock on the door. It is repeated.*)

SCROOGE (*Snaps*): Well, come in, come in. The latch isn't on. (*The door opens and the* SOLICITOR *enters.*)

SOLICITOR (*Advances a few steps and looks first at* CRATCHIT *and then* SCROOGE): Scrooge and Marley's, I believe? (*As he says this, he refers to a paper he is carrying.*) Have I the pleasure of addressing Mr. Scrooge, or Mr. Marley?

SCROOGE: Mr. Marley has been dead these seven years. He died seven years ago, this very night.

SOLICITOR (*As he crosses to front of* SCROOGE's *desk*): Then I have no doubt his liberality is well represented by his surviving partner. (*He draws forth an identification paper and shows it to* SCROOGE, *who doesn't bother to look.*) At this festive season of the year, Mr. Scrooge, we try to make some slight provision for the poor and destitute, who suffer greatly at the present time. Many thousands are in want of common comforts, sir.

SCROOGE: Are there no prisons? (CRATCHIT *listens, while working.*)

SOLICITOR: Plenty of prisons.

SCROOGE: And the workhouses, are they still in operation?

SOLICITOR: They are, unfortunately. I wish I could say they were not.

SCROOGE: And the Poor Law, it is still in full vigor?

SOLICITOR: It is, sir. (*He takes out a pen.*)

SCROOGE: I was afraid, from what you said, that something had occurred to stop them in their useful course. I am glad to hear it.

SOLICITOR: We chose this time to help these unfortunates, because it is a time when want is strongest. What shall I put you down for?

SCROOGE: Nothing!

SOLICITOR: You wish to be anonymous?

SCROOGE: I wish to be left alone. I don't make merry myself at Christmas, and I can't afford to make idle people merry. I help to support the establishments I have mentioned: and those who are badly off must go there.

SOLICITOR: Most of them would rather die than do that.

SCROOGE: Then let them do exactly that, and help decrease the surplus population.

SOLICITOR: Obviously you are not interested in the misfortunes of others. (*He puts his pen in his pocket.*)

SCROOGE: It's enough for a man to understand his own business, and not to interfere with other people's. Mine occupies me constantly. Good day, sir.

SOLICITOR (*Politely*): Merry Christmas, Mr. Scrooge. (SCROOGE *pays no heed, and returns to his papers. The* SOLICITOR *crosses to door. In passing, he turns to* CRATCHIT.) Merry Christmas. (CRATCHIT *nods and with his lips forms the words: "Merry Christmas." The* SOLICITOR *exits.* CRATCHIT *takes out his watch—a large one—and looks at it. He winds it and puts it away, at the same time he looks at* SCROOGE.)

SCROOGE: It is but twelve minutes past five o'clock, Cratchit. Your work day ends at six.

CRATCHIT: I know, sir, but I have to stop at the greengrocer's and the poulterer's before I get home, and they close at six sharp.

SCROOGE: Oh, very well. (CRATCHIT *hurriedly puts away his ledger and inkstand and papers. Then he climbs off the stool and prepares to leave.*) You'll want all day tomorrow, I suppose?

CRATCHIT: If quite convenient, sir.

SCROOGE: It's not convenient, and it's not fair. If I was to stop half-a-crown for it, you'd think yourself ill-used. And yet you don't think me ill-used when I pay a day's wages for no work.

CRATCHIT (*As he puts on his hat*): It's only once a year, sir.

SCROOGE: A poor excuse for picking a man's pocket every twenty-fifth of December. But I suppose you must have the whole day. Be here all the earlier the next morning.

CRATCHIT: Indeed, I will, Mr. Scrooge. (*As he starts to exit.*) And Merry Christmas, sir. (*He exits.*)

SCROOGE: Humbug.

CURTAIN

*　*　*

SCENE 2

TIME: *Ten o'clock the same night.*

SETTING: *A corner of* SCROOGE's *bedroom. It takes in the upper left section of the stage. This area is dimly lit, while the rest of the stage is in darkness. The furnishings are a small bed and a chair.*

AT RISE: SCROOGE *is asleep on the bed. There is a pause, and then from the darkened right can be heard the sound of thumping footsteps and dragging chains.* SCROOGE *stirs uneasily. The sound stops, then is resumed. Into the lighted area steps* MARLEY'S GHOST. *A long chain is clasped around his middle; the chain is so long, it drags on the floor.* MARLEY *stops at the foot of the bed, and as he does,* SCROOGE *suddenly sits up.*

SCROOGE: What do you want with me?

MARLEY: Much.

SCROOGE: Who are you?

MARLEY: Ask me who I was.

SCROOGE: Who were you, then?

MARLEY: In life I was your partner, Jacob Marley.

SCROOGE (*Looks at him doubtfully*): Can you—can you sit down? (MARLEY *moves to chair and sits.*)

MARLEY: You don't believe in me.

SCROOGE (*Now he has lost his fear*): I don't!

MARLEY: Why do you doubt your senses?

SCROOGE: You're nothing but a stomach-ache—an undigested bit of beef, a blot of mustard, a crumb of cheese. There's more of gravy than of grave about you. Humbug!

MARLEY: You are wrong. I am the ghost of Jacob Marley.

SCROOGE: Then why do you come to me?

MARLEY: It is required of every man that the spirit within him should walk among his fellow men and travel far and wide; and if that spirit goes not forth in life, it is condemned to do so after death. (*He rattles his chains, and moans.*)

SCROOGE: You are fettered. Tell me why?

MARLEY: I wear the chain I forged in life. I made it link by link, yard by yard. Of my own free will I wore it. Is its pattern strange to you? You also wear one, Ebenezer. Only you still are forging yours.

SCROOGE: Can't you speak some words of comfort, Jacob?

MARLEY: I have none to give. I cannot rest, I cannot linger anywhere. Many weary journeys lie ahead of me.

SCROOGE: Seven years dead and traveling all the time?

MARLEY: The whole time. No rest, no peace. Incessant torture of remorse. I travel on the wings of the wind. Oh, such was I, an unheeding man.

SCROOGE: But you were always a good man of business, Jacob.

MARLEY (*Wrings his hands*): Business! Mankind was my business. The common welfare was my business; charity, mercy, forbearance and benevolence were all my business. The dealings of my trade were but a drop of water in the ocean of my business. At this time of year, I suffer most.

SCROOGE: You do speak strangely, Jacob.

MARLEY (*Rises*): Hear me. My time is nearly gone.

SCROOGE: I will, but don't be hard upon me.

MARLEY (*Points a finger at* SCROOGE): I am here to warn you that you have a chance of escaping my fate.

SCROOGE: You were always a good friend to me.

MARLEY: You will be haunted by Three Spirits.

SCROOGE: I—I think I'd rather not.

MARLEY: You will be haunted by Three Spirits. Without their visits you cannot hope to escape my fate. Expect the first when the bell tolls one.

SCROOGE: Couldn't I take them all at once, and have it over with?

MARLEY: Expect the second when the bell tolls twice and the third when it strikes three times. And heed them when they appear. (*He backs away from the lighted to the unlit portion of the stage. His voice is heard from the darkness.*) You will not see me any more, but remember what has passed between us. Try and escape my miserable fate. (SCROOGE, *his mouth open, watches as* MARLEY *disappears. Then the lights black out. There is a pause, and the lights come up again in the area surrounding* SCROOGE'S *bed. He sleeps restlessly. Off in the distance, one stroke of a steeple bell is heard. Into the lighted area steps the* FIRST SPIRIT. *It is dressed in white and has a young face, and in its hand it holds a sprig of holly. Suddenly* SCROOGE, *as though bidden, sits up.*)

SCROOGE: Are you the spirit whose coming was foretold to me?

SPIRIT 1 (*Gently*) : I am.

SCROOGE: Who are you?

SPIRIT 1: I am the Ghost of Christmas Past.

SCROOGE: Long past?

SPIRIT 1: No. Your past.

SCROOGE: What business brings you here?

SPIRIT 1: Your welfare. (*He holds out his hand.*) Rise! And walk with me.

SCROOGE (*Rises and slips on his dressing gown. He crosses over to* SPIRIT.) : Where are we going?

SPIRIT 1: Out into the night . . . on wings of air.

SCROOGE: I am a mortal. I'm liable to fall.

SPIRIT 1 (*Places his hand on* SCROOGE's *heart*): Bear but a touch of my hand there, and you shall be upheld in more than this. (*The lights black out. A pause and then the lights come up. In the center at a small desk sits a young boy, bent over a book. He faces downstage.* SCROOGE *and the* FIRST SPIRIT *stand downstage right.*)

SPIRIT 1: Do you recognize this deserted study hall?

SCROOGE: It looks familiar. Who is that lad?

SPIRIT 1: It is the Christmas holiday, and this is the second year he has been left behind. (*The boy wipes away a few tears.*) No place to go for Christmas.

SCROOGE: Poor chap. I wish—but it's too late.

SPIRIT 1: You wish what?

SCROOGE: There were some boys singing carols outside my counting house yesterday. I drove them away. (*As the boy raises his head.*) He's looking up. Why . . . why, it's myself as a boy. Yes, and this is the school I attended. I was so lonely.

SPIRIT 1: Do you remember this, too? (FAN *enters from right. She rushes to young* EBENEZER SCROOGE.)

FAN: Dear, dear brother. (*He rises and hugs her.*) I have

come to take you home, Ebenezer. To bring you home, home.

EBENEZER (*Wistfully*) : Home, dear Fan!

FAN: Yes, home for good. Father is ever so much kinder than he used to be, and now home is a wonderful place. Yesterday I asked him if you couldn't come home to us, and this morning he sent me here in a coach. It's outside in the drive. (*He puts his arms around her.*) And we're to leave right away, and you're never coming back.

EBENEZER: Will we always be together?

FAN (*As they exit to right*) : Always together, Ebenezer, from now on. (*Blackout center area*)

SPIRIT 1: Your sister was a delicate creature, but always kind and thoughtful. A girl with a big heart.

SCROOGE: So she had.

SPIRIT 1: She died a young woman, leaving behind her one child.

SCROOGE: Yes. My nephew Fred.

SPIRIT 1: He visited you yesterday.

SCROOGE (*Uneasily*) : So he did. May we leave here?

SPIRIT 1: Yes, for there is another shadow. (SCROOGE *and the* SPIRIT *stand there. The area in the center lights up. Old* FESSIWIG *is seated at the desk. He is looking through some papers.*)

SCROOGE: Why, bless my soul!

SPIRIT 1: Do you know him?

SCROOGE: Know him! Of course. Bless his heart! It's old Fessiwig alive again. Why, I was one of his apprentices. He taught me my business. A fine man, old Fessiwig! (FESSIWIG *lays down the papers. He takes out his watch and looks at it.*)

FESSIWIG (*Looks to his right*) : One of you boys, come here. (EBENEZER SCROOGE, *now a young man, enters.*)

EBENEZER: Yes, Mr. Fessiwig.

FESSIWIG: Do you know the day, Ebenezer Scrooge?

EBENEZER: Indeed, yes, sir. It's the afternoon before Christmas.

FESSIWIG: To be sure, to be sure! And no more work for the day, not a tap of it. Understand! Now, up with the shutters, Ebenezer.

EBENEZER: Yes, sir.

FESSIWIG: Tonight we'll dance and sing and play. There'll be no talk of business, or of profits or losses. Mrs. Fessiwig and my daughters have the finest of foods ready.

EBENEZER: I've been smelling those wonderful odors all day.

FESSIWIG (*Rises*): Off we go, then. (*As they exit.*) We'll keep Christmas as it should be kept. (*They exit. The lights in center go out.*)

SPIRIT 1: A silly man.

SCROOGE: Mr. Fessiwig wasn't a silly man. He was kind and generous. If only I could speak to him.

SPIRIT 1: My time grows short. There is still another shadow.

SCROOGE: I've seen enough.

SPIRIT 1: Are you sure, Ebenezer? I think not. (*The lights black out and come up again downstage right where* SCROOGE *and the* SPIRIT *are standing, and center.* EBENEZER SCROOGE, *now a young man, faces* BELLE, *a pretty girl of 18.* EBENEZER'S *face now wears the signs of avarice.*)

SCROOGE: Why—why, it's Belle.

SPIRIT 1: The beautiful girl you were to marry. And there you are, in your prime. Now your face reflects the signs of greed. There is a restless motion to your eyes. Belle noticed it.

BELLE (*To* EBENEZER): It matters very little to you. Another idol has displaced me. I hope it comforts you in time to come.

EBENEZER: What idol do you refer to, Belle?

BELLE: A golden one.

EBENEZER: There is nothing in this world as hard as poverty.

BELLE: You fear the world too much. You hold money more important than me or anything else.

EBENEZER: I have grown wiser, but it hasn't changed my attitude toward you.

BELLE: But it has. You are changed. I am going to grant your wish, and let you free to go your way.

EBENEZER: Have I ever asked to be freed?

BELLE: Not in so many words, Ebenezer, but it is what you wish. I hope you will be happy in the life you have chosen. (*She starts to exit right.*) Goodbye, Ebenezer.

EBENEZER (*He takes a step toward her.*): Belle! (*She exits. He shrugs and then exits left. The light in the center blacks out.*)

SPIRIT 1: Today, Belle is a happy woman, surrounded by her children and grandchildren.

SCROOGE: Spirit, show me no more. Show me no more. I cannot bear it.

SPIRIT 1: My time has ended, Ebenezer. Listen for the stroke of two. (*The* SPIRIT *steps from the lighted area and exits right. The lights black out. When they come up again, the area at upper left, surrounding* SCROOGE's *bed is lit.* SCROOGE *tosses about on the bed.*)

SCROOGE (*Moans*): Show me no more. I cannot bear it. Show me no more, I beg you. (*There is a pause, and then, coming from the distance can be heard the steeple bell as it strikes twice. The* SECOND SPIRIT *steps into the lighted area. He is a big, robust man and is dressed in a green cloak.*)

SPIRIT 2 (*He has a booming voice.*): Ebenezer Scrooge! Ebenezer Scrooge. (SCROOGE *sits bolt upright.*) I am the Ghost of Christmas Present. Look upon me.

SCROOGE: You're practically a giant, yet you have such a young face. I have never seen the like of you before.

SPIRIT: I have many brothers—more than eighteen hundred, one for each Christmas.

SCROOGE: You are here to take me with you? (*The* SPIRIT

nods.) Conduct me where you will. (*He rises and crosses over to the* SPIRIT.)

SPIRIT 2: I trust you will profit by your journey. Touch my robe. (SCROOGE *does. The lights in this area black out. There is a pause, and then the area downstage right is lit, revealing* SCROOGE *and the* SPIRIT.)

SCROOGE: Where are we, Spirit?

SPIRIT 2: You shall see. (*The area from right to center is lit up to reveal a table and some chairs. Seated are* MRS. CRATCHIT *and three of her children:* PETER, DICK *and* TOM.)

SPIRIT 2: A very poor house, as you can see.

SCROOGE: Indeed, it is. Who, may I ask, lives here?

SPIRIT 2: An underpaid clerk named Bob Cratchit. The woman is Mrs. Cratchit, and those are three of her children. There are two others.

MRS. CRATCHIT: What has become of your precious father and Tiny Tim? And Martha wasn't half as late last Christmas Day by half an hour.

MARTHA (*Enters from right*): And just who is using my name in such a manner? (*She crosses to them. The boys rise, ad lib happily as they do.*)

MRS. CRATCHIT (*Rises*): Dear Martha. (*She hugs her.*)

MARTHA (*As she hugs each of the children*): My goodness, such affection. Merry Christmas to all of you.

MRS. CRATCHIT (*As* MARTHA *removes her shawl and bonnet, which she hands to one of the children, who exits*): You dear child, how late you are.

MARTHA: We'd a great deal of work to finish up last night, and we had to clear away this morning.

MRS. CRATCHIT: Well, never mind, so long as you are here. (MARTHA *sits next to her.*) Lord bless you.

PETER: Guess what! We're having the most wonderful goose for dinner.

DICK (*Who has just entered again*) : Of course it isn't a very big one.

TOM : And we have plum pudding.

PETER : With sauce.

MARTHA : How wonderful! (*A sound can be heard from right.*)

TOM : Here come Father and Tiny Tim.

DICK : Hide, Martha, hide. (MARTHA *goes to corner and stands in the shadow.* BOB CRATCHIT, *carrying* TINY TIM *and his crutch, enter from right.*)

CRATCHIT (*As he puts* TINY TIM *down*) : Why, where's our Martha?

MRS. CRATCHIT : Not coming.

CRATCHIT : Not coming! Not coming on Christmas Day! (MARTHA *runs down and puts her arms around him.*) Martha! (*He kisses her.*)

MARTHA : I'm so glad to be home. (*She goes to* TINY TIM *and kisses him.*) Tiny Tim, how are you?

TIM : I've been to church. (CRATCHIT *hands his muffler and hat to one of the boys.*)

MRS. CRATCHIT : There's some punch ready. Go get it. Boys, help your sister. (*All the boys and* MARTHA *exit right.* CRATCHIT *stands rubbing his hands.*) And how did Tiny Tim behave?

CRATCHIT : As good as gold and better. He told me, coming home, that he hoped the people in church saw he was a cripple, because it might be pleasant to them to remember on Christmas Day who made the lame beggars walk, and the blind men see. (*Both* CRATCHITS *exchange knowing looks.* CRATCHIT *leans forward and pats his wife on the hand.*)

SCROOGE : That little chap with the crutch. . . .

SPIRIT 2 : Tiny Tim?

SCROOGE : Has he been crippled long? (*The* SPIRIT *nods.*) Can't the doctors help him?

SPIRIT 2: Bob Cratchit can't afford a doctor, not on fifteen shillings a week salary. He has many mouths to feed. (MARTHA, TINY TIM, PETER, TOM *and* DICK *enter. They are carrying an assortment of old cups and glasses, and* MARTHA *holds a pitcher, which she sets on the table.*)

CRATCHIT: Ah, your mother's famous Christmas punch, the finest in all England.

MRS. CRATCHIT: You pour it, Bob.

CRATCHIT: Have your cups and glasses ready. (*He picks up the pitcher and, one by one, fills the cups and glasses; and as he does, the following sequence takes place.*) Your dear mother, as usual, has outdone herself. What better way to start off the day than with a fine bit of punch.

TIM: I'm hungry.

MRS. CRATCHIT: Directly we finish this, we'll have dinner.

CRATCHIT: Now, are we all ready? I propose a toast.

MARTHA (*Echoes*): A toast!

CRATCHIT: I propose two toasts. First the founder of this feast-to-be. I give you Mr. Scrooge.

MRS. CRATCHIT: Mr. Scrooge, indeed. I wish I had him here. I'd give him a piece of my mind to feast upon, and I hope he'd have a good appetite for it.

CRATCHIT: My dear! The children . . . Christmas Day.

MRS. CRATCHIT: I'll drink his health for your sake and the day's, and not for his. Long life to him! A Merry Christmas and a Happy New Year! He'll be very merry and very happy, I have no doubt. (*The* CRATCHITS *drink in silence, and obviously with no enthusiasm.*)

CRATCHIT: And now a toast to us: A very Merry Christmas to all of us! God bless us! (*The others echo: "God bless us."*)

TIM: God bless us, every one. (*The area where the* CRATCHITS *are blacks out; downstage left stays lit.*)

SCROOGE: Tell me, Spirit, will Tiny Tim live?

SPIRIT 2: I see a vacant seat in the chimney corner, and a crutch without an owner, carefully preserved. If these shadows remain unaltered by the Future, the child will die.

SCROOGE: Oh, no, Spirit. Say Tiny Tim will live, that he will be spared.

SPIRIT 2: Why concern yourself about him? Isn't it better that he die and decrease the surplus population?

SCROOGE: But he and these others must be helped.

SPIRIT 2: Are there no prisons, and the workhouses, are they still in operation?

SCROOGE: Do not taunt me.

SPIRIT: Come, we must go.

SCROOGE: Answer me.

SPIRIT: We have still another stop. (*The lights come up in the center, revealing* FRED *and* PEG, *his young wife. They are dressed for walking.*)

FRED: Cold, my dear?

PEG: Just a bit, but I don't mind.

FRED: We'll be home in another few minutes. This walk will make us hungry.

PEG: Not too hungry, I hope.

FRED: Don't worry, Peg. I'm sure there'll be more than enough to eat. (*He puts his arm around her waist.*)

SCROOGE: Is that his wife?

SPIRIT 2: Yes, the niece you've never bothered to meet.

PEG: Christmas is such a wonderful day, and not a humbug, as your precious uncle claims.

FRED: He believed it, too, more's the pity.

PEG: It's hard to have pity for such a man.

FRED: I feel sorry for him. However, his offenses carry their own punishment, and I have nothing to say against him.

PEG: Funny, his not wanting to bother with us. All we ask is his company, nothing more.

FRED: He's the only one who suffers by his ill whims.

PEG: One thing: he's losing a fine dinner by it.

FRED: Let's hurry home, dear. (*They exit right. Their area is blacked out.*)

SCROOGE: She seems a nice enough sort, don't you think? I should like to meet her, I believe.

SPIRIT 2: You had your chance, Ebenezer Scrooge. Now, I must leave you. The time is drawing near.

SCROOGE (*Holds on to him*): Please, kind Spirit, don't leave me, not right now. I wish to talk . . . to ask your advice.

SPIRIT 2: Are you sure you need advice, Ebenezer? After all, are you not a rich man, a man of intelligence, a man who knows his own mind?

SCROOGE: No, no!

SPIRIT 2: Goodbye, Ebenezer. Wait for the stroke of three. (*He exits right. The lights go out. They come up again in the area covering* SCROOGE'S *bed, and reveal him asleep. The steeple bell tolls three times. On the last stroke, the* THIRD SPIRIT *steps into the light. He is tall and is shrouded in a long black cloak. He stops at the foot of the bed.* SCROOGE *moans, and then sits up.*)

SCROOGE: The third and last one. The Spirit of Christmas Yet to Come. (*The* SPIRIT *nods. He raises his hand in a beckoning gesture.* SCROOGE *rises.*) Where will you take me? What will I see? (*He crosses to the* SPIRIT.) Have I anything to fear? You are about to show me shadows of the things that have not happened, but will happen in the time before us. Is that so, Spirit? (*The* SPIRIT *inclines its head.*) Lead on, then, for the night is waning fast, and it is precious time to me. (*The* SPIRIT *raises his arms in such a manner that, clad as he is in a black cape, he looks like a huge bird. He envelops* SCROOGE, *hiding him from view. The lights black out. When they come up again, they light up the downstage right and right center areas.* SCROOGE *and the* SPIRIT *stand in the first area and two* BUSINESSMEN *in the second.*)

MAN 1: When did he die?

MAN 2: Last night, I believe.

MAN 1: I thought he'd never die.

MAN 2: I wonder what he has done with all his money?

MAN 1: I haven't heard. Left it to his company, perhaps. One thing is certain, he didn't leave it to charity.

MAN 2: Are you going to his funeral?

MAN 1: Not unless a free lunch is provided.

MAN 2: I'm not that hungry, thank you. (*The light covering their area blacks out.*)

SCROOGE: Spirit, this man those men were discussing, who is he? (*The* SPIRIT *does not answer.*) Whoever he is, or was, he left no sympathy behind him. He must have been much disliked. (*The lights come up again on the area that had been occupied by the* BUSINESSMEN. MRS. CRATCHIT *is seated on a chair sewing.* MARTHA *is seated at her mother's feet.*)

MARTHA: You shouldn't work in this bad light, Mother. Your eyes already are strained.

MRS. CRATCHIT (*She puts down her sewing.*): I'll stop for a while, for I don't want to show a pair of red eyes to your father when he comes home. It's time he was here.

MARTHA: Past it, rather. But these days he walks slower than he used to.

MRS. CRATCHIT: I've known him to walk with Tiny Tim upon his shoulder very fast, indeed. He was so light to carry and your father loved him so, it was no trouble.

MARTHA: Poor Father! He's aged so these past few months. (BOB CRATCHIT *enters from right.*)

MRS. CRATCHIT: You're late tonight, Robert.

CRATCHIT (*Quietly*): Yes, I'm late.

MARTHA: I'll fetch you some tea, Father. (*She exits right.*)

MRS. CRATCHIT: You went there today, Robert?

CRATCHIT: Yes, I wish you could have gone. It would have done you good to see how green a place it is.

MRS. CRATCHIT: I'll go with you one of these days.

CRATCHIT: I promised him I would walk there every Sunday. My poor Tiny Tim. At last he got rid of his crutch. (*MRS. CRATCHIT rises and embraces her husband. The light covering them blacks out.*)

SCROOGE: Why did Tiny Tim have to die? If only someone could have helped him. (*Suddenly he clutches the SPIRIT.*) Spirit, the dead man those men were talking about, who was he? Who was he? (*The SPIRIT points to upper left. The area surrounding SCROOGE's bed lights up. The bed is empty.*) You mean it was I? I was the man! Oh, no, Spirit, no! Hear me. This can't happen. It mustn't be allowed. I am not the man I was. I will not be the man I must have been but for this lesson. I will honor Christmas in my heart. I will try and keep it alive all the year. I will live in the Past, the Present and the Future. I will not shut out the lesson that all three Spirits have taught me. (*As SCROOGE speaks, the SPIRIT raises his black arms until they again resemble a pair of wings. He steps from the light and exits right.*) Oh, tell me there is hope, that I may sponge away my selfish past. (*The lights black out, including the area covering SCROOGE's bed. There is a pause and when the lights come up again, SCROOGE is in his bed, tossing about.*) Tell me there is still hope. I will be a different man. (*Suddenly he sits up. He looks around.*) Where am I? Why, I'm in my own bed. (*The sound of church bells is heard from the distance.*) Right in my own bed. Those bells! It must be Christmas Day. Christmas Day. I wonder. (*He hops out of bed and exits right. There is a pause and SCROOGE enters again, accompanied by a young* BOY.) Now tell me, what day is today?

BOY: Today! Why it's Christmas Day, of course.

SCROOGE: And to think the Spirits have done it all in one night.

BOY: What's that, sir?

SCROOGE: Do you know the poulterer's in the next street?

BOY: I should hope I did.

SCROOGE: An intelligent boy! A remarkable boy! Do you know whether they've sold the prize turkey that was hanging in the window?

BOY: The one as big as me?

SCROOGE: What a delightful boy. Yes, the one as big as you.

BOY: It's hanging there now.

SCROOGE: Is it? Go and buy it.

BOY: You're pulling my leg.

SCROOGE (*Reaches into his dressing gown pocket and takes out some money*): Indeed I'm not. Here is the money. Go buy it and deliver it to Bob Cratchit, who lives on Golden Street in Camden Town.

BOY (*As he takes the money*): Cratchit . . . Golden Street . . . Camden Town. I understand. (*He looks at the money.*) But, sir, there will be considerable money left over, almost a half a sovereign.

SCROOGE (*Chuckles*): Keep it, my boy, keep it.

BOY: Oh, thank you, sir.

SCROOGE: And, boy. (*The* BOY *pauses.*) Don't let Mr. Cratchit know who sent the turkey. It's a surprise. And something else. A very Merry Christmas to you. (*Blackout. The area in center is lighted. It reveals* FRED *and* PEG.)

PEG: We'll be ready for dinner in another half-hour.

FRED: Fine! I'm as hungry as the proverbial bear. (*A knock on the door at right is heard.*)

PEG: If it is someone looking for charity, do what you can.

(FRED *exits right. From offstage he can be heard saying:* "*Who is it? You!*" SCROOGE *and* FRED *enter.*)

SCROOGE (*As he crosses to center*) : This took a lot of courage, but here I am. Well, nephew, introduce me to your wife.

FRED (*Still stunned*) : Uncle Ebenezer, this is Peg.

SCROOGE (*As she is about to curtsey*) : That's no way to greet an uncle. (*He gives her a resounding kiss.*) That's the way to greet an uncle. Are you a good cook, Peg?

PEG : Quite good!

FRED : She's a wonderful cook.

SCROOGE : I'm sure she is. I've accepted your invitation for Christmas dinner. (*He puts an arm around each of them.*) From now on both of you had better plan on seeing a great deal of me. (*He notes their surprised looks.*) I'll explain it all later. Right now let me say I'm a changed man. (*The lights black out. There is a pause and the lights come up to reveal* SCROOGE's *office.* SCROOGE *is seated at his desk. There is a pause during which* CRATCHIT *sneaks in from right.* SCROOGE *glances at him and then at his watch.*) Well, Cratchit, what do you mean by coming to work at this time of day? You are eighteen and one-half minutes late.

CRATCHIT (*As he removes his hat and scarf*) : I'm sorry, sir, I overslept.

SCROOGE : Overslept, eh! A poor excuse.

CRATCHIT : Please, sir, it happens but once a year. I was making rather merry yesterday.

SCROOGE : Step this way. (CRATCHIT *crosses to him.*) Now, I'll tell you what, my friend. (*As he speaks, he rises.*) I am not going to stand this sort of thing any longer. (*He claps* CRATCHIT *on the back.*) Therefore, I am going to raise your salary. (*He again slaps* CRATCHIT *on the back.*) A Merry Christmas, Bob. A merrier Christmas than I have given you for many a year.

CRATCHIT: Are you well, sir?

SCROOGE: Couldn't be better. And this afternoon we'll discuss how I can best help you and your family, especially Tiny Tim. He'll get well. I'll see to that. (*Briskly*) Now, make up the fire and buy another coal scuttle before you dot another "i".

CRATCHIT: You seem in unusually fine spirits.

SCROOGE: Spirits! I should be, for I was visited by three of the nicest and wisest spirits that ever walked the earth.

CRATCHIT: God bless you, sir. And, as Tiny Tim would say, God bless us, every one. (*As the curtain falls, from offstage can be heard the group of young boys singing "God Rest Ye Merry Gentlemen."*)

THE END

A Christmas Carol

by Charles Dickens

Adapted for radio by WALTER HACKETT

SOUND: *Church clock striking three times.*

CHORUS (*Young Voices*): *They sing a chorus of "God Rest Ye Merry Gentlemen." At its climax*:

SOUND: *Door opens.*

SCROOGE (*Barks*): Stop it! Stop it, I say! (*Singing stops*) Get away from here. We'll have no singing around here. Understand me! No singing!

BOY: A Merry Christmas, sir.

SCROOGE: Get away, I say.

2ND BOY: No need to wish 'im a Merry Christmas. That's Old Scrooge.

MUSIC: *A contemporary Christmas ballad. Forte and fade under.*

NARRATOR: Yes, that is Old Scrooge . . . Ebenezer Scrooge. It is the afternoon before Christmas Day in the year of our Lord 1844. Despite the bitterly cold weather, all of London is in a festive mood. But there is no happy expression on Ebenezer Scrooge's lined face, as he closes the front door of his warehouse and returns to his office. (*Music out*) He throws a glowering look at his clerk, Bob Cratchit. Satisfied that the poor wretch is hard at work, Scrooge adjusts his spectacles. Then without warning . . .

SOUND: *Door (away) opens.*

FRED: A Merry Christmas, Uncle. God save you!

277

SCROOGE: Bah! Humbug!

FRED: Christmas a humbug? Surely, you don't mean that, Uncle.

SCROOGE: Merry Christmas, indeed! What right have you to be merry? You're poor enough.

FRED: What right have you to be dismal? You're rich enough.

SCROOGE: What's Christmas time to you but a time for paying bills without money; a time for finding yourself a year older, and not an hour richer. If I had my way, every idiot who goes about with "Merry Christmas" on his lips would be boiled with his own pudding and buried with a stake of holly through his heart. You keep Christmas in your own way, and let me keep it in mine.

FRED: I came here to ask you to spend Christmas Day with Peg and me.

SCROOGE (*Flatly*): No!

FRED: But we want nothing from you, Uncle, other than your company. (*Pause*) Won't you change your mind and have dinner with us?

SCROOGE: Good afternoon, Fred.

FRED: A Merry Christmas.

SCROOGE: Good afternoon.

FRED: And a Happy New Year.

SCROOGE: Bah! Humbug!

MUSIC: *A brief bridge, up and out.*

CRATCHIT: Er, pardon me, Mr. Scrooge, but there is a gentleman here to see you.

SCROOGE: What about, Cratchit?

CRATCHIT: He didn't say, sir.

GENTLEMAN: Ah, good afternoon, sir. Have I the pleasure of addressing Mr. Scrooge or Mr. Marley?

SCROOGE: Mr. Marley, my former partner, has been dead these seven years. He died seven years ago, this very night.

GENTLEMAN: Then I have no doubt his liberality is well represented by his surviving partner.

SCROOGE: What do you want?

GENTLEMAN: At this festive season, Mr. Scrooge, we try and make some slight provision for the poor and destitute. Many thousands are in want of common necessities.

SCROOGE: Are there no prisons?

GENTLEMAN: Oh, plenty of prisons.

SCROOGE: And the workhouses, are they still in operation?

GENTLEMAN: I wish I could say they were not. How much shall I put you down for, Mr. Scrooge?

SCROOGE: Nothing!

GENTLEMAN (*Puzzled*): Nothing?

SCROOGE: Exactly! Let these deserving people of yours go to the establishments I have mentioned.

GENTLEMAN: Most of them would rather die than do that.

SCROOGE: Then let them do that, and help decrease the surplus population. I'm busy. Good afternoon to you.

GENTLEMAN (*Quietly*): Very good, Mr. Scrooge. Merry Christmas to you.

SOUND: *Door (off) open and close.*

SCROOGE (*Grumbles*): Charity! Pah! Humbug!

CRATCHIT: Er, Mr. Scrooge, sir.

SCROOGE: Well, what is it, Cratchit?

CRATCHIT: I was wondering—

SCROOGE: You were wondering if you could go home.

CRATCHIT: Yes, sir. It's getting late.

SCROOGE: Yes, go on. You'll want all day tomorrow, I suppose?

CRATCHIT: If quite convenient, sir.

SCROOGE: It's not convenient, and it's not fair.

CRATCHIT: It's only once a year, sir.

SCROOGE: A poor excuse for picking a man's pocket every twenty-fifth day of December. I suppose you must have the whole day. But be here all the earlier the next day. Understand?

CRATCHIT: Yes, sir. And Merry Christmas.

SCROOGE: Christmas! Humbug!

MUSIC: *A Christmas theme, up and under.*

NARRATOR: A few minutes later Scrooge leaves his warehouse and makes his way to his melancholy chambers, a gloomy suite of rooms. By the light of a single flickering candle, he eats his cold supper. And then to save lighting his stove, Ebenezer Scrooge retires for the night. (*Music out*) The minutes tick away. Scrooge sleeps uneasily, tossing from side to side.

SOUND: *Chains being dragged across the floor.*

NARRATOR: Suddenly he awakes with a start. Walking toward him, and dragging a heavy chain, is a gray, dim figure of a man. It stops at the foot of the bed.

SCROOGE (*Frightened*): Who are you? What do you want with me? (*Pause*) Who are you?

MARLEY: Ask me who I *was.*

SCROOGE: You're . . . you're . . .

MARLEY: Yes, in life I was your partner, Jacob Marley.

SCROOGE: But it cannot be so. You're dead.

MARLEY: You don't believe in me.

SCROOGE: No. You're nothing but an undigested bit of beef, a blot of mustard, a crumb of cheese.

MARLEY: You are wrong, Ebenezer. I am the ghost of Jacob Marley.

SCROOGE: Why do you come to me?

MARLEY: It is required of every man that the spirit within him should walk abroad among his fellow men and travel far and wide; and if that spirit goes not forth in life, it is condemned to do so after death.

SCROOGE: No, no, I don't believe it.

MARLEY: It is then doomed to wander through the world.

SCROOGE: You are chained, Jacob. Tell me why?

MARLEY: I wear the chain I forged in life. I made it link by link, and yard by yard. I wore it of my own free will. Is its pattern strange to you?

SCROOGE (*Trembling*): I don't understand.

MARLEY: This chain I wear is as heavy as the one you are now forging.

SCROOGE: You talk strangely, Jacob.

MARLEY: For seven years I have been dead—traveling the whole time. No rest, no peace. Only remorse.

SCROOGE: But you were always shrewd, Jacob.

MARLEY: Aye, too shrewd.

SCROOGE: A good man of business.

MARLEY: Business! Mankind was my business. The common welfare was my business; charity, mercy, forbearance and benevolence were all my business. But I heeded none of these. Instead, I thought only of money.

SCROOGE: And what is wrong with making money?

MARLEY: That is your fault, Ebenezer, as it was mine. That is why I am here tonight. That is part of my penance. I am here to warn you . . . to help you escape my fate. You have one chance left.

SCROOGE: Tell me how this chance will come!

MARLEY: My time draws near. I must go. Tonight you will be haunted by three spirits. The first will appear when the bell strikes one; expect the second at the stroke of two, and the third as the bell tolls three.

SCROOGE: Couldn't I take 'em all at once, and have it over with?

MARLEY: No. And heed them when they appear. (*Fading*) Remember it is your last chance to escape my miserable fate.

MUSIC: *A bit ominous. Forte and fade out under* NARRATOR.

NARRATOR: As Scrooge stares in frightened silence, the wraithlike figure of his deceased partner dissolves into space. Then, exhausted by the ordeal, Scrooge drops off to sleep. Twelve o'clock comes. Time passes. Then:

SOUND: *Off in the distance, steeple clock strikes once.*

NARRATOR: The curtains of Scrooge's bed are drawn aside, but by no visible hand. There by the bed stands an unearthly visitor . . . a strange figure—like a child. Its hair is white, and in its hand it holds a sprig of fresh green holly. Scrooge stares and then speaks.

SCROOGE: Are you the spirit, whose coming was told me by Jacob Marley?

1ST GHOST (*A gentle voice*): I am.

SCROOGE: Who, and what are you?

1ST GHOST: I am the Ghost of Christmas Past.

SCROOGE: Long past?

1ST GHOST: No. Your Past. Rise and walk with me.

SCROOGE: Where?

1ST GHOST: Out through the window.

SCROOGE: But we are three stories above ground. I am only a mortal.

1ST GHOST: Bear but a touch of my hand upon your heart and you shall be upheld in more than this.

SCROOGE: What are we to do?

1ST GHOST: *I* am going to help reclaim you. Come! Walk with me out into the night . . . into the past.

SOUND: *Wind. It sweeps in; hold and then fade out.*

SCROOGE: Tell me, Ghost of Christmas Past, where are we?

1ST GHOST: Look down, Ebenezer, and remember back.

SCROOGE (*Amazed*): Why . . . why, of course. The river . . . the meadows . . . and—why, there's my old school. I went there as a lad. But there is no one about.

1ST GHOST: It is Christmas holiday. Let us look into this study hall.

SCROOGE: Empty, except for a young boy sitting at a desk, his head in his hands. Left behind. He . . . he's crying. Poor chap! No place to go at Christmas. Ah, now he's looking up.

1ST GHOST: Do you recognize him?

SCROOGE (*Stunned*): Why, it's—

1ST GHOST: What is his name?

SCROOGE (*Slowly*): Ebenezer Scrooge. (*Pause*) I wish— But it's too late now.

1ST GHOST: What is the matter?

SCROOGE: Nothing, nothing. There were some boys singing Christmas carols outside my warehouse door yesterday afternoon. I drove them away.

1ST GHOST: Let us see another Christmas.

SOUND: *Wind up briefly and out.*

1ST GHOST: It is a year later . . . another Christmas.

SCROOGE: And again there is the school.

1ST GHOST: That boy standing in the driveway, pacing up and down.

SCROOGE: It is I.

1ST GHOST: And what do you see?

SCROOGE: A coach coming up the driveway. Now it has stopped, and a little girl gets out. Look, she is hugging me. It's Fan, my sister.

1ST GHOST: Listen to what she says.

FAN: I've come to bring you home, dear brother. Father's not mean any more, and he says you're never coming back here, and from now on we'll always be together. (*Fading*) Just think, together for the first time in four years.

1ST GHOST: Your sister was a delicate creature . . . kind . . . big-hearted.

SCROOGE: So she was, so she was. She died comparatively young.

1ST GHOST: She left one child behind her.

SCROOGE: Yes. Fred, my nephew.

1ST GHOST (*Mildly*): He was in to wish you a Merry Christmas yesterday.

SCROOGE: Yes. Yes, he did so. Please take me back.

1ST GHOST: Not yet. There is one more shadow.

SCROOGE: No more. I do not wish to see it.

1ST GHOST: You must.

SOUND: *The wind sweeps in full again, then out.*

1ST GHOST: The years have passed. In this house below. Look, there sits a young girl, a beautiful girl.

SCROOGE: It's Belle.

1ST GHOST: The girl you were to marry. And there you sit next to her, a young man in your prime. Only now your face begins to show the signs of avarice. There is a greedy, restless motion in your eyes. Listen to what she is saying to you.

BELLE (*She is about 18*): It matters very little to you. Another idol has displaced me, a golden one. You hold money more important than me or anything else, for that matter. And I'm going to grant your wish: free you from marrying me. (*Fading*) That is the way you wish it, Ebenezer. I feel sorry for you.

SCROOGE: Spirit, show me no more.

1ST GHOST: Today, Belle is a happy woman, surrounded with her fine children. Those children might have been yours if you hadn't been so selfish.

SCROOGE: Take me back. Haunt me no more! I beg of you, don't!

MUSIC: *Ethereal theme. Forte and fade under for* NARRATOR.

NARRATOR: The steeple clock has just finished striking the second hour of Christmas Day. Scrooge finds himself back in his bedroom. Slowly his door, though bolted, swings open.

MUSIC: *Out.*

2ND GHOST (*A big, booming voice*): Good morning, Ebenezer.

Welcome me. I am the Ghost of Christmas Present. Look upon me.

SCROOGE: You're practically a giant. Yet you have a young face.

2ND GHOST: Have you never seen the like of me before?

SCROOGE: Never.

2ND GHOST: I have many brothers, over eighteen hundred of them, one for each Christmas since the very first.

SCROOGE: And you are here to take me with you?

2ND GHOST: Yes. I trust you will profit by your journey. Touch my robe, Ebenezer.

SOUND: *Wind. Up full and out into:*

CHORUS (*Mixed voices*): *Singing a chorus of a Christmas hymn. As they near conclusion, fade them under for:*

SCROOGE: Those people in this church, they seem very happy.

2ND GHOST: They are, for they are giving thanks for all the joys brought to them during the year.

SCROOGE: And the crew of that ship over there. . . . Look, they are shaking hands with the captain.

CHORUS: *Out.*

2ND GHOST: Wishing him a Merry Christmas. But come! We have not much time left, and there is still another place we must visit. It is a very poor house in a very poor section of London. This one directly below us.

SCROOGE: Indeed it is. Who, may I ask, lives here?

2ND GHOST: An underpaid clerk named Bob Cratchit.

SCROOGE: The Bob Cratchit who is employed by me?

2ND GHOST: The very same.

SCROOGE: That woman . . . those four children.

2ND GHOST: His wife and family.

SCROOGE: Coming up the stairs right now. That's Cratchit. He's carrying a young boy.

2ND GHOST: His fifth child . . . Tiny Tim.

SCROOGE: He carries a crutch.

2ND GHOST: Because he is crippled.

SCROOGE: But the doctors—

2ND GHOST: Cratchit cannot afford a doctor, not on fifteen shillings a week.

SCROOGE: But—

2ND GHOST: Sshhh! Listen.

SOUND: *Door opens.*

CRATCHIT (*Heartily*): Good afternoon, everyone.

TIM: And a most Merry Christmas.

MRS. CRATCHIT: Father . . . Tiny Tim.

THE OTHER CRATCHITS (*They ad lib*): "Merry Christmas," "Welcome," "Tiny Tim, sit next to me," "Father, let me take your muffler."

MRS. CRATCHIT: And how did Tiny Tim behave at church?

CRATCHIT: As good as gold, and better.

TIM: I was glad to be able to go to church. That's because I wanted the people to see that I'm a cripple.

MRS. CRATCHIT: Now that's a peculiar thing to say, Tiny Tim.

TIM (*Eagerly*): No, it isn't. That's because I was in God's House, and it was God who made the blind able to see and the lame able to walk. And when the people at church saw me and my crutch, I was hoping they would think of what God can do, and that they would say a prayer for me.

MRS. CRATCHIT: I . . . I'm certain they must have prayed for you.

TIM: And one of these days I'm going to get well, and that'll mean I can throw away this crutch, and run and play like the other boys.

CRATCHIT (*Softly*): You will, Tim—one of these days. (*Heartily*) And now, Mother, the big question. When will dinner be ready?

BIZ: *Ad libs from the children.*

MRS. CRATCHIT: It's ready now: just about the finest goose you have ever seen. Martha, you carry it in. Tom, you fetch the potatoes and turnips. Dick, Peter, set the chairs around the table.

TIM: And I'll sit between Father and Mother.

CRATCHIT: This is going to be the best Christmas dinner anyone could hope for. (*Fading*) And I'm the luckiest man in the world, having such a fine family.

SCROOGE: It isn't a very big goose, is it? I could eat the whole bird myself, I believe.

2ND GHOST: It is all Bob Cratchit can afford. His family doesn't complain. To them, that meagre goose is a sumptuous banquet. And more important, much more important, Ebenezer.

SCROOGE: Go on.

2ND GHOST: They are a happy and united group. Look at their shining faces. Listen to them.

BIZ: *The* CRATCHITS *ad libbing in happy fashion,*

CRATCHIT: What a superb dinner we have had . . . the tempting meat, the delicious dressing.

TIM: And the plum pudding, Father. Don't forget that.

CRATCHIT: That pudding was the greatest success achieved by Mrs. Cratchit since her marriage.

BIZ: *The children laugh.*

MRS. CRATCHIT: Thank you for the compliment. I must confess it was good.

CRATCHIT: And now for the crowning touch. The punch!

BIZ (*Ad libs of*): "The punch!" "Good!" "Oh!"

CRATCHIT: Here we are. Get your glasses. You, Peter . . . Dick . . . Tom . . . Martha . . . Tiny Tim . . . and last, but far from least you, Mother. And not to forget myself. (*With finality*) There!

TIM: A toast!

CRATCHIT: First the founder of this feast, the man who has made it possible. I give you Mr. Scrooge.

MRS. CRATCHIT (*Bristling*): Mr. Scrooge, indeed. I wish I had him here. I'd give him a piece of my mind to feast upon, and I hope he'd have a good appetite for it.

CRATCHIT (*Warningly*): My dear, the children! Christmas Day.

MRS. CRATCHIT: He's a hard, stingy, unfeeling man. You know he is, Robert, better than anybody else.

CRATCHIT (*Mildly*): My dear. Remember, Christmas Day.

MRS. CRATCHIT: I'm sorry. Very well, I'll drink his health. Long life to him! A Merry Christmas to him! To Mr. Scrooge.

FAMILY (*Chorusing*): To Mr. Scrooge!

CRATCHIT: And now a toast to us: A Merry Christmas to us all. God bless us!

FAMILY: God bless us.

TIM: God bless us every one.

MUSIC: *"Noel"—Forte and fade under.*

SCROOGE: Spirit, tell me if Tiny Tim will live.

2ND GHOST: I see a vacant seat in the chimney corner, and a crutch without an owner, carefully preserved. If these shadows remain unaltered by the Future the child will die.

SCROOGE: No, no. Oh, no, kind Spirit! Say he will live, that he will be spared.

2ND GHOST: Why concern yourself about him? Isn't it better that he die and decrease the surplus population?

SCROOGE: But these poor people must be helped.

2ND GHOST: Are there no prisons? And the workhouses, are they still in operation?

SCROOGE: Do not taunt me.

2ND GHOST: It is time for us to go.

SCROOGE: No, I wish to remain.

2ND GHOST: I can remain no longer. Touch my robe and we shall go.

SCROOGE: No! No, I say! Spirit, don't desert me. I need your help.

MUSIC: *Up briefly and under.*

NARRATOR: As Ebenezer Scrooge comes to his senses, he discovers himself standing on the street, outside of his lodgings. A heavy snow is falling, blanketing a sleeping London. The wind has died down. It is still early Christmas morning.

MUSIC: *Out into:*

SOUND: *Steeple bell off in distance striking three times.*

3RD GHOST (*Warningly*): Ebenezer . . . Ebenezer Scrooge.

SCROOGE: You are the third and last.

3RD GHOST: I am the Ghost of Christmas Yet to Come.

SCROOGE: You are about to show me shadows of the things that have not happened, but will happen in the time before us. Is that so, Spirit?

3RD GHOST: Yes, Ebenezer, that is correct.

SCROOGE: I tremble at going with you. I fear what I am to see.

3RD GHOST: Come, Ebenezer.

SOUND: *Wind up full and out.*

SCROOGE: Why do we stop here on this street corner, Spirit?

3RD GHOST: Those two men standing there, do you know them?

SCROOGE: Why, yes, I do business with them.

3RD GHOST: Their conversation is interesting.

MAN 1: When did he die?

MAN 2: Last night, I believe.

MAN 1: I thought he'd never die.

MAN 2: What has he done with his money?

MAN 1: I haven't heard. Left it to his company, perhaps. Well, one thing is certain, he didn't leave it to charity.

MAN 2: Are you going to his funeral?

MAN 1: Not unless a free lunch is provided.

MAN 2 (*Fading*): A very good point . Can't say that I blame you.

SCROOGE: Spirit, this dead man they were discussing, who is he?

3RD GHOST: I will show you.

SOUND: *Wind up briefly and out.*

SCROOGE: This room, it's too dark to see.

3RD GHOST: In front of you is a bed. On it lies a man—the body of the man those men on the street were discussing.

SCROOGE: And no one has come to claim this body?

3RD GHOST: No one, for he left not a friend behind him. Come closer and look into his face.

SCROOGE: No.

3RD GHOST: Look!

SCROOGE: Spirit, this is a fearful place. Let us go.

3RD GHOST: Look at the face of this unclaimed man.

SCROOGE: I would do it if I could. But I haven't the power. Let me see some tenderness connected with a death. If I don't, that lonely body in this dark room will ever haunt me.

3RD GHOST: Yes, I know of such a home, one where there is tenderness connected with death. Over here on this poor street and in this dismal house.

SCROOGE: But this house— Why, yes, I've been here before. Bob Cratchit, my clerk lives here. There is Mrs. Cratchit and her eldest daughter, Martha.

MARTHA: Your eyes, Mother, you'll strain them working in this bad light.

MRS. CRATCHIT: I'll stop for a while. I wouldn't show weak eyes to your father when he comes home. It's time he was here.

MARTHA: Past it rather. But these days he walks slower than he used to, Mother.

MRS. CRATCHIT: I have known him to walk with Tiny Tim upon his shoulder very fast, indeed. He was very light to carry and your father loved him so, it was no trouble.

SOUND: *Door handle.*

MRS. CRATCHIT: There is your father now at the door.

SOUND: *Door opens and shuts.*

MRS. CRATCHIT: You're late tonight, Robert.

CRATCHIT: Yes, I'm late.

MARTHA: I'll get some tea for you, Father.

CRATCHIT: Thank you, Martha.

MRS. CRATCHIT: You went there today, Robert?

CRATCHIT: Yes. I wish you could have gone. It would have done you good to see how green a place it is.

MRS. CRATCHIT: I'll see it soon.

CRATCHIT: I promised him I would walk there every Sunday. My poor Tiny Tim. At last he got rid of his crutch.

MRS. CRATCHIT (*Fading*): Yes, at last he did. Our poor Tiny Tim.

SCROOGE: Tell me, Spirit, why did Tiny Tim have to die?

3RD GHOST: Come, there is still another place to visit.

SOUND: *Wind. Up and out.*

SCROOGE: A graveyard. Why do we pause here?

3RD GHOST: That tombstone . . . read the name on it.

SCROOGE: Before I do, answer me one question. Are these the shadows of the things that *will* be, or are they the shadows of the things that *may* be, only?

3RD GHOST: The inscription on the tombstone.

SCROOGE: It reads . . . (*Slowly*) "Ebenezer Scrooge." No, Spirit. Oh, no, no! Hear me! I am not the man I was. I will not be the man I must have been but for this lesson. I will honor Christmas in my heart.

3RD GHOST: But will you?

SCROOGE: Oh, yes. I will try and keep it alive all the year. I will live in the Past, the Present and the Future. I will not shut out the lesson that all three Spirits have taught me. Oh, tell me there is hope, that I may sponge away the writing on this stone.

SOUND: *Wind up strong. Hold and out into: Joyous church bells, tolling Christmas Day. Hold under.*

SCROOGE (*Moans, as though coming out of a dream*): Tell me there is hope, that I may sponge away the writing on this stone. (*Coming to*) Eh, what am I holding on to? The bedpost. I am in my own bed . . . home. Those bells! It must be Christmas Day. Christmas Day—I wonder if it really is. We shall see. I'll open the window.

SOUND: *Window being raised.*

SCROOGE: You boy, down there.

BOY (*Away*): Eh?

SCROOGE: What day is today, my fine lad?

BOY: Today! Why, Christmas Day, of course.

SCROOGE: And to think the Spirits have done it all in one night.

BOY: What did you say, sir?

SCROOGE: Do you know the poulterer's in the next street?

BOY: I should hope I did.

SCROOGE: An intelligent boy! A remarkable boy! Do you know whether they've sold the prize turkey that was hanging in the window?

BOY: The one as big as me?

SCROOGE: What a delightful boy. Yes, the one as big as you.

BOY: It's hanging there now.

SCROOGE: Go and buy it. I am in earnest. Here is the money. Catch. (*Pause*) Deliver it to Bob Cratchit, who lives on Golden Street in Camden Town.

BOY: But, sir, there will be considerable change left over.

SCROOGE (*Chuckling*): Keep it, my boy. Keep it.

BOY (*Delighted*): Oh, thank you, sir.

SCROOGE: And, boy.

BOY: Yes, sir.

SCROOGE: Don't let Mr. Cratchit know who sent the turkey. It's something of a surprise. And something else.

Boy: Yes, sir.

Scrooge: A very Merry Christmas to you.

Music: *A Christmas hymn. Up and under.*

Sound: *Knock on door. Repeated. Door opens.*

Fred: What is it? (*Pause*) Why, bless my soul!

Scrooge (*Heartily*): Yes, yes, it is I—your Uncle Scrooge. I've come for dinner. Now let me in. I have a present for your good wife. From now on I'm going to be one of your most persistent guests. I've changed, my boy: you'll see!

Music: *Up and under for* Narrator.

Narrator: Scrooge was better than his word. He did everything he promised, and infinitely more. He became a persistent visitor to his nephew's home, and even took Fred into business with him. He raised Bob Cratchit's salary to a figure that left that bewildered gentleman gasping; and to Tiny Tim, who did not die, he was a second father. He provided doctors for the little lad, and very soon Tiny Tim will have his wish: he will be able to throw away his crutch and run and play like the other boys. As for the three Spirits, Ebenezer Scrooge never saw them again. That was due to the unchallengeable fact that Scrooge, for the rest of his days, helped keep alive the spirit of Christmas. And so, as Tiny Tim observed, God bless us every one.

Music: *Up full to close.*

THE END

Production Notes

Pink Roses for Christmas

Characters: 2 male; 3 female.

Playing Time: 25 minutes.

Costumes: Everyday modern clothes. Tillie wears a house dress with an apron.

Properties: Silverware and dishes for table setting. Pink candles in holders, four place cards, newspaper, shawl, wrapped packages, matches, pink roses, arranged for a centerpiece.

Setting: Upstage rear stands a buffet on which the candles are placed. A door, up left, leads out. Another door, down right, leads to the kitchen, and there is a door right center leading upstairs. Downstage center stands the dining table, set for four people.

Lighting: No special effects.

Musical Note: If desired, "Silent Night" is softly played at rise of curtain.

No Room at the Inn

Characters: 13 male; 1 female; extras.

Playing Time: 30 minutes.

Costumes: The players wear the traditional flowing garments of the Orient, not necessarily white. The Boy is dressed in a short tunic. Sandals are worn by all.

Properties: Pitchers, staffs for the Shepherds, three coffers.

Setting: On two sides of the stage, rear and left, runs the wall of the courtyard. This is about six feet high and is broken by two arched gateways. One arch is at the center of the rear wall and leads to the stables. It has a wooden gate. The other arch is at the center of the left wall and is the entrance to the inn yard from the highway. It has no gate. On the right of the stage is the wall of the inn. There is a door in the center of the wall; to the right of the door, a bench; to the left, a small window. The stage is bare save for the bench and at the rear left a circular well-curb of stone wide enough to use as a seat. Above the wall only the sky may be seen.

Lighting: Red overheads and footlights are used in Scene 1, with most of the light from the overheads concentrated at left or perhaps additional red spots shining from the left wings. For Scene 2 dark blue overheads and footlights are desirable. A white spot from offstage can be placed to shine directly over the stable to represent the star; or the desired effect can also be attained by hanging a silver star above the stable and using a white spot on it.

Note: This play can be combined effectively with a musical program by preceding and following it with the singing of carols. One verse of a carol could be sung also while the curtain is lowered to denote passage of time. Nothing longer should be introduced here as it would break the continuity of the play.

Appropriate carols are "O Little Town of Bethlehem," "While Shepherds Watched Their Flocks," "Away in a Manger," "We Three Kings," "Silent Night," "All My Heart this Night Rejoices," "It Came upon a Midnight Clear," "First Noel," "In Bethelehem 'neath Starlit Skies," "Adeste Fidelis."

PUPPY LOVE

Characters: 3 male; 4 female.
Playing Time: 30 minutes.

Costumes: Modern dress.

Properties: Cards, wrapping paper, boxes, string, greens, small tree, a large stuffed toy dog, wrapped packages, red bow, tag, lights for tree, trays, plates of cakes, teacups, teapot.

Setting: The living room of the Bradley home. It is attractively and comfortably furnished with chairs, tables, bookcases, etc. Upstage center are two card tables. Downstage right, near a large armchair, is a small tea table.

Lighting: No special effects.

SILENT NIGHT

Characters: 4 male; 5 female.

Playing Time: 25 minutes.

Costumes: Herr Pastor Mohr wears dark shabby clothes, probably odd trousered with a smoking jacket, in the first scene. In Scene II, he is wrapped in an old faded afghan. In Scene III he would be in his best clothes ready to conduct the Christmas services. Herr Gruber is dressed in dark clothes also, less shabby than Herr Mohr's. He wears a long flowing black tie. In Scene II he enters in heavy black over-coat with fur collar, fur hat, brightly colored muffler, and wears gloves. In the last scene he also is in holiday attire. Frau Mohr is large and blonde, wearing a plain house dress with large clean white apron tied in a big bow at the back. Joseph is in brown knickers, brown shoes and stockings, and a green sweater. The Organist is in plain dark suit with dark tie. The four daughters are all in white; the choir in regulation attire.

Properties: Large bookcases, many books for their shelves, a large oak table, a large over-stuffed armchair, several shabby straight-back chairs, a footstool, paper, a quill pen with inkwell, a worn rug, lamps, five candles, a tray, two cups of chocolate, some rolls on a plate, a piano or organ where available, folding chairs, a printed program.

Setting: Scene I is an interior set, with dark panelling half way up the walls. In the rear are double windows, curtained plainly. Bookcases line the other walls up almost as high as the panelling. Odd pictures and paintings, too dark and dreary to recognize, are scattered about the upper walls. To the right of the double window is a practical door. In left center wall is an open fireplace with electric logs, or simulated fire. Through the window snow can be seen to be falling, and part of the windows are frosted, with cakes of ice surrounding the rims. The large overstuffed easy chair is directly before the fireplace. There are two floor lamps, and a large painted one on the table. Scene II is the same with papers littering the floor, and a tray with chocolate also on the floor beside the door. Scene III is the stage of the Church. This may be played on a bare stage or with a rich green cyclorama. Floral decorations, and candelabra may be added, to give a more festive air. The snow may be small pieces of white paper realistically cut, soap flakes, or camphor. These should be dropped from behind and above the windows; and an electric fan playing upon them will give a very realistic effect. If this is impractical, heaps of "snow" may be piled or painted on the two window ledges. Or the window curtains may be drawn so that the storm cannot be seen. Paper may not be used on Gruber, when he enters during Scene II, as it will not brush off correctly.

Lighting: Scene I: Amber and white footlights, and overheads dim, for twilight effect; gradually dimming to dusk. Scene II: Brighter white and amber footlights, light pink overhead to dawn. Scene III: Footlights and overheads up bright white. Spots on Organist in audience, and on four daughters as they sing; other lights dimming to rise up full at end of song.

Note: Where organ is not available change lines to read "piano" and carry along logically from that.

Santa Goes to Town

Characters: 10 female.

Playing Time: 35 minutes.

Costumes: All characters wear modern everyday dress. Midge and Sprat need Santa Claus costumes, with pants, coat, boots, mittens, cap with false face attached. Katie wears maid's uniform. Miss Sharp wears a hat and coat.

Properties: Dancing costumes and Santa Claus costume to strew around room; box of doughnuts; five Christmas packages of assorted shapes and sizes; spectacles for Miss Sharp and oxford glasses for Miss McGill; doll; sack for Santa to fill; sleighbells, broom, mop, carpet sweeper, suitboxes, wheelchair.

Setting: Dressing room. One door left, two right, window at rear. Several folding chairs, strewn with costumes that spill onto floor. Screen with costumes flung over it. Clothes tree with costumes dangling from hangers on it.

Lighting: No special effects.

The Perfect Gift

Characters: 10 males; 2 females.

Playing Time: 30 minutes.

Costumes: The traditional Oriental costumes.

Properties: Small wooden figure and a knife for David. Staffs, a red apple, several eggs, some nuts for shepherds.

Setting: The court before the inn at Bethlehem. A wall, six or seven feet high, at the rear of the stage and at the left. In the middle of the rear wall, an arched portal facing the stable. The right side of the stage is the front wall of the inn. Near the middle of this there is a door. In the center of the stage stands a bench.

Lighting: Dim at first, growing gradually lighter as day approaches. Very bright at the end.

Note: In order not to break the continuity of the play, only three or four lines of a carol should be sung at any time, except at the rise of curtain and at the fall, when carols may be given in full.

Suggested Carols: "It Came upon a Midnight Clear," "Silent Night," "While Shepherds Watched Their Flocks," "O Little Town of Bethlehem."

THE PERAMBULATING PIE

Characters: 5 male; 5 female.

Playing Time: 30 minutes.

Costumes: Modern dress.

Properties: Bags, groceries, cardboard sign, boxes, large pie tin wrapped in waxed paper, sweater, Christmas greens, baskets, small jar, card and check in envelope.

Setting: A room in the Community House. The only furnishings are several large tables and a few chairs.

Lighting: No special effects.

THE CHRISTMAS SNOWMAN

Characters: 4 male; 3 female.

Playing Time: 30 minutes.

Costumes: Modern dress. The children wear hats and coats and boots when they enter. Jenkins and Sarah should be dressed in black. Mr. Weatherby also wears black.

Properties: Tray, teapot, cup, paper, long overcoat, cane, two hats, pencil, axe.

Setting: The library in Mr. Weatherby's home. Upstage center is a large fireplace with high bookcases full of books on either side of it. There is a large mirror over the fireplace. In the center of the right wall is a French window leading to the outside. Against the wall are more cases of books. In the center of the left wall is a door leading to the rest of the house. Upstage from the door is a small table with a telephone, pad of paper and pencil on it. Near the fireplace at right is a large chair with a small table in front of it with a chess board and chess men set up on it as though someone were in the middle of a game. Bric-a-brac is placed around the room, and on the mantel is a large china cat. Other chairs and tables are placed around the room, and pictures are hung on the walls.

Lighting: No special effects.

NAOMI-OF-THE-INN

Characters: 8 male; 7 female; offstage choir.

Playing Time: 30 minutes.

Costumes: Simple costumes of the period. Elisabeth, Salome, and their husbands are well dressed. In Scene 2 Naomi and Martha wear cloaks.

Properties: Water-jug.

Setting: Scene 1: The courtyard and entrance of the Inn. At back center is the doorway of the Inn. There is a bench a little to left of the door. If possible, two or three palms are placed about the stage. Scene 2: All that is needed is a wall running along one side of the stage.

Lighting: As indicated in text, in Scene 2, a soft, white light beams on the wall.

ANGEL IN THE LOOKING-GLASS

Characters: 3 male; 5 female.

Playing Time: 20 minutes.

Costumes: Modern dress. Lucy wears a white flowing robe typical of the angel's costume in a Christmas pageant.

Properties: Pins, tape measure, halo.

Setting: Before the curtain there is a large full-length mirror placed on one side of the stage. The stage itself is divided into three "apartments." In the Youngs' apartment are two chairs and a table. In Aunt Martha's apartment are an over-stuffed chair and two hassocks. In Zorlova's apartment are a chair and a modernistic dressing table. On the dressing table is a telephone. Note: this play may be produced without any scenery at all; the apartments may be indicated by signs.

Lighting: No special effects.

THE BROTH OF CHRISTKINDLI

Characters: 5 male; 3 female; carolers may be male or female.

Playing Time: 15 minutes.

Costumes: The carolers are dressed in medieval costumes; long hose, short full pants and long dark tunics. Christkindli wears a long white gown with full flowing sleeves, and a golden crown on her head. The rest of the characters are dressed in appropriate peasant costumes.

Properties: Cloak, small bag, candle, plate of cakes, ladle, bowl, cups, star.

Setting: A room in a peasant cottage in Switzerland. Upstage center is a fireplace, and in the fireplace on some logs is a small pot. On one side of the fireplace is a large cupboard, on the other a gaily curtained window. Small chairs are in front of the fireplace. Downstage right is a small decorated Christmas tree, and near the tree a low table.

Lighting: No special effects. A spotlight might be turned on the Angel as she enters.

HAPPY CHRISTMAS TO ALL

Characters: 3 male; 3 female.

Playing Time: 20 minutes.

Costumes: Dr. Moore wears a long black coat of clerical cut, and spectacles on his nose. At first he wears slippers, but changes to shoes when he goes out. He also then puts on an overcoat, a black stove-pipe hat, and a black woolen muffler.

He wears gloves. Mrs. Moore wears a white apron over her dark house dress. She wears a neat white cap on her head. The boys are dressed in warm winter clothes, as is the girl. Emily is smartly dressed according to the fashion of the early Nineteenth century. At end children wear white flannel nightgowns.

Properties: Books, quill pen, paper, tall red candle, covered basket, packages with Christmas wrappings, simulated turkey, black toy kitten, newspaper, bowl and spoon.

Setting: There is an old-fashioned desk upstage right. Left upstage is a fireplace where light may be hidden to represent a fire. Over the fireplace is a mantel. The room is cheerful. There are several comfortable chairs scattered about the room, and a table in the center. There is a pile of books on the desk. There is an armchair near the fireplace with a footstool in front of it. There is a window and door in the rear wall, and a door in the left wall beyond the fireplace.

Lighting: Lighting is furnished by candles which are on the fireplace mantel. At the end of each scene, just before the reading of the poems, the light may be dimmed.

JINGLE BELLS

Characters: 3 male; 4 female.

Playing Time: 25 minutes.

Costumes: Everyday modern dress.

Properties: Christmas tree ornaments, strings of popcorn, pocket-knife for Jack, white costume with shiny beads and sequins sewed on it, cardboard suitbox, snow shovel, group of presents wrapped expensively, coats for Jack, Diana, Elsie, Ginny, Danny and Mother, scarfs, mittens, etc., for family.

Setting: There are entrances at right and left, the right leading to the front of house and the left to the back and upstairs. The room is homey and pleasant, furnished with comfortable chairs and sturdy maple tables. Upstage is a large Christmas tree partly trimmed. The tree has electric lights which have not yet been connected and turned on. It is also trimmed with modern ornaments mixed with old-fashioned ones as well as some strings of popcorn. On the floor near the tree is a box of Christmas tree ornaments. On a table against the left wall is a telephone and on another table near an armchair at left is a bowl of popcorn. On a table at right is a new-looking book with a bright jacket.

Lighting: No special effects.

THE FRIDAY FOURSOME PACKS A BOX

Characters: 7 female.

Playing Time: 25 minutes.

Costumes: Everyday clothes. Susan wears a maid's uniform.

Properties: Large, wooden box with lid; four packages for Shirley; four hosiery boxes and a spool of ribbon for Beverly; four differently shaped packages for Elise; four packages for Annette. Tissue paper and four packages for Dora and for Polly. (These packages are much more attractively wrapped than those of the other girls'.) Large silver tray with silver service. Small cards. Christmas tree ornaments.

Setting: Sunroom in Dora's home. There is a large window at back and on the right a little down the room is a small settee with a hassock. Left of the window is a coffee table with a chair nearby. At lower left is a chaise longue and at lower right a desk with chair. In front of the window is a beautifully bedecked Christmas tree and around its base are heaped gaily-wrapped packages. There is a door down right leading to the hall and one down left leading to another room. Between the door at right and the settee is a large wooden packing box.

Lighting: No special effects.

The Best Gift of All

Characters: 5 female; mixed extras.

Playing Time: 10 minutes.

Costumes: The children are all in plain costumes of ancient drape and varying in color. Naomi will be easily distinguishable from the others by the tattered condition of her dress. The Angel is in traditional costume of white robe, with wings.

Properties: A carved box, a vase, a beautifully bound book, a jar of honey, a carving, miscellaneous boxes and packages of different sizes to serve as gifts, a shiny red apple, a large rock or rough bench for Naomi to sit on, and a variety of shrubs, real or simulated.

Setting: A road leading to Jerusalem. A painted backdrop with hills, trees, and a bright blue sky with fluffy white clouds; or a plain white cyclorama.

Lighting: Overhead and footlights up full white. Baby spot follows Angel's movement on stage, and another picks up Naomi as she looks up with a smile at Curtain.

Everywhere Christmas

Characters: 15 male; 9 female; male and female extras.

Playing Time: 15 minutes.

Costumes: Ted and Ginny are dressed in pajamas. The Old Man wears shabby clothes over a regular Santa Claus costume. The Dutch children wear appropriate costumes with wooden shoes. The French children wear wooden shoes. Eagle Feather may wear an Indian costume. Pedro is in Mexican dress. The other children may wear everyday, modern clothes or some costume suggestive of their country. The Elves may be dressed in brown shorts and jerkins and wear pointed caps. The Fairies are dressed in white or pastel colors. The Gingerbread Children may wear brown pants and brown shirts or a more elaborate costume may be made.

Properties: Candles, long stockings to hang on the fireplace, a toy bank, a penny, a plum pudding (this can be made out of cardboard), holly, ivy and mistletoe, a Yule log, a lantern, musical instruments, a large urn, Christmas tree, lights, a piñata, long pole, something suggestive of a sheaf of grain, a large bag or pack for the Old Man, wrapped packages, a hat for the Old Man.

Setting: A fireplace stands upstage against the center of the wall. There are windows on either side of it. A door, leading outside, is on the left; an inner door, right. There are easy chairs on either side of the fireplace. A few occasional chairs are placed here and there. A toy bank is on the mantelpiece and two empty stockings hang over the fireplace. Lighted candles or Christmas lights stand in the windows and on the mantle.

Lighting: All lighting is supplied by candles.

The Littlest Fir

Characters: 4 male; 1 female; 2 others either male or female.

Playing Time: 10 minutes.

Costumes: The Fir trees are dressed in long, green robes with pointed green hats, and each carries a suitable sized branch. The Mother, Father and children wear everyday clothes.

Properties: Packages, string of Christmas tree lights.

Setting: No setting is required, but if desired a backdrop of a home may be used. Set should be so arranged that the string of lights placed on the Littlest Fir can be quickly plugged into an electric outlet or an extension cord.

Lighting: Where indicated in script, Christmas lights are turned on.

Mrs. Santa's Christmas Gift

Characters: 1 male; 1 female; elves may be either male or female.

Playing Time: 10 minutes.

Costumes: Santa is dressed in the traditional red suit. Mrs. Santa wears a long, full skirt, white blouse, and apron. The elves are dressed in tight-fitting costumes of red and green, and wear little pointed caps with bells.

Properties: Long sheet of paper, pencil, red ribbon, large box in which is a huge watch with a long gold chain, tray of cakes.

Setting: Santa's workshop. Part of the stage is littered with bits of wood, paper, ribbon and greens. Long tables may be placed along the upstage wall, and on the tables hammers, saws and other tools can be seen. In one corner is a decorated Christmas tree, and under the tree are ten small packages. A large cupboard is upstage right, and above the cupboard is a clock.

Lighting: No special effects.

The Unhappy Santa

Characters: 2 male; 1 female.

Playing Time: 15 minutes.

Costumes: Santa is in traditional dress. Jane and Billy are in pajamas.

Properties: Santa's sack, doll carriage, toy train, two boxes, one containing brightly colored socks, the other a scarf.

Setting: In the center of the room is a gaily trimmed Christmas tree. Under it are a number of packages wrapped in Christmas wrappings, a doll carriage, and toy train.

Lighting: None required.

The Christmas Train

Characters: 8 male; 2 female; male and female extras.

Playing Time: 10 minutes.

Costumes: Suggestive toy or animal costumes.

Properties: None required.

Setting: None required.
Lighting: No special effects.

CANDY CANES

Characters: 4 male; 1 female.

Playing Time: 10 minutes.

Costumes: Santa wears the traditional costume. The elves are
  dressed in long pants, matching jerkins and pointed caps.
  Dorothy and Grandfather wear everyday, modern clothes.

Properties: Bag for Santa, letter, red mitten with white cuff,
  pad of paper and pencil.

Setting: Very little is required. A box covered to look like a
  tree stump is near the center of the stage. Two trees, and
  more if desired, made of boxes, posts or cardboard, are on
  stage.

Lighting: No special effects.

A CHRISTMAS CAROL

Characters: 19 male; 5 female; male extras.

Playing Time: 30 minutes.

Costumes: Costumes are typical of England in the early nineteenth century. Illustrated books of Dickens' works will give
  examples. Scrooge wears a long dressing gown over his suit
  during the Spirits' visits. Marley's Ghost wears a suit, and
  white make-up. A chain of papers, ledger books, etc., is tied
  around his waist. The First Spirit is dressed in white and
  carries a sprig of holly. The Second Spirit is dressed in
  green and wears a green cloak. The Third Spirit wears a long
  full black cloak.

Properties: Scene 1: Papers, ledger, wood, watch, inkstand, pen.
  Scene 2: Papers, crutch, cups, glasses, pitcher, sewing, money.

Setting: Scene 1: The counting house of Ebenezer Scrooge in
  London. Upstage left is Scrooge's desk. Upstage right is

Cratchit's desk. Upstage center is a window. Scene 2: Upstage left is Scrooge's bedroom; the furnishings are a small bed and a chair. Then, at center, there is a school room with a small desk. Fessiwig also sits at this desk. For the scene with Belle, the desk is taken away. The Cratchit home is represented by a table and some chairs. The scene with Fred and Peg takes place in the center and requires no scenery. The Businessmen also stand in the center. A chair is then placed in the center for the Cratchits. The scene with Peg and Fred requires no furnishings. As the play ends, the two desks of Scrooge's counting house have been moved back on the stage.

Lighting: Scene 1: The stage can be a little dark, to give a gloomy effect. If possible, light should come through the window. Scene 2: Spot lights and other lights are turned off and on as indicated in the play.